The Splendor of Recognition

An Exploration of the *Pratyabhijñā-hṛdayam*, a Text on the Ancient Science of the Soul

Swami Shantananda

with Peggy Bendet

An Exploration of the *Pratyabhijñā-hṛdayam*,
a Text on the Ancient Science of the Soul

The Splendor of Recognition

A Siddha Yoga® Publication / Published by SYDA Foundation, South Fallsburg, NY

Published by SYDA Foundation
PO Box 600, 371 Brickman Rd, South Fallsburg, NY 12779-0600, USA
(845) 434-2000 *www.siddhayoga.org*

Art Direction: Stephen Magner
Inside Page Design and Typography: Christel Henning
Cover Design: Susan Moriguchi
Cover Photograph: © Sambra Photo/Photonica
Print Production: Ana Carolina Kapp
Production Assistance: Robert Alter, Cynthia Briggs, Joël Dubois, Julian Elfer, Allen Kent, Vera Mezina, Valerie Sensabaugh, and Maria Syldona
Sutra Pronunciation CD: Producer, Molly O'Neill; Recording Engineer, Barbara Froscher; Production Engineers, David Cook and David Kingsley.

Printed in the United States of America

First published 2003

11 10 09 08 07 06 05 04 03 5 4 3 2 1

Library of Congress Cataloging-in-Publication Data
Shantananda, Swami
The splendor of recognition : an exploration of the Pratyabhijñā-hṛdayam : a text on the ancient science of the soul / Swami Shantananda with Peggy Bendet.
p. cm.
Includes bibliographical references and index.
ISBN 1-930939-00-0
1. Kashmir Śaivism — Doctrines — Early works to 1800. 2. Soul (Hinduism) I. Bendet, Peggy. II. Title.
BL1281.1547.S53 2003
294.5'2 — dc22

2003015594

To my beloved master Gurumayi Chidvilasananda,
who is for me the one source of inspiration and wisdom
in the ever-joyful play of divine Consciousness:

I offer this book in gratitude and celebration
on the twentieth anniversary
of your accession to the Guru's seat.

Acknowledgments

WITH IMMENSE REVERENCE AND GRATITUDE, I bow to my spiritual masters, Gurumayi Chidvilasananda and Baba Muktananda, from whom I have received the illuminating grace and insight that enabled me even to consider commenting on a work so fundamental as the *Pratyabhijñā-hṛdayam.*

I bow as well to the text's author, the sage Kshemaraja, for widening my vision on the path of divine recognition. It is my sincere wish that my commentary honors and reflects the knowledge held by him and by all of the great Śaiva masters from Kashmir: Utpaladeva, Abhinavagupta, Vasugupta, and others.

In my own study, I have been taught by many exceptional individuals, people who shared most generously their knowledge and their love of this tradition. My gratitude goes to the late Swami Tejomayananda, who guided the first Siddha Yoga study groups on Śaivite texts, and to professors Debabrata Sensharma and Paul E. Muller-Ortega, who have deepened my understanding through their writings and lectures and in our conversations. I want to offer special thanks to Carlos G. Pomeda, a dedicated student of Sanskrit and Śaivism who reviewed the text and supervised the translation of these sutras based on his master's degree thesis, *The Heart of Recognition: Kshemaraja's Pratyabhijñā-hṛdayam,* at the University of California, Berkeley.

To Peggy Bendet, my co-writer, I am heavily indebted for her long hours of patiently, diligently and lovingly giving body to my thoughts in words and drawing from me my personal experiences of these esoteric matters to ensure that I made the teachings relevant to seekers.

I prepared the original manuscript of this book in Spanish, my mother tongue, and it was through the meticulous work of Jorge Arditi, professor of the sociology of knowledge at the State University of New York, Albany, that my work was translated into English. The journalist Patrick Tierney was translator of the book's original Introduction.

Many others contributed tremendously to the creation of this book. The researchers included Harry Spier, Swami Anantananda, Swami Siddhananda, Surabhi Cannon, Judy Williams, Juliana Carvalho, and Christopher D. Wallis. The reviewers, who offered tremendously valuable insights and suggestions, were Stratford Sherman, Marilyn Goldin, Swami Ishwarananda, Swami Indirananda, Swami Akhandananda, Nancy Fales Garrett, Penelope Clyne, Laura Duggan, Liane White,

Susan Baker, Jonathan Shimkin, Kathryn Downing, Sandy Swindal, Karen Sweezy, Carol Overy, Anjali Yajnik, Margaret Simpson, Professor John Palka, Christopher D. Wallis, Kurt Joachim Reinelt, and Debra Schneider-Franz. Production of the book was skillfully overseen by our managing editor Pamela Williams and coordinating editor Anne Malcolm, and the manuscript was prepared with the generous assistance of Jennifer Bernstein. Judith Levi, stepping in at the eleventh hour, put together the index.

This book was first conceived as a series of articles published by *DARSHAN*, a Siddha Yoga monthly magazine. I wish to thank the various *DARSHAN* editors—including Swami Durgananda, Jane Ferrar, Ed Levy, and Lise Vail—for their assistance in polishing my initial thoughts on the first ten sutras and to offer my special thanks to Sanskrit scholar Sharada Patel, who undertook the English translation of those sutras.

Finally, my heartfelt gratitude goes to the generous donor who underwrote publication of this book, a gift that springs from a deep commitment to the Siddha Yoga teachings.

Contents

Foreword

IT IS A DELIGHT AND AN HONOR to be invited to say a few words about Swami Shantananda's new book on Kshemaraja's classic aphoristic text. Swamiji is someone whom I feel fortunate to count both as a friend and as an inspired companion and guide on the great path of Siddha Yoga *sādhana.*

Though it is usually considered impolite in India to speak about, or even to refer to, the life circumstance of a swami prior to his or her having taken the vows of monkhood, in this case I feel I have dispensation to do so since Swamiji has himself mentioned some of this in this book. I believe that Swamiji is the only member of his traditional order of Indian swamis to have been born and reared in Puerto Rico. He was encouraged by his family in his original studies in European art history, which led him to do graduate work in that discipline in London. This was followed, as he tells us, by a fateful and prolonged stay in India and by his encounter there with the Siddha Guru Swami Muktananda. After accepting the invitation of Swami Muktananda to take the vows of monkhood in a traditional ceremony in 1977, Swami Shantananda has dedicated his entire life to the practice and teaching of Siddha Yoga. Upon the passing of Swami Muktananda in 1982, Swamiji accepted Gurumayi Chidvilasananda as his Guru. His discipleship to Gurumayi for the last twenty years, as evidenced by his service and his commitment to her worldwide teaching mission, is truly superb.

I was first privileged to meet Swamiji in 1989, when I was invited to Shree Muktananda Ashram to participate in the teaching of a four-day course on the philosophy of Śaivism. One of my fellow teachers in this course was Swami Shantananda. I soon came to realize in our many conversations, often held in rapid-fire Spanish, that Swamiji was an ecstatic and amazing being. Despite his very real humility, it was evident that his years of dedicated practice had awakened and engendered in him a profound condition of inner attainment. His particular blending of a depth of insight with personal balance and light-hearted humor was both infectious and highly appealing. Over the years, our friendship has blossomed in many long conversations on topics of Śaivism, the arts, and passionate discussions of the personal adventures and challenges in the spiritual life. I am always fascinated to hear Swamiji recount stories of his own search for spiritual enlightenment. For Swamiji has an intimate way of telling a story that takes one straight into the situation, and then, at the culminating moment, one knows for certain that the experience he is describing is authentic—because one can palpably taste its power.

SWAMI SHANTANANDA IS AN EXEMPLAR of the spiritual life, and of the particular path to the Supreme that is known as Siddha Yoga. Because of this, in *The Splendor of Recognition,* Swamiji is modeling for us at least four distinct and significant ways in which to go about the process of studying a spiritual classic such as Kshemaraja's *Pratyabhijñā-hṛdayam.* Putting it differently, we might say that these four avenues are specific,albeit interconnected, approaches that have allowed such a text as this to open itself to Swamiji's deep and considerable understanding. They are, as it were, the sources for the spiritual authenticity and even, one could dare to use the word, authority that this book carries. These four "approaches" involve initiation; discipleship; sustained study and contemplation over time; and, finally, a deep, continuous engagement with and unfolding of the spiritual experience of the Self. As a result, the reader of this book receives not only an introduction to the philosophy of Śaivism as it is given in the *Pratyabhijñā-hṛdayam,* but also a view of the role and function this philosophy ascribes to such a text in the emergence of the experience of the supreme Self.

For this reason, anyone who wishes to understand the Śaivism of Kashmir will find this an extremely significant offering. The very process of *sādhana* and of *siddhi*—that is to say, of the conscious disciplined path of walking toward the supreme Absolute, as well as the process of ultimate recognition and establishment in an abiding and stabilized condition of such ultimate Reality—are only possible when the mind is saturated and imbued with the *śiva-dṛṣṭi,* the supreme viewpoint of Śiva. Thus, in this tradition, scriptural study of a very particular sort is central to enlightenment. In this regard, Swamiji's book itself serves as an elegant model of the deep study of a sacred text, study that occurs from within the perspective of an active and intelligent cultivation of *sādhana*.

For instance, Swamiji shares with us generously in this book with regard to the stirring of grace by his two masters. Over time, again and again, he has received the infusion of grace, the *śaktipāta-dīkṣā* or *guru-kṛpā* that both initiated and sustained the active impulse of his *sādhana*. It is this transmission of grace that first awakened his interest in these sorts of studies, and it is precisely the awakened *kuṇḍalinī* energy that resulted from this initiation that Swamiji sees as the illuminative fire of wisdom that has allowed him to steep and saturate himself in the study of and insight into the teachings of Śaivism. In this sense, it is also Swamiji's sustained discipline—his constancy in discipleship and in the practice of the prescriptions of *sādhana* as given to him over the last thirty years by his Gurus—that has stood as the foundation of this very process of study. It is, then, on the basis of grace, and of his own sustained efforts to cultivate the spiritual fruits inherent in this grace, that Swamiji has given himself to the contemplative study of the precise aphoristic formulations of Kshemaraja in the *Pratyabhijñā-hṛdayam*.

Here we should comment that, though he quite modestly mentions the absence of formal academic or scholarly credentials on his part, nevertheless what Swami Shantananda *does* bring to bear on the text is understood, from a traditional point of view, to be much more crucial than mere scholarly or intellectual training could ever be. In a more traditional sense, the *adhikāra*, the "entitlement" or "permission" to study a text, derives (precisely as Kshemaraja himself tells us) from *dīkṣā* and *sādhana* rather than from purely intellectual, scholarly knowledge. Above all, it is the unfolding reality of a direct, experiential realization of the great Self that serves as the basis for a capacity to understand what this text is describing. From the vantage point of these realizations, the otherwise abstract realities of the text become concrete and direct.

Nothing can substitute for this kind of study: extended over time, repetitively engaging again and again with this text in an act of devotion, and so penetrating ever more deeply into the levels of mysterious teaching that are densely embedded into these twenty beautiful aphorisms. The authority of this book is thus rooted in Swamiji's thirty years of dedicated daily practice of traditions of *sādhana* that are directly connected to, and certainly thoroughly imbued with and inspired by, the same currents of teaching and lineage that run through Kshemaraja's work. One might therefore say without exaggeration, that it is the lively voice of the divine Citiśakti hailed in the first sutra which is present and operating in Swamiji's own voice in this book.

READING THIS BOOK, written as it is with such delightful ease, mastery, lucidity, and modesty, one might be deceived into thinking that the efforts involved in the pursuit and cultivation of the above four "approaches" is an easy matter. This is not the case. Nevertheless, the difficulties involved in gaining the insights that Swamiji here conveys to us in such abundance, and the difficulties involved in the very fashioning and writing of a book of this nature (nearly twenty years in the making, I am told), are all, as in any great work of art, carefully concealed. Rather, the reader is offered an open doorway into the highest teachings of the Indian philosophical and spiritual tradition. With grace and modesty, with clarity of expression and simplicity of organization, Swamiji has created a sort of divine bridge across which many spiritual seekers will be able to walk into the great domain of the teachings of the Śaivism of Kashmir. Undoubtedly, this is but one text in a tradition that is now known for its exquisite body of revealed and exegetical literature. Yet here Swamiji has offered to us the kernel and the core! Just as Kshemaraja tells us in his title, the *hṛdaya,* the essential teachings.

Swami Shantananda's commentary on the *Pratyabhijñā-hṛdayam* signals a new moment in the evolution of the Western encounter with the esoteric traditions of medieval Śaivism, a moment in which many decades of dedicated practice combine with many years of careful and traditional study of a scripture to give rise to a quite beautiful result: a book that makes accessible to many what otherwise (as Swamiji himself says in his own Introduction) would remain inaccessible to most. As well, this book represents part of the continuing legacy of Swami Muktananda's announced and explicit agenda in his own spiritual mission to assist in the presentation of the knowledge of the Śaivism of Kashmir to the West. It has been long, though never commonly, known that it was Swami Muktananda's own personal engagement with and love for the texts of this tradition that helped to prompt the revival of their study through the publication of new translations and commentaries. This work has been continued and significantly expanded by Gurumayi Chidvilasananda through her establishment of the Muktabodha Indological Research Institute, an international organization of scholars dedicated to the preservation of India's spiritual traditions and texts. It is a credit to the true greatness of this contemporary Siddha Guru that one of her long-time disciples has been able to accomplish what is so readily evident in these pages: the fusion of direct experiential knowledge with the prolonged study and contemplation of a spiritual text.

Thus, the reader of this new book can expect to be guided—lovingly, with great clarity, and with great authority—into the deepest understandings of the intricacies of the Śaivism of Kashmir. If a reader pursues such study and dedicates himself or herself to its cultivation over time, then it is certain that the sorts of profound unfoldings, realizations, and insights offered here by Swamiji can become both a living reality and a rooted truth in the reader's own awareness. Such a process will in itself teach the reader about the powerful connections between such a study of a scriptural text and the unfolding of the deep, inner realizations of *sādhana.*

To my mind, the core of the gift that Swamiji here offers us in this book centers on these two dimensions. In *The Splendor of Recognition,* Swami Shantananda has given us his accessible and insightful commentary on the meaning of these famous Śaivite sutras. As well, he guides the willing reader into what is equally valuable and extraordinary: a deeper understanding of the potency of scriptural study as he himself has undertaken it. The result is beyond splendid—it is luminous, it is bright with a joyous relishing of the deep teachings and truths of this spiritual tradition.

Paul E. Muller-Ortega
Professor of Religion
University of Rochester
January 1, 2003

The Sutras

	SANSKRIT
1	*citiḥ svatantrā viśva-siddhi-hetuḥ*
2	*svecchayā svabhittau viśvam unmīlayati*
3	*tan nānā anurūpa-grāhya-grāhaka-bhedāt*
4	*citi-saṃkocātmā cetano'pi saṃkucita-viśvamayaḥ*
5	*citir eva cetana-padād avarūḍhā cetya-saṃkocinī cittam*
6	*tanmayo māyā-pramātā*
7	*sa caiko dvirūpas trimayaś caturātmā sapta-pañcaka-svabhāvaḥ*
8	*tad-bhūmikāḥ sarva-darśana-sthitayaḥ*
9	*cidvat tac chakti-saṃkocāt malāvṛtaḥ saṃsārī*
10	*tathāpi tadvat pañca-kṛtyāni karoti*
11	*ābhāsana-rakti-vimarśana-bījāvasthāpana-vilāpanatas tāni*

ENGLISH

Consciousness, in her freedom, brings about the attainment of the universe. 1

By the power of her own will, she [Consciousness] unfolds the universe upon a part of herself. 2

That [Consciousness becomes] diverse because of the division of reciprocally adapted objects and subjects. 3

Even the individual, whose nature is Consciousness in a contracted state, embodies the universe in a contracted form. 4

Consciousness herself, having descended from the expanded state, becomes the mind, contracted by the objects of perception. 5

One whose nature is that [the mind] experiences *māyā*. 6

And so he is one, is of two forms, consists of three, is fourfold, and is of the nature of the seven groups of five. 7

The positions of all philosophical systems are stages of that [Consciousness]. 8

That which is full of Consciousness, due to contraction of its powers, becomes a transmigratory soul, covered by impurities. 9

Even then, [the transmigratory soul] performs the five acts like [Śiva]. 10

These [five acts take place in the form of] illuminating [the object], enjoying it, knowing it, planting a seed [of limiting memories], and dissolving [those limitations]. 11

12 *tad-aparijñāne svaśaktibhir-vyāmohitatā saṃsāritvam*

13 *tat-parijñāne cittam-eva*
antarmukhī-bhāvena cetana-padādhyārohāt citiḥ

14 *citivahnir avarohapade channo'pi*
mātrayā meyendhanaṃ pluṣyati

15 *balalābhe viśvam ātmasāt karoti*

16 *cidānanda-lābhe dehādiṣu cetyamāneṣv api*
cidaikātmya-pratipatti-dārḍhyaṃ jīvanmuktiḥ

17 *madhya-vikāsāc cidānanda-lābhaḥ*

18 *vikalpakṣaya-śaktisaṃkocavikāsa-*
vāhacchedādyanta-koṭinibhālanādaya ihopāyāḥ

19 *samādhi-saṃskāravati-vyutthāne*
bhūyo bhūyaś cid-aikyāmarśān nityodita-samādhi-lābhaḥ

20 *tadā prakāśānanda-*
sāra-mahāmantra-vīryātmaka-pūrṇāhantāveśāt sadā
sarva-sarga-saṃhāra-kāri-nija-saṃvid
devatā-cakreśvaratā-prāptir bhavatīti śivam

12 The condition of a transmigratory soul is delusion, [brought about] by his own powers when he is not fully aware of that [his authorship of the five acts].

13 [However,] when one is fully aware of that [authorship of the five acts], the mind itself becomes Consciousness by rising to the state of full expansion through inward-facing contemplation.

14 The fire of Consciousness, even though [it is] hidden when it has descended to the [lower] stage, partly burns the fuel of that which is knowable.

15 On attaining strength, one makes the universe one's own.

16 The state of liberation while living is the unwavering experience of oneness with Consciousness, even while one perceives the body and so on, [a state that ensues] on the attainment of the bliss of Consciousness.

17 The bliss of Consciousness is attained through expansion of the center.

18 In this regard, the means [for expansion of the center] are dissolution of thoughts, contraction and expansion of one's power, cessation of the flow [of the incoming and outgoing vital energy], awareness of the point at the beginning and the end, and so on.

19 The permanent attainment of *samādhi* [is established by] contemplating one's identity with Consciousness again and again in the state following meditation, which is full of the imprints of *samādhi.*

20 Then, by entering the perfect I-ness, whose nature is the potency of the great mantra and the essence of the bliss of the light of Consciousness, one attains lordship of the wheel of the deities of Consciousness that carry out all manifestation and reabsorption. This is Śiva.

Introduction

A Journey of the Soul

THE *Pratyabhijñā-hṛdayam* IS A TEXT THAT SUPPORTS the journey of the soul. This scripture, which is the focus of our study, helps us to understand the gifts we've been given on the spiritual path. Even more significantly, it helps us explore that path to its very end.

The text was written by the Kashmiri sage Kshemaraja in the eleventh century C. E. Kshemaraja is a prolific writer who is considered by scholars to be the foremost disciple of Abhinavagupta, who is himself thought to have been a genius of the highest order and the greatest of all the teachers of the philosophy now known as Kashmir Śaivism. We know very little about the lives of these Kashmiri sages. Kshemaraja is believed to have been Abhinavagupta's cousin and to have lived with him as a student. More importantly, we know that Kshemaraja was exceedingly learned, studied closely with his master, and that he wrote brilliant commentaries on both the *Śiva-sūtra* and the *Spanda-kārikā* as well as other core texts of the tradition. Of the Kashmir Śaiva texts that have been translated into English thus far, most of the commentarial work has been from Kshemaraja.

It seems apparent that he composed the sutras of the *Pratyabhijñā-hṛdayam* and commented on them as an act of compassion to summarize and synthesize what he himself had learned from the tradition and from his own teacher. As Kshemaraja says in his introduction to the text:

> In this world, there are some devoted people who are undeveloped in reflection and who have not taken pains in studying difficult works like logic and dialectics. They nevertheless aspire after *samāveśa* [to merge] with the highest Lord, which blossoms forth with the descent of Śakti. For their sake, the truth of the teaching of *Īśvara-pratyabhijñā* [Recognition of the Lord]* is being explained briefly.[1]

I take exception with the venerable Kshemaraja on just one point: in giving the tenets of Śaivism briefly, he does not necessarily make them accessible—at least not to me. Perhaps they were more easily understood in their original historical context, but as for me, I have struggled for years to unravel this text.

The first question that comes up when one is studying a Śaiva scripture is, simply, why? Why do it? Why embark on a course of study that's

* Kshemaraja refers to the main source of inspiration for the *Pratyabhijñā-hṛdayam:* the *Īśvara-pratyabhijñā-kārikā.* This is the foundational text of the Pratyabhijñā School, written in the tenth century by Utpaladeva to establish logically the main tenets of his nondual philosophy.

going to be long and, at times, exceedingly difficult when, by the very language and examples employed, it seems that the material has so little connection with one's life in the modern world?

There are many possible answers: Contemplating scriptural concepts can bring discipline and refinement to the mind and an elevating focus to even the most mundane moments of one's life. By memorizing or by pondering the meaning of the twenty sutras of the *Pratyabhijñā-hṛdayam,* you can share the consciousness of great souls—an unarguably elevating and enriching experience. And these are just some of the benefits.

My own favorite reason for studying scripture is one I learned from my spiritual master, Gurumayi Chidvilasananda, concerning the way such an endeavor gives context and impetus to the spiritual journey. Gurumayi, a contemporary teacher who cherishes the traditional Indian forms of scriptural study, addressed this question one day about a decade ago. She had invited a group of students she was training as teachers, myself included, to meet regularly and contemplate one of India's most venerated philosophical texts. Each of these sessions began with one student reading aloud that day's sutra in Sanskrit and English. The reader offered a commentary, and the other students followed, each in turn adding his or her own understanding to what had been said.

One day, we explored an aphorism concerning the origin of scripture. The previous sutra had identified God as the source of the world, and this sutra, building on that foundation, said, "From its womb, the source of scripture"[2]—which meant to me that God is not only the universal mother, not only the creator of the world, but also the fount from which scripture springs. Then, as is quite common in this sort of inquiry, we considered an alternative reading of this same sutra:

"Scripture is the womb." From this, I understood that the power contained in sacred texts is itself a form of revelation, a key to understanding God and his creation.

Gurumayi listened to the students' comments on this profound scriptural statement, and then she offered a new dimension to our contemplation. She said that everyone in the world should become familiar with the understanding contained in this aphorism, because that very knowledge would change people's view of their spiritual paths. "People worry about not having spiritual experiences," Gurumayi said. "If they understood the meaning of this sutra, then they could take comfort in it. For the sutra says that everything is contained in God—our own Self, everything we are, is already there. This means that when the time is right, everything in *sādhana* will unfold of its own accord."[3]

In other words, on our spiritual quest nothing need be rushed or pushed. The effort that is most advantageous for *sādhana* is to study, to learn, and to apply—to put into action the teachings of those scriptural texts that explain the very meaning of *sādhana*. *Sādhana*, a term that denotes both the spiritual path and the spiritual practices that we employ as we move along that path, is a concept so interwoven with my own life that it's a part of my moment-by-moment awareness and, certainly, my daily vocabulary. For a spiritual seeker, to understand *sādhana* better is to understand better the very meaning of life. So, scriptural study has everything to do with our lives. Contemplation of a scripture can serve as a vantage point from which to view what happens to us, as a touchstone to help us through difficult moments, and as a foundation for an understanding that can help us turn our experience of life into knowledge and that knowledge into wisdom and joy.

This opportunity for scriptural study that Gurumayi shared with a small number of her students at the Siddha Yoga ashram in Ganeshpuri, India, she later opened to the entire *saṅgham.* In 1997 at the closing of the Siddha Yoga Global Conference in her ashram in South Fallsburg, New York, she announced to meditation teachers and leaders of meditation centers that the following year, instead of the usual conference topics, the entire community would undertake the study of a scripture. Gurumayi spoke eloquently of the benefits of such contemplation, saying that with scriptural knowledge, one's tongue refuses to complain about God's universe, one's ears refuse to hear negativities. She added:

> Your heart will be permeated with the knowledge of the all-pervasive Truth. In each face, you will be able to see the light of God. In each difficulty, you will see the Blue Pearl* shining. Your vision will change completely. As you study the scriptures, your experience of the great *śakti* [the power of God] will become more concrete. You will understand it in a very different way.[4]

The text that was chosen for study the following year was the very one we are undertaking here: the *Pratyabhijñā-hṛdayam.*

The Selection of This Text

Pratyabhijñā-hṛdayam is usually translated as *The Heart of Recognition*—the recognition of one's own deepest nature, of the heart of one's being. Gurumayi once asked me to write on the philosophy of Kashmir

* The Blue Pearl *(nīlabindu)* is a bright point of conscious light in all living creatures that is both the source and seat of the essential Self. For a more detailed description, see Swami Muktananda's *Play of Consciousness* (South Fallsburg: SYDA Foundation, 2000).

Śaivism, and I knew immediately that the text I wanted to focus on was the *Pratyabhijñā-hṛdayam.* This was the text that Gurumayi's own spiritual master, Swami Muktananda, had himself put forward as the best opening for our study of this philosophical tradition.

Baba Muktananda was the Siddha Guru who first taught Kashmir Śaivism widely in the West. The *Pratyabhijñā-hṛdayam* is a scripture Baba Muktananda frequently quoted, the one he most often directed his students to learn, and, in the final two years of his life, it was the subject of two of his lecture series. At the beginning of one of these talks, Baba said:

> In the Sanskrit language, *hṛdaya* is the heart, so this text is the heart of all philosophies. This book contains only twenty aphorisms. Although it has only twenty aphorisms, I have been studying it for the past thirty years, and I'm still reading it today.[5]

Baba identified the *Pratyabhijñā-hṛdayam* as one of the three major texts of Kashmir Śaivism, along with the *Śiva-sūtra* and *Spanda-kārikā,* and of all of them he most often recommended the *Pratyabhijñā-hṛdayam* for study. Why? Its brevity makes it the easiest, Baba used to say, and yet in spite of its length, it is complete. He once said:

> A person who understands these twenty aphorisms doesn't have to know a twenty-first. He doesn't have to know anything else in this world.[6]

From the late 1970s on, Baba spent much of his public time presenting the teachings of Kashmir Śaivism. He once described it as a philosophy for our times. He meant, I think, that Kashmir Śaivism is relevant to us because it is inclusive, it is comprehensive, it is understandable, and, more than anything else, it is generous. It affirms not only our own divine nature—there are other Indian philosophies that also attest to this—but the divinity of everything else as well, in this world and in any other world that we can explore, hear of, or even just imagine. The Śaiva sages of this tradition say that everything is God, and so everything and everyone is worthy of love and respect.

In Kashmir Śaivism, the divine splendor that is the Self—lying at the center, at the very heart, of all creation—is evoked by the word *hṛdaya.* Gurumayi uses the image of the heart as a leitmotif of her teachings on the Self. Just by having the awareness of this Self, Gurumayi tells us, we can create paradise in this very life. By "paradise," she implies a culture of kindness and mutual support, of generosity and humanity in our treatment of one another—a culture in which we live from the heart. Gurumayi says:

> Entering the heart is like coming into the center of the sun. There is no more you; there is nothing except the iridescent force of that light. When you are in the center of the sun, there is no way to block its light. It streams through you and around you. So by entering your own heart, you make the whole world a better paradise.[7]

And how do we attain this sublime state of affairs? It happens through a sea change in our own awareness that comes with an inner awakening. The Kashmiri Śaiva sages describe how a living flame of Consciousness is passed from the spiritual master to the disciple, bringing about this awakening as an act of pure grace.

My Introduction to Śaivism

In that respect, I suppose you could say that my own introduction to Śaivism occurred about thirty years ago when I first arrived at the ashram in Ganeshpuri, though philosophical knowledge was not something I was seeking at the time. I went because in those days it was fashionable to go to India on a spiritual quest. I had finished my schooling in Europe, and a trip to the East attracted me as the next step. I met a swami in an ashram near the Ganges in the Himalayan foothills, and he told me about Swami Muktananda, whom he described as "a great guru who lives in Ganeshpuri." When I first saw Baba Muktananda, he looked more like an artist to me, with his dark glasses and fluid gestures. He was handsome and dynamic. I liked him, and I liked the ashram itself. I had always lived a thoroughly undisciplined life, and here I was getting up every morning long before sunrise, trying to chant unfamiliar Sanskrit texts, working in the gardens—and yet feeling perfectly happy. This intrigued me, but still it wasn't an experience I felt it necessary to prolong.

After several weeks, I followed what I perceived to be the tradition of the place: I approached Baba as he sat in the courtyard in the late morning, thanked him for allowing me to stay in his ashram, and told him that I would be leaving the following day. He asked me where I was planning to go, and I replied that I wanted to visit the saints and ashrams and tourist attractions of South India. Baba said, "It's natural that you want to see so many beautiful things in India. Recently I went to a temple in my native region of Karnataka that I had never seen before. There were many people there taking notes and taking photographs of the beautiful sculptures." At this, he turned and began speaking to somebody else.

Notes and photographs? For a full minute, I remained standing before Baba, contemplating those words. For some reason, my mind couldn't seem to wrap itself around the significance of that image. And then it came to me—Baba was describing exactly what I had been doing in his ashram: taking photographs and making notes in my journal! I asked myself what I wanted to gain from this trip to India. Was I going to temples just to admire the architecture? And why was I in the ashram? Was I just a tourist, or had I come for some deeper pursuit?

The moment I had that thought, Baba turned back to me. He asked, "Have you observed any difference in the quality of your meditation while you were in the ashram?"

"Certainly, I have," was my reply. "You have a very nice meditation room. . ."

Baba said, "Why do you want to leave when you are beginning to attain something? It's better for you to remain here as long as you can so that you can consolidate what you have gained. Then you can leave."

I opted to stay, of course. A moment later, I asked Baba a question about a mantra I had received, a mantra I'd found ineffective for meditation. Baba told me, "Forget about it." He promptly handed me a card, which he'd extracted from a stack beside him on the platform where he sat. The card, large and ceremonial in appearance, was imprinted with the mantra *Oṃ Namaḥ Śivāya.** I took the mantra into that very nice meditation room. It was there that I did receive something, something profound.

Sitting on a cushion, repeating *Oṃ Namaḥ Śivāya* silently in my mind, I noticed the letters of the mantra begin to dissolve. I could perceive the words as pure energy, as a vibrant and intelligent power. This mantric power, which had a presence, also had an intention. I could feel it move to the base of my spine and proceed, gently, up the spine until it reached the top of my head. There it seemed that the power of the mantra opened

---

* *Oṃ Namaḥ Śivāya* is the initiation mantra given by the Siddha Yoga Gurus; it can be translated as "I offer my reverence to Śiva." Śiva is here understood as the Consciousness that is the Self of all.

itself out, like the petals of a blossoming lotus, and then slowly began to close again, wrapping itself almost tenderly around my mind. I had the very clear impression that this energy formed a grip on my mind and, then quite literally, put it to the side. Although I didn't open my eyes, it seemed as if I could see my mental activity neatly bundled beside me on the meditation cushion.

At that point, I became totally serene. It was almost as if I'd entered an inner space, a space that contained no images, no emotions, no mental conversations, no thoughts at all. Yet this space was not empty. It was filled with something, but what was it? All I was aware of at the time was a pervasive sense of sweetness.

After an hour and a half, I once again began to think, and one of the first things that came up in my mind was bewilderment. What was this all about? My mind wasn't at all active in that meditation—I could actually see it being held—and so what was the power by which I saw my mind? It was definitely a conscious experience. I knew what had happened, but how did I know?

I wasn't aware of it at the time, but the very process of formulating these questions was the beginning of that "consolidation" Baba had suggested that I undertake.

In those days, the early 1970s, Baba used to hold informal question-and-answer sessions three times a week. Some fifty of us who were living in the ashram then would gather in the shady veranda outside his apartment. People submitted questions on slips of paper, and when the translator read out your question, you would raise your hand. I never asked a question about this meditation experience, but again and again in these sessions, I heard Baba speak about the Self, the innermost being.

He always said the nature of this Self is *citiśakti,* a conscious power that pervades the entire universe. He described *citiśakti* as our own awareness. He called it the Witness, the consciousness that allows us to perceive things around us without getting involved in them. After hearing Baba speak like this a number of times, finally it dawned on me that he was describing exactly what I had experienced that day in meditation. It was a moment of *aha!* for me, an *Oh, THIS is who I am!*

This revelation was the turning point of my life, the inspiration for the years of *sādhana* that have followed, the identification I was making when I took vows as a monk, and it was also my impetus for studying the scriptures and writing this book. I said earlier that the Kashmiri sages speak of a passage of power, of *śakti,* from Guru to disciple, bringing about an awakening of consciousness. This initiation is the means, the scriptures say, of overcoming the first form of ignorance, *pauruṣa-ajñāna,* the innate ignorance we have of our own nature. It is not, however, enough. Even though I'd glimpsed the truth of my own being by using a Siddha Guru's mantra (one of the classic ways in which a Guru imparts spiritual power), I had no idea of the significance of what I'd experienced until Baba explained it to me. In doing so he was addressing the second form of unknowing, *bauddha-ajñāna,* which is intellectual ignorance.

Experience means very little without understanding. It is for this reason that we listen to the words of great beings and read the scriptures, turning the teachings over in our mind, comparing them to our own experience. In some ways, this intellectual knowledge is even more important than innate knowledge because once we understand the nature of our own being, we can always make the right effort to experience it; but without that understanding, even if we have the experience, we won't cherish it, we won't hold it—in time we may not even be able to remember that it happened.

With this in mind, let us look a little more closely at the *Pratyabhijñā-hṛdayam.*

In Twenty Concise Statements

In my attempts to understand certain concepts in Kshemaraja's commentary on the sutras, I have turned to the revealed scriptures of this tradition and to the writings of other sages—Baba and Gurumayi, as well as those who authored commentarial works. I was seeking further explanation, alternate interpretation, additional context. What I found in this search is that there is enormous richness in Kashmir Śaivism.

During the time this philosophy was being formulated, from the ninth through the eleventh centuries, the Śaiva sages of Kashmir developed a number of different philosophical schools based on older revealed texts, or Āgamas. They did not call them "Kashmir Śaivism." This is a modern term we use to refer to all these expressions of philosophical activity. They were originally called *śāsana* (teachings) or *śāstra* (scripture). There were at least five different monist systems active in Kashmir during that period: the Kaula, the Krama, and the Trika, as well as the two truly native Kashmiri schools, the Spanda and the Pratyabhijñā. Because Kshemaraja lived toward the end of this two-hundred-year period, he received the benefit of all of these points of view—and he included them all in his summary work, the *Pratyabhijñā-hṛdayam.*

Therefore, at times, in order to truly understand a phrase of his commentary or even just one word of a sutra, it is necessary to follow the meaning back to the original system from which it was drawn. For me, the doctrinal breadth of *The Heart of Recognition* has accounted for some of the challenge of my study and for at least part of my enjoyment of the text. A number of the gems, the understandings that have come to me in my study, are contained in this book. It was impossible, however, to include everything—impossible ultimately even to touch on all of the positions and suppositions, the axioms and principles that are identified and implied in the twenty concise statements of the *Pratyabhijñā-hṛdayam.* And even if I could have included them all, I would not wish to. Once when I was speaking to Gurumayi, I told her about my excitement in discovering a modern commentary that gave an extremely clear elucidation of one of the more abstruse aspects of Indian philosophy. I was describing at some length the brilliance of the author and some of the subtleties of his explanation. Gurumayi listened to me patiently, and when I paused in my commentary, she said, very gently, "Swamiji, don't get lost in that *vidyāraṇya,* that forest of knowledge."[8]

Gurumayi often tells her students that rather than acquiring vast tracts of scriptural information, what matters most is putting the teachings into action. With this illuminating instruction in mind, what I seek to do here is discuss the teachings I feel bear most directly on my own experience of spiritual practice and of life.

A Guide to Scriptural Study

In India until just a few hundred years ago, books were written by hand and, as a consequence, were very rare. Scriptures were presented orally, and though it was up to the disciple to learn by heart what he'd heard, Gurus condensed their teachings into succinct statements that could be remembered easily. This is the reason for the sutra form itself. A sutra is supposed to be the most concise statement possible for a teaching or cluster of teachings. As the student recites the sutra, the associated ideas are meant to come up in his mind with the ease and spontaneity of the unfurling of a rolled carpet. This may or may not be the case with some sutras, but it is nonetheless the premise underlying the course of study undertaken here.

Someone once asked me to suggest an approach he could take to scriptural study. I gave it some thought and formulated what I considered to be the essence of my own method of study. Here are, roughly, the steps I outlined:

1. Before you begin reading a commentary, recite the verse or sutra itself at least three times in the original language. (To help readers with this step, we are including a CD with the Brahmin priest Shri Vivek Godbole repeating all twenty sutras in Sanskrit.)

2. Read the commentary slowly, so that you don't miss something not initially apparent to you.

3. Take note of any word or phrase or sentence that you would like to consider in greater depth. Hold it in your mind as you go about your day. Refer your experience to it—an action, an interchange, a perception. Give yourself room for *aha!* moments. And then go back to the book.

4. Before you start exploring any particular teachings in a chapter, finish reading the entire commentary, so that you have the full context.

5. When you finally bring your focus to the phrase or idea you have selected, think about it. Ask questions: *What does the passage mean*

to me? What is the meaning of each word? What is the relationship between the individual words and the whole concept?

6. Look up the words or concepts in other sources from that particular philosophical tradition; perhaps there is another author or book that might shed some light on these for you. Particularly, look them up in the writings of your own spiritual teacher.
7. Then, sit quietly, invoke your teacher (or God in the form you most easily love), and ask for grace to unravel the meaning for you. Write down your understanding.
8. Ask yourself what you are going to do with this understanding. This is the most significant step: *How will I live my new understanding? How will I take it into my life?*

After enumerating these steps, I could see that something was still missing. I thought a little further, and it occurred to me that there was another principle, one so basic to my life that it had slipped my mind entirely. Since the moment I received spiritual awakening, I have dedicated myself to the pursuit and the attainment of the Self. In my life, every other priority is secondary to that one great goal. So before I begin reading any book, whether it's the *Bhagavad-gītā* or the *Śiva-sūtra* or the great text that we are undertaking here, I approach it with the light of my intention; I ask of the book: *How can this knowledge support me in what I have decided to do?* This is the tack I strongly recommend to all readers.

In the long view, it is also important to revisit a text. As we mature, our ability to comprehend the profound teachings that are presented to us naturally deepens. There is always more joy to be experienced when one reads a scripture once again. Baba Muktananda continued to study the scriptures throughout the whole of his life, even though he lived in the exalted state from which these texts were written. He once told me that he had read the *Śiva-sūtra* eighty times, and he said this with such obvious pleasure that I knew he would never stop reading the *Śiva-sūtra* or, for that matter, any other of the great texts of this tradition.

Some Definitions

In this study, we explore some concepts that require our understanding, at the outset, of a few basic terms. In the scriptures of India there are several thousand names for Reality, which is sometimes referred to as "he," sometimes as "she," and sometimes "it." Nonetheless, all these names indicate the same principle. One of the names given this luminous principle is Paramaśiva, Supreme Śiva. The prefix *parama* means "supreme" and the name Śiva is "the auspicious one" and is traditionally associated with kindness and friendliness and a benign disposition. Supreme Śiva is the one who bestows grace on humanity and is, thus, the highest source of benevolence. The basic tenet of this philosophy is that the whole of creation—all the principles, worlds, and beings in the entire universe—are fashioned ultimately by and of this one Reality, Paramaśiva. This, of course, includes you and me.

In Kashmir Śaivism, the awareness of the divinity of our own nature, of our heart, is called *pratyabhijñā.* This is more than just a Sanskrit word; it is a technical term of this philosophical system. By this I mean that a simple definition is not sufficient to convey the full meaning. *Pratyabhijñā* is often translated as "recognition," which implies recalling, remembering—as if on visiting France for the first time and seeing the

Eiffel Tower, one might recall having seen it in photographs and thus recognize it. This form of recognition is a purely mental operation. The act of *pratyabhijñā* spoken of by the Śaiva sages, and particularly by the tenth-century sage Utpaladeva who is the founder of this school of Śaivism, is something much more than an act of mental recall or perception. The *pratyabhijñā* that Utpaladeva describes means coming to the awareness of your own divine consciousness and, in that awareness, understanding that this sensibility has always been with you. This is not a thought but an immediate certainty, a sense of familiarity or rightness. For instance, when I had the experience in the meditation hall that I described earlier, while I was immersed in the experience, I wasn't at all surprised by it. It felt to me as if I had always been in that state. That was a glimmer of *pratyabhijñā*. In the final stages of *sādhana*, one recognizes the experience of God as one's own innermost being. Commenting on Utpaladeva's treatise, the *Īśvara-pratyabhijñā-kārikā*, Abhinavagupta states that the Self is a fact of everybody's direct experience. *Pratyabhijñā* arises where the two experiences, the knowledge of the Lord as supreme power and the awareness of one's own Self, are unified in one's experience: "Certainly, I am that very Lord."[9] In the same vein, we could say that the purpose of studying *Pratyabhijñā-hṛdayam* is to have *pratyabhijñā*, to recognize one's own Self as God. The experience is gloriously luminous and brimming with ecstasy—hence the title for our book, *The Splendor of Recognition.*

Once again, I want to caution you: This recognition is not just an exercise of the intellect. We can say the words, "I am Śiva," and if we say them several times, we will recall having said them before. This is not *pratyabhijñā*. For most of us the attainment of *pratyabhijñā* involves much more than just planting the seed. True attainment requires preparing the ground, nourishing the soil and tilling it; watering the seed so that it gestates, so that it sprouts and puts down roots; and then making sure the shoot receives enough sunlight so that it will grow. Then we can take nourishment. Then there's new life.

This is not to say that you are not in this very moment God. The full capacity for Self-realization is within each one of us right now. Gurumayi says this repeatedly. She never once said that we will be God at some future time; she only says, "You are the Lord," and then exhorts us to know that reality, to live in it at this very moment. For me, the most exciting aspect of Śaivism is precisely this: the power of our own awareness to create an extraordinary reality in every moment of our life. This is why we do *sādhana.*

Within this book, the reader will find anecdotes from my own spiritual journey and teachings from both of my beloved Gurus and from other saints and sages. While this is not a book about my own spiritual path, at times it might seem to be. The Siddha Yoga path is the foundation of my own spiritual practice, and the Siddha Yoga Gurus are my spiritual guides, and so when I comment on a spiritual text like the *Pratyabhijñā-hṛdayam,* I naturally have a great deal to say about Siddha Yoga.* This is the way I understand this scripture. I would never have thought to undertake such a bold enterprise had it not been for Gurumayi's invitation to do so. The credit for whatever is meritorious in this work must go to her unfailing grace.

In several places, I have spent some time in defining Sanskrit terms, but I must caution you that I am not a Sanskrit scholar. Throughout

* For those who wish to know more about Siddha Yoga tradition, please turn to Appendix A, "The Lineage of Masters."

the book, I have depended on the translations and expositions of others: both of Baba and Gurumayi, and of contemporary scholars such as Jaideva Singh, whose translation of the text was the one I first studied, and also of Paul E. Muller-Ortega and Mark S. G. Dyczkowski, whose lucid explanations of various aspects of Śaivism have greatly expanded my knowledge. I have tried to identify any material borrowed from others, but if there are places where I have been less than meticulous in this, I ask for the reader's forgiveness. My intention was not to mislead or to establish myself as a scholar. My primary focus is on the application of these sutras, on their relationship to spiritual work.

The book is meant for those who have tasted Kashmir Śaivism, who feel they have gained from that endeavor, and who wish to do as Baba invited me to do so many years ago—to stay with the study and to consolidate what they have learned. Everything that is defined and discussed, everything we consider or contemplate in these pages is only for the sake of *pratyabhijñā,* only for the sake of our coming to experience the splendor of our own heart.

Now, to Begin

Since ancient times in India, it has been traditional to begin a session of scriptural study by reciting mantras to invoke the highest power and ask for knowledge to be revealed. Kshemaraja opens his *Pratyabhijñā-hṛdayam* with verses praising Lord Śiva who performs the five acts in the eternal play of Consciousness: the creation, sustenance and dissolution of the universe, and the concealment and graceful revelation of Truth.

You are invited to entreat the great power with this mantra each time you open this book for contemplation. The translation follows.

Oṃ namo mangalamūrtaye
atha pratyabhijñā-hṛdayam

namaḥ śivāya satatam
pañca-kṛtya-vidhāyine
cid-ānanda-ghana-svātmaḥ
paramārthāvabhāsine.
Oṃ śāntiḥ śāntiḥ śāntiḥ

Om. Salutations to the embodiment of auspiciousness.
Now, the heart of recognition.

Salutations always to Śiva,
who performs the five acts,
makes the Highest Reality shine forth,
and illuminates the Supreme Goal:
one's own Self, a mass of bliss and Consciousness.
Oṃ. Peace, peace, peace![10]

1

Consciousness: The Creative Power of the Universe

Sutra 1

चितिः स्वतन्त्रा विश्व सिद्धि हेतुः

citiḥ svatantrā viśva-siddhi-hetuḥ

Consciousness, in her freedom,
brings about the attainment of the universe.

citiḥ:	Consciousness
svatantrā:	free, independent, self-reliant
viśva:	the universe
siddhi:	accomplishment, attainment
hetuḥ:	cause

As I embark on this commentary, a long-forgotten scene arises in my memory: I am about ten, standing on a balcony of my family's house, gazing with awe at the black chasm of the night sky. The house is in a valley of sugarcane fields on the eastern coast of Puerto Rico, and the stars shine with astonishing clarity, arrayed across the sky like a vast canopy of lights. The sight fills me with a sense of the immensity of all that lies before me, and I find myself wondering, *What is it that's out there? Is God looking at me from behind the sky?*

This ten-year-old's awed response to the luminosity of the universe is one that every human being has experienced at some time. It is the state from which the primordial questions of all philosophical traditions arise—the archetypal calls that come from deep within the human psyche. The finite mind glimpses infinity and, trying to encompass the experience with words, asks to know the nature of this numinous, mysterious Reality. The first sutra of the *Pratyabhijñā-hṛdayam* deals with this very theme.

Sutra 1 discusses the creative force of the universe. From a devotional point of view, it addresses the heart's longing to know the nature of God. The sutra offers an explanation of Reality—the nature of Reality and its relation to the world and to us, as human beings.

We can consider the rest of the sutras to be expansions of the first. For this reason, I've covered a number of fundamental concepts in this first commentary—more than with any other single sutra. My suggestion to the reader is that you treat each of the five main sections that follow as separate units, pausing between them if necessary to consider the material that's just been presented. These are subtle matters, and there is no need to speed through them.

Citi: The Great Light of Consciousness

In the *Pratyabhijñā-hṛdayam,* the highest Reality is most often designated by the term *citi.** Many Sanskrit words contain a rich collection of meanings that derive from their roots, and *citi* is no exception. *Citi* is one of the feminine forms of the root *cit,* which implies "to perceive, to observe, to appear, to understand," and "to know." That is to say, *citi* is that which is endowed with the power to know and to perceive; it is that which makes other things appear. And how does *citi* do this? *Citi* "makes" things appear in the sense that an object can only appear—or exist—in our experience when it is held in the field of our awareness. Each of these definitions of the term *citi* highlights capacities and activities associated with knowledge, with being conscious. For this reason, we usually translate the word *citi* as "consciousness." Also, Śaivism assigns feminine attributes to this power and gives it the name Citi since, as the sutra implies, she is the highest Goddess, the mother of all creation. Like a caring mother, Citi lovingly nurtures and supports the universe. It is Citi, supreme Consciousness, that is the central theme of this text.

What do we mean by the term "consciousness?" We could say that consciousness is simply awareness, the same power of attention, of intelligent knowing that we use in every moment of our waking lives. Most of us have a deeply held belief that there must be more to it than this—the supreme Consciousness that creates the universe must be substantially different from our own individual awareness. But is it really so? The *Pratyabhijñā-hṛdayam* says very clearly that if you want to understand

* The word *citi* is pronounced chit-ee. Further guidance on pronunciation can be found in "A Note on the Sanskrit" on page 402.

the highest Reality, you must first understand yourself. You yourself are your doorway to Reality. It is through your own consciousness that you can know supreme Consciousness.

You can do this right now, simply by turning your attention inward, toward itself—by becoming *aware* of yourself. You may feel that you are already quite naturally aware of yourself. After all, you know that you exist. No one needs to say to you, "Have you noticed that you're alive?" This is something that is so obvious that most people never even think about it. And yet now that you *are* thinking about it, how do you know that it's true? You could ask yourself, *Who is asking the question?* If you conclude that the question is coming from your mind, then take it a step further and ask, *Who is experiencing the mind?* If, for instance, your mind stops for a moment, when it starts moving again, ask yourself, *Who is it that knew the mind was quiet?*

Anyone who is accustomed to contemplating along these lines will have had some experience of an identity beyond the mind, beyond the personality with its name and nationality and cultural biases. That deeper sense of "I," which has never changed, which was with you in your childhood and has remained unaltered in every instance since, is pure Consciousness. It is *citi*.

There is a great deal of richness to be mined through this contemplation. Someone once asked Baba Muktananda which practices he recommended for spiritual development, and Baba told the person that self-discovery was the only place to begin:

> For your spiritual development, all you need to know is your Self. If you get to know your Self, you will get to know everything. The first and foremost question is: "Who am I?" Everything else

> comes later. Self-discovery is the root of all actions, all duties, all religious practices. First, know your own inner Self.[11]

This contemplation, that Consciousness is our own inner nature, does not arise specifically until later in the sutras, and yet it is the foundation of sutra 1, of all the sutras, and of spiritual practice. The discovery—or I should say, *rediscovery*—of our deepest nature is the entry point to our quest. What we are looking for, we find, is the Self.

Many people tell me that they find the term "Self" to be abstract. I'm often asked, "What is the Self? What does it look like? How can I know if I'm experiencing the Self?" The Śaiva sages have given us some ways to identify this divine power we know as the Goddess Citi and as the Self, and these are what we turn to now.

Light and the Awareness of Light

In his commentary on sutra 1, Kshemaraja hints at two aspects of Consciousness that we can explore in order to gain a clearer vision of Citi's nature: *prakāśa* (light) and *vimarśa* (awareness).*

Consciousness is light—not a light that can be seen with the eyes, but the light by which the eyes see. This light is the capacity of Consciousness to illumine and reveal, to make things appear and manifest. The term that designates this light is *prakāśa*. The word *prakāśa* derives from the Sanskrit prefix *pra*, which means "to go forth," and from the root verb *kāś*, which means "to shine, to be brilliant," and also "to be visible, to

---

* The concept that Consciousness has these two aspects is introduced by Utpaladeva in his *Īśvara-pratyabhijñā-kārikā* (1.5.2-3 and 1.5.11,13) to describe the nature of Reality and the means by which a human being obtains knowledge of that Reality. *Prakāśa* and *vimarśa* are notions so basic to the understanding of Kashmir Śaivism that Kshemaraja doesn't address them directly in the *Pratyabhijñā-hṛdayam* but assumes knowledge of them and builds from that.

appear, to see clearly." *Prakāśa,* then, is that which shines and radiates, illumines and reveals, that which brings objects forth, making them manifest.

The luminosity of *prakāśa* is what determines existence, the Śaiva philosophers tell us. The objects we perceive appear in their specific natures through the agency of the Great Light. *Prakāśa* is their source, that is, the ground from which they originate. This luminosity is, furthermore, the raw material of creation. What we perceive as fire or earth, metal, water, or any other material is nothing but a manifestation of the light of Citi, something we look at more closely in sutra 2.

This light of Consciousness is inextricably linked to the second aspect, *vimarśa,* awareness, which can be viewed as the reflection of that light on itself—the capacity of Consciousness to know herself.

Vimarśa is derived from the prefix *vi,* which means "apart" or "in two parts," and the root verb *mṛś,* which implies "to touch, to be sensitive or aware" and also "to consider, to reflect, to examine." *Vimarśa* is the capacity by which we can touch—that is, feel, know, examine—this miraculous universe that has been created, and we can then reflect on our perceptions and make them meaningful. In fact, perception isn't even truly possible unless we reflect on the meaning of what we perceive. Without *vimarśa, prakāśa* would be nothing more than inert light.

For me, one vivid image of the interplay between *prakāśa* and *vimarśa* is the miracle that is taking place at some point in the world in every moment: the dawning of a new day. When I was young, I used to love to watch the day's first traces of sunlight touch the valley where I lived. In the soft glow of the morning, I could begin to distinguish the contours of the distant hills, the silhouettes of the trees and rooftops, the wide expanse of the sugarcane fields that covered the valley like a carpet. Once the sun itself appeared on the horizon, the light would brighten, clarifying the lines of the landscape and bringing forth its vivid tropical colors. It seems to me that the light of *prakāśa* performs this function within us.

Prakāśa is the initial flash of form, the moment of watching the dawn before the labeling and reactions begin. *Vimarśa,* whose emergence is virtually simultaneous, is the discernment and discrimination by which you recognize what you are seeing. It's the knowledge, for instance, that one sweep of color or shadow is a tree, a specific kind of tree, a particular tree with which you have history, about which perhaps you have some feeling. *Vimarśa* is your awareness—even though you can't perceive this with your physical eyes—that the tree is quivering with life in every moment, from the roots to the very last leaf. It is also your capacity to know that you are looking at the tree, your ability to watch the movement of your own mind as you do so.

About the exquisite play between light and awareness, Gurumayi writes:

> The light of your awareness
>   is a glorious boon from God.
> It is your protection, your guide,
>   your wealth, your liberation.
> When you lose an object in the dark,
>   you can find it with a candle
>   or a flashlight. You can turn on a lamp.
> But when you lose your thoughts,
>   ideas, intentions, and goals
>   in the dark field of your mind,
>   how will you regain them?
> Only the light of your awareness
>   can illumine the field of your mind.[12]

Awareness is, of course, just another word for consciousness—small "c" individual consciousness. It's this capacity, which we all possess, that allows us to ponder the nature of supreme Consciousness, to ask ourselves: *How do I know Consciousness is real? What proof do I have that it even exists?* The answers don't lie in logical argument or scientific justification. As I said earlier, we ourselves are the entry point to the rediscovery of our foundational nature. It is by the power of awareness that we know, *I am alive, I exist.* The evidence of this awareness stands by itself as clear as water.

Please observe that we aren't discussing an abstract philosophical concept. We are simply giving a label—awareness, *vimarśa*—to an experience shared by all human beings.

This capacity for self-knowledge is, of course, vital to anyone on a spiritual quest. Anytime you ask yourself questions that take your awareness inside— *Who is seeing through my eyes? Who is experiencing the mind?* all the way to that ultimate question, *Who am I?*—you're exploring your own being through the power of self-reflection. You are coming in touch with *prakāśa* through the agency of *vimarśa.* The capacity by which we know ourselves is the same power by which supreme Consciousness enfolds herself to know herself.

At this point, we've discussed two distinct potentials for *vimarśa:* the power of Consciousness to know herself and her power to discern and distinguish between the various forms of the universe. There is a third potential, just as significant as the other two and simultaneous in its appearance: the power to create a universe.[13] Here, too, we can perhaps most easily understand how *vimarśa* operates on the cosmic level by examining what we already know about ourselves as individuals.

The sages of Śaivism tell us that we cannot truly perceive an object without discriminating and understanding what it is for us. Then our understanding itself so colors and flavors our experience of that perception that in the process of discerning what an object is, we have, for all intents and purposes, created it anew. Thus our very perception of the universe is, inevitably, an act of creation. This means that the world of our experience, the world in which we live and act and feel, is our own manifestation. We explore this extremely significant phenomenon further in the discussion of sutra 5.

Classically, *vimarśa* is compared to a mirror or a reflective pond, for it is in this metaphor that we can best distinguish all three functions of awareness. Like a mirror, *vimarśa* shows us ourselves and our creation. Each of us has a face—this is *prakāśa,* existence—but until we see that face reflected back to us through the capacity of *vimarśa,* we have no idea what our face looks like. Thus, the Śakta text *Kāma-kalā-vilāsa* says of *vimarśa:*

> She, the primordial Śakti, who excels all and who in her own true nature is eternal, limitless bliss, is the seed of all the moving and motionless things which are to be, and is the pure mirror in which Śiva experiences himself.[14]

Here *prakāśa,* which is pure illumination, is personified as Śiva, while *vimarśa,* the power of self-enfolding knowledge that both creates and knows its own creation, is personified as Śakti. A recurrent term in Śaivism, *śakti* is associated with power, energy, capability, strength, and might. It is this power of *vimarśa,* Śakti, that provides the mirror in which Śiva may see his own greatness reflected—and in which we, as well, may see ours.

As this passage indicates, there is yet another highly significant perspective from which we can view *prakāśa* and *vimarśa.*

The Primordial Couple

You'll recall that in the Introduction, the name we gave the ultimate Reality is Paramaśiva. The sages of Kashmir Śaivism tell us that as Paramaśiva begins to contemplate the creation of a universe—I like to imagine that Reality turns its face toward manifestation—there is an appearance of Śiva and his power Śakti, symbolizing the primordial couple. Together, never apart, Śiva and Śakti express the initial vibratory movement, the *spanda* of wanting to become the creation. In them there is the intention to manifest, though this intention is as yet unexpressed.

The attention of Paramaśiva as he turns toward his manifestation is a power, a vibrant yet extremely subtle resonance. This is why, in the texts of Śaivism, Śiva is represented through his *citśakti,** the power to illumine, to give existence and form, to bestow an appearance to things—in short, *prakāśa.* Śakti is represented in her aspect as *ānanda-śakti,* the power of bliss, for she not only experiences the immense satisfaction of being perfect, full, and ecstatic, but that very bliss has driven her to take the form of all created things. *Ānanda-śakti* is pure Consciousness, aware of who she is, the power that imparts knowledge

* This is in spite of the fact that earlier we identified Citi, Consciousness (also known as Citiśakti), as the Goddess. As was also said in the Introduction, Reality is sometimes identified as *he,* sometimes as *she,* and also as *it*—and yet ultimately all represent the same principle. As the power of illumination, *citśakti,* which is feminine (as all *śaktis* are), is the power that constitutes Śiva's true nature. The power is feminine; the power holder masculine. The two are inseparable, in the same way that I am inseparable from my capacity to experience bliss.

in creation—*vimarśa*—and, at the same time, she is the kernel of our experience of love.

The intrinsic nature of Consciousness is *prakāśa-vimarśa*—a marriage of clear perception and right understanding, in short, Śiva and Śakti as one. These two aspects are ever united. We say they are two only so that we can describe them. When we speak of one, we know that it includes the essence of the other. Joined, *prakāśa-vimarśa* is the fullness of divine Consciousness. The entire universe emerges from Citi's splendor without altering her nature in the least, without her being dimmed in the slightest. This fullness makes Citi aware of the perfection of her contentment. If something were taken from her, she would remain perfect; if something were added to her, she would still remain perfect. Citi knows that she contains within herself all possible creations and that she alone is Reality. Being aware of this wholeness, she experiences an immense bliss: *ānanda.* It is for this reason that knowledge of the Self is always accompanied by immense happiness.

The Bliss of Consciousness

Since *prakāśa* gives rise to *cit,* the principle of conscious existence, and *vimarśa* results in *ānanda,* bliss, Reality can be known as *cidānanda,* the bliss of Consciousness. One of the boons of spiritual practice and study under the guidance of an enlightened Guru is that one discovers and rediscovers, experiences and re-experiences this truth at all stages of *sādhana.*

I recall a time at Gurudev Siddha Peeth when we had been chanting a mantra for three consecutive days. I was feeling very expanded, literally reeling with joy. While the chant continued in the temple, I went out to the courtyard, where Baba was sitting with a group of his students gathered informally around him. I sat down at the back to meditate on the exquisite sensation of inner joy that I was experiencing. With no forewarning, this joy seemed to explode right out of my body, streaming from me in all directions. Then, wondrously, the objects I perceived through my five senses became imbued with vibrant luminosity.

There was an effervescence of sparkling bliss arising from my body, and when I looked up at Baba, I could see the same bliss pouring from him. Infinitesimal bubbles of ecstasy seemed to percolate from the floor of the courtyard, from the walls, from each person and tree and bird that I could see. For the time this awareness of ecstasy lasted, my sense of being a limited person dissolved into the expansiveness of *cidānanda.* I knew that I wasn't separate from God nor different from God's creation, nor were God's movements in any way distinct from my own. I experienced myself as one mass of radiant, blissful Consciousness, and the sensation was utterly delicious. In that moment, blissful within my own being like the Goddess Citi, I also experienced a sense of total freedom.* I was *svatantrā* in the midst of my own universe.

The Absolute Freedom to Create a Universe

Svatantrā means "free, independent, self-reliant." Or more precisely, following the meaning of the prefix *sva* (one's own) and the noun *tantra*

* It is important to remember that these various experiences of enlightenment that I am describing from my own *sādhana* occur for every seeker. During the time of our *sādhana,* such experiences seem to wax and wane, and they are often separated by periods of apparent dryness. The goal of *sādhana* is to reduce and then eliminate the interstices so that finally, like our Gurus, we experience uninterrupted *cidānanda.*

(depending on), we could say that in being *svatantrā,* Citi depends on only herself. Supreme Consciousness has *svātantrya,* complete freedom to do or not to do, to assume any form or not to assume a form at all. Citi can manifest herself as any finite form, and at the same time she can remain infinite; she can be beyond limitations, and she can become all limitations. She can do all of this alternately or simultaneously, as she wishes. Consciousness depends solely and exclusively on herself. Nothing hinders her freedom since there is no power apart from her. *Svātantrya* is the will set free. It is irrepressible volition. The definition of Reality as *svātantrya-śakti,* "the power of freedom," is one of the distinctive characteristics of Kashmir Śaivism, and it is a key to *sādhana* as well.

The implicit message of sutra 1 is this: Just as Citi is free and unencumbered in the expression of her will, we too are free from dependence on outer circumstance. As we look at our own lives, we may feel that we are not free. We may feel that we do not have sufficient freedom of will, that we cannot in fact determine the circumstances of our lives or even choose our own associates. This is because most of us think of freedom as the ability to have what we want. The Siddhas, on the other hand, are more likely to describe personal freedom as the capacity to want what we have —to experience joy in the face of any circumstance and, thus, to exercise our own will to choose what God has willed for us. There is, paradoxically, tremendous freedom in such a stance—and we know this not by thinking about it or speaking of it, but through our direct experience in such a moment. These experiences of autonomous joy, which can arise in even the most disagreeable circumstances, are often what inspire a person to commit to a spiritual quest. We want to understand this joy, to fathom its source, to experience it all the time. In her book *The Yoga of Discipline,* Gurumayi says:

> The very fact that you are a seeker means you want to know the Power behind the universe. You want to unearth the mysterious laws behind events. You want to understand the independent joy that you come across every now and then. Think of a time when, all of a sudden, you were happy. You didn't do anything to make yourself happy, but you were happy. This happiness is called *svayambhū*, spontaneous. It is self-born joy. As a seeker you want to know what causes this.[15]

Taking this still further, the Śaivites create no separation between supreme Will and the individual will. These sages say our own power of will is the divine Will in a contracted form. In other words, when we are able to cleanse this power of the mind, we can experience the full glory of *citiḥ svatantrā.* As our *sādhana* progresses and the mind is cleansed of egoistical motivations, we become increasingly aware when we are and are not aligned with divine Will. This process is described in greater detail in our exploration of destiny in sutra 9. For now, it's enough to say that when our will is clear and specific, it is possible for us to carry through our vision, to bring into being what we intend to do. Baba Muktananda says:

> A human being has the freedom to become anything. By his own power he can make his life sublime or wretched. By his own power he can reach the heavens or descend to the depths. In fact, the power of a human being is so great that he can even transform himself into God. God lies hidden in the heart of every human being, and everyone has the power to realize that.[16]

This is the essence of the *Pratyabhijñā-hṛdayam*—the understanding that true Self-realization is to become fully *svatantrā,* fully free. It is not enough to have a glimpse of divine splendor in our lives from time to time. We must become that divine splendor.

Sutra 1 says that this *citiḥ svatantrā* is the cause *(hetu)* of the attainment *(siddhi)* of the universe *(viśva)*. For Kshemaraja, the term *viśva,* with which he designates the universe, has a more specific and technical significance as well: *viśva* also refers to the entire array of *tattvas.*[17] We discuss the *tattvas* in sutra 4; for now we can say that they are creative principles, encompassing all entities, manifest and unmanifest, and that together they constitute the universe. The word *siddhi* also indicates fulfillment or accomplishment, and refers to the actions by which Consciousness carries forward and accomplishes or attains her creative aims. Citi is *hetu,* "the cause," of manifestation—which includes not only creation but also maintenance and reabsorption as well. These are the three main processes that occur in the universe: coming into being *(sṛṣṭi),* continuing existence *(sthiti),* and dissolving or retreating into repose *(saṃhāra).* Again, these are concepts we look at in greater detail later. In his commentary, Kshemaraja has this to say about the appearance, and disappearance, of the world:

> It is only when Citi, the ultimate consciousness-power, comes into play [literally, she raises her eyelids] that the universe comes forth into being and continues as existent; when she withdraws its movement [when she lowers her eyelids], the universe also disappears from view. One's own experience bears witness to this fact.[18]

I particularly cherish the sage's metaphor of the eyelids. For me it's a vivid reminder that our knowledge of Reality is based on our own day-by-day experience. The sage is saying that when we open our eyes and become aware of the world around us, we are creating our world. And at night, as we close our eyes in sleep, we're dissolving that same world. Just as the Goddess Citi creates a universe, so do we create one every day in our own experience.

If you have ever undergone sensory deprivation for some time—it doesn't have to be all of your senses, just one is enough—and then felt the bliss that comes when that sensory appetite is slaked, you may also have some glimmer of the bliss of Citi in her creation of the universe. Recall what it is like to eat food when you are truly hungry or the flavor that water can have—the delight you can take in its very wetness—when you have been thirsty for some time. This opening and closing of our senses is exactly what Citi does in the creation of the universe. This is never clearer than when you see the delight an infant takes in playing peek-a-boo. You hide and then you leap out, or possibly just hide your face behind your hands and then pull your hands down—and the child is enchanted! A world is hidden; it emerges; it is hidden again . . . What is most astonishing is that an infant almost never tires of this game. The hands can come up and go down, come up and go down almost indefinitely, and the child never stops being entranced. Why? In this simple game, the child is playing as God plays. The act of creation is simultaneously an act of perception. When I perceive something, I am creating it for myself. The creation exists as long as I retain it in my perception, and when I dissolve what I perceive, for me it ceases to exist. (And, since no one else perceives it in quite the same way, we can say that it has also ceased to exist as a fact.)

In his book *Mukteshwari,* Baba Muktananda refers to this fundamental truth of human life, addressing himself as if speaking to a seeker:

Because of your existence,
Creation exists.
If you do not exist,
nothing exists.
Muktananda, first know your Self.

What are you looking for
east and west,
north and south,
above and below?
Muktananda, the whole universe
you alone are, you alone are,
you alone are.[19]

When I first read the words *you alone are,* I was seized by a feeling of immense loneliness. I thought, *I'm all by myself.* Later it occurred to me that this is not a message of emotional and psychological isolation. This *you* Baba refers to is the essence of creation in all its magnificence. The experience of union, the sense that we are all one, is precisely the kind of aloneness Baba is talking about. Simply stated, Baba is addressing the supreme Self in you, as you. He is saying that you and the universe are the same principle, and further, for this glorious creation to exist, you must be present. In other words, you—your inner being, the Self—can generate a universe out of your own Consciousness. This is precisely the message of sutra 1: Consciousness is the cause of the universe. Only Consciousness is capable of creating the cosmos, and only Consciousness can be the material from which that cosmos is made. Everything depends on Consciousness. The creative capacity of all individuals, of all of nature, has its source in Citi and derives its power from Citi. There is no manifested thing that, in and of itself, has the capacity to know Consciousness without engaging its own power of Consciousness. Only Consciousness can know herself, as well as everything that takes form within her.*

Our Self and Our World

When we begin to understand and to perceive everything as Consciousness, as one Reality—or as a reality of One—an unsettling thing happens: the world itself seems unreal at first. Or, at least, it seems grounded in a strange reality. We think that if everything is *citiśakti,* then the universe does not exist, for what then is different from Consciousness? In other words, if God is the only Reality, then how could you or I exist, or our families, or the world we inhabit? But isn't that absurd! The world does exist. We know that. We're living in it. Yet if the world exists, as our senses tell us, and it is nothing but Consciousness, as the Śaivite sages suggest, then why is one thing different from another? Is every manifestation equally real? And how does Consciousness become the world?

To establish the causal connection between the Creator and the creation, Śaivism offers an explanation very much its own: Supreme Consciousness, through her own free will, contracts herself to assume the manifold forms and objects that make up creation. In Sanskrit, contraction or condensation is called *saṃkoca.* It operates on much the same principle as water freezing to become ice or vaporizing to become steam or humidity. Though these forms are different—one liquid, one solid,

* Kshemaraja alludes to this in his commentary on sutra 1: "Therefore space, time, and form, which have been brought into being and are vitalized by it *[cit]* are not capable of penetrating its real nature"; trans. Jaideva Singh, *The Doctrine of Recognition* (1990), p. 46.

one vaporous—in essence they are the same; their molecular composition is unchanged. If ice is melted or vapor condensed, the substance is water once again. In a similar metaphor, the sage Abhinavagupta seems to bring out the sweetness of *ānanda* in its free and purposeful gesture of condensing into the world we experience:

> As a sweet watery juice will become thick and thicker still, lumpy sugar and refined sugar are all only sugarcane juice, so all phenomena are merely different states of Śiva, the Lord in his universal aspect.[20]

The difference between this process and the condensation of Citi to create the solid forms of the universe is that the creative act of Consciousness happens outside of time and free from the limitations of space and form, within which the laws of cause and effect operate. As she exercises her *svātantrya-śakti,* her power of free will, the one Reality projects her light like an explosion of fireworks on a dark night, sending forth brilliant sparks that assume the countless forms that inhabit the cosmos. It is in these objects and worlds—in creation itself—that we encounter the parameters of time, space, and the natural laws of cause and effect. Prior to creation, the sages say, there is only the undifferentiated potential of the Goddess Citi. While there may be tremendous differences in the language and metaphors employed by science, many theoretical physicists appear to hold somewhat parallel views—particularly concerning the absence of natural laws at the point at which creation occurs.*

* The eminent physicist Stephen Hawking suggests that creation occurs as the "event horizon," on which all objects appear, emerging from what he calls "the singularity," that point when space and time are born. Beyond this singularity, Hawking says, the natural laws of the universe have no foundation. One source for Hawking's theories is his classic *A Brief History of Time* (New York: Bantam Books, 1988).

The act of manifestation is the coming forth of what is already contained in the undivided oneness of Consciousness. In a classic analogy, Kshemaraja clarifies this point:

> The entire universe is already contained in Supreme Consciousness or the highest Self even as the variegated plumage of a peacock is already contained in the fluid of its egg. *Vimarśa* is the positioning of the Self that leads to manifestation.[21]

A modern metaphor for the peacock's plumage is the way every aspect of one's genetic inheritance—stature, the color of the eyes and hair and skin—is contained in the DNA molecules. *The positioning of the Self* is a reference to a quality of Consciousness that we might call creative vibration. In its original, pure state, *vimarśa* (discernment) is a reflected brilliance that throbs with a movement of extreme subtlety.

The sage Vasugupta calls this primordial vibration *spanda,* the pulsation by which Consciousness becomes the source of all creation. This will come up again in the course of our study. For now, Kshemaraja is saying that the vibrations of *spanda* pulsate from the heart of *vimarśa,* which is Consciousness's awareness of herself. This movement is described with the adjective *kiṃcit calanā,* which means "an infinitesimal stirring," or "the very slightest and most tremulous movement." Of course, with the term "movement," we are usually referring to a motion at least as tangible as a pulsation, like an electric wave moving from socket to cable. The *kiṃcit calanā* of Consciousness, which is beyond space and time, is a vibration so extraordinarily subtle that its motion is not at first externally directed. These vibrations occur without interruption, in a throbbing motion of contraction and expansion through which the cosmos appears and disappears. When you blink, your own universe appears and disappears from sight—and we do this every six or seven seconds, so it happens thousands of times each day. It is through *spanda* that the cosmic eyes of Consciousness open *(unmeṣa)* and close *(nimeṣa)* and the universe unfolds and refolds itself in a rhythm of creation and dissolution. The universal pulsation of *spanda* happens at dizzying speed, ceaselessly renewing its manifestation.

As yogis, it is significant for us to know that the world in which we are living at this point in time is not the same as the world that existed just a moment ago. This cosmic process is not unlike what occurs within each of us, individually. This is why spiritual transformation is always possible for us, why it's a possibility for us all. Rather than holding on to notions that fossilize our lives into undesirable patterns—grudges, visceral fears, noxious habits, or even just the opinion that we can't change—we have the power to align our intentions and activities with the rhythms of the *spanda,* and thereby to tap the source of genuine contentment. For me this is the most significant message of this sutra: like unencumbered Consciousness, we as individuals possess the freedom to establish a universe in which we can live blissfully. Recognizing this gives us access to a part of our nature that is innate, though often forgotten.

The Triad of Knowledge

Citiśakti casts herself into creation. She becomes innumerable forms, and each of these forms is a world unto itself. In other words, each individual being in creation is the center of his or her—or its!—own world of experience. Each one is what is known in Śaivism as the knowing subject, the *pramātā.* And for each subject, everything else is an object of knowledge, a *prameya.* Further, the relationship that each subject has to its world, to its "objects," is established through the act of perception, *pramāṇa.* These three—the knower, the known, and the act of knowing—are seen as the triad of knowledge, and together they form the fundamental structure of any creation.

These three forms of knowledge arise out of the fragmentation of the natural attributes of *prakāśa-vimarśa* (illumination and creative awareness) in the contraction of Consciousness. The metaphor of light that we used earlier applies perfectly here. The subject is the light that illumines, the object is that which is illuminated, and the relation between them is a function of the illuminative power—knowledge. In the Āgamas, the revealed scriptures of this tradition, the subject or the knower is likened to fire, a luminous and illuminative element whose flames devour everything they touch. It is said that all forms, or objects, are fuel for fire and are reduced by fire to ash. In the same way, Citi reduces the perception of differences to a vision of unity.

When Brahmin priests make offerings to the fire in sacred rituals such as the *yajña,* this sacrifice and the accompanying mantras and prayers are consumed by Agni, the lord of fire, the light that bears witness to ritual actions. Agni carries these offerings to the deities, the powers of the cosmos who, thus propitiated, rest satisfied and are inclined to offer blessings. Likewise, an individual becomes tranquil and blissful in the Self after digesting the world of diversity. The blessing bestowed is immense joy. The Āgamas often identify knowledge, *pramāṇa,* with the sun, which derives its light from fire and illumines all things in the world, making them perceivable to the subject. The known, *prameya,* is like the moon, which becomes visible as it receives and reflects the sunlight. Just as moonlight has a nectarean nature, the objects of perception can also give off nectar, which can lure us, binding us to the things of this world.

To the yogi, however, what is most important here is the knowing subject, for it is the subject that is both the origin and goal of all cognitive acts. In other words, if you, as the knower, are not present, there is no experience of the world. This is what Baba is referring to in the line *If you do not exist, nothing exists.* In any and every situation, both the object and the knowledge of that object depend on the perceiving subject. Abhinavagupta makes the same point in slightly different terms:

> Nothing perceived is independent of perception, and perception differs not from the perceiver; therefore the [perceived] universe is nothing but the perceiver.[22]

We might ask, just who is this perceiver on whom the entire universe rests?

The word *pramātā* means "one who understands, one who holds authority" and "one who measures." That is to say, the Self. Enshrouded in the limiting conditions of a body and a mind, the supreme Self no longer perceives the total unity of free Consciousness, but perceives only separate measurable units. When we walk through the woods and see the trees, smell the fragrance of wildflowers, hear birdsong, and feel the cool water of a stream running over our feet, we are having fragmentary experiences of Consciousness; we are aware of what can be measured and classified. In spite of the limited nature of our ordinary perception, however, the perceiver never ceases to be Consciousness. Just as fire radiates light, the Self sends forth the modulated vibrations of *spanda* that swiftly move to seize the experiences that we have of this world. As a center of untainted Consciousness, the subject is the true authority of knowledge, the one who understands what is truly happening, the one who makes sense of the world, within and without. This is only natural, since it is this same Consciousness that creates everything it perceives.

In my own experience, understanding the subject has been the most significant lesson of the spiritual journey. Until I became aware of my own awareness in meditation, I didn't know myself as a conscious being. Like most people, I took my own consciousness for granted, much as I took the presence of the material world for granted. Once I began to meditate, I began to experience my ability to perceive my own life. Then my awareness of that perception began to change my relationship with what I saw—with my reactions, for instance, and my own emotions. I became a witness of my life. I began to take things less personally, and so I could relate to the world around me in a more meaningful way.

So that you can either develop or strengthen your ability to witness your world from another perspective, I invite you to undertake a contemplative exercise. First take a few deep breaths, inhaling and exhaling fully. Then let your breathing return to normal. Now, without straining your attention, begin to perceive yourself in your surroundings. Try not to focus on particular details but on the sense of space itself. Ask yourself: *Is my consciousness in this space? Or is this space in my consciousness?*

We will revisit this contemplation further on, and so there is no need to complete our discussion of it here. Besides, it's very useful to sit with a question like this. As I found, the delicious *aha!* of experiencing the answer is much more edifying than just hearing it.

The Highest Reward of Life

Near the end of his commentary, Kshemaraja makes an expansive gesture that Sanskrit scholars often take great pleasure in: that is, he makes a semantic shift, putting forward secondary meanings for some of the words and thus, with great skill, altering and enhancing the interpretation of the sutra. It seems clear that his intention is to bring forward the ultimate purpose for having the recognition of Citi. In his new interpretation, the word *siddhi,* which was "attainment," now becomes "yogic attainment." Thus, sutra I becomes:

Consciousness, in her freedom,
brings about the attainment
of [the true nature of] the universe.

In this interpretation, Kshemaraja calls upon two subsidiary meanings of the word *siddhi* that evoke yogic attainment: bliss and liberation. Thus, the phrase *viśva-siddhi* of the sutra now signifies *bhoga,* the enjoyment of the universe in its true nature, which we now see as the blissful play of Citi. By extension, *viśva-siddhi* is transformed into the experience of *mokṣa,* liberation from the limitations assumed by Consciousness. When we speak of limitations, we refer to our identification with the sufferings of life and the feeling that makes us believe we are insignificant and bereft of happiness.

Here Citi plays the revealing role of grace by which we recognize our freedom and the incomparable joy of the Self. Citiśakti, of her own free will, irradiates the darkness in which we were engulfed and bathes us in her exquisite brilliance. The yogic attainment of both enjoyment of the world *(bhoga)* and liberation *(mokṣa)* as unrestrained and joyful expressions shows us that Consciousness herself is the *summum bonum,* the goal of the greatest well-being and the highest reward of life. In this attainment, creation is respected as a sacred place, for it has helped us to reach the ultimate end and it continues to be the divine playground of Citi.

This may sound magnificent, but how do we get there? What do we have to do to reach the goal? In answer to this question, Kshemaraja gives another turn to the sutra; he takes the word *hetu,* which was "the cause," and reads it as "the means"—in this case, the means to recognition, to divine knowledge. The sutra now reads:

**The universe is the means
to attain the realization
of Consciousness in her freedom.**

Our individual universe is now seen as the indispensable instrument for yoga. The *siddhi,* or attainment, consists in merging all the perceptions that we experience as separate from us in the space of the knower and thereby identifying with all that we "know." We will thus realize the true nature of our universe as the play of Consciousness in her full freedom. In this interpretation, sutra 1 is telling us that any experience is a potential means for gaining full knowledge of the supreme Self. Ordinary people get lost in the objects of the world, in wanting and not wanting various people and situations and all manner of things, both material and subtle. In the face of overwhelming distraction, they forget their own truth. Yogis, on the other hand, remain alert; they keep their attention on the union that is the fundamental relationship between themselves and the world. We find the essential intention of this effort summarized in a verse of the *Vijñāna-bhairava,* one of the Āgamas Kshemaraja quotes in his commentary on this sutra:

> The consciousness of object and subject is common to all the embodied ones. The yogis, however, have the distinction that they are mindful of this relationship [between them].[23]

The majority of the greatest expounders of Śaivism in Kashmir were yogis who observed a regular domestic routine, with wives and children and the responsibilities of supporting their families. Their students, men and women alike, felt that the world did not interfere with their inner search for attaining God. By their example, we can see that whatever our role may be—and there are many in our world!—the journey of the spirit is undertaken in this body and in this life. This opportunity is a precious gift of the Goddess Citiśakti. The sages of Kashmir Śaivism encourage us to approach every moment as an opportunity to experience the bliss of Consciousness. Understanding that Citi has created this universe, we can take the view that life itself is the divinely offered means—the only means!—for the realization of the supreme goal.

2

The Mirror of Consciousness and Its Countless Reflections

Sutra 2

स्वेच्छया स्वभित्तौ विश्वम् उन्मीलयति

svecchayā svabhittau viśvam unmīlayati

By the power of her own will, she [Consciousness] unfolds the universe upon a part of herself.

sva: own*
icchayā: by her will
sva: own
bhittau: on a part, a portion, a wall-like surface
viśvam: the universe
unmīlayati: causes to appear, unfold or manifest

---

* Due to *sandhi*, the grammatical conventions that govern adjoining Sanskrit words, when *sva* (own) and *icchayā* (by her will) appear together in that order, they're combined as *svecchayā*. This sort of spelling change, which frequently arises in the sutras, stems from the necessities of pronunciation.

IN THE SECOND SUTRA, Kshemaraja expands our understanding of the freedom that Consciousness has to create a universe, stating that she acts of her own volition *(svecchayā)*, free from the impediment or influence of any will other than her own. How do we know this is true? Because Citi causes the universe to appear *(unmīlayati)* upon a part of her own being *(svabhittau)*. The significance of this term *svabhittau* is tremendous. Citi unfolds this universe upon only a fraction of herself; with all that the universe is, still Citi herself is greater.

In the first sutra, we learned that Citi is the cause of the universe. In the second, Kshemaraja tells us that she is the *only* cause: she is not only the maker of the universe, she is also the material from which it is fashioned.

The question of creation has always fascinated me. For a number of years I studied art history, and at one point, when I was in my twenties and living in Madrid, I asked a well-known artist to paint my portrait. As he worked—the back of the canvas toward me—I couldn't see what he was painting. Instead I watched the play of expressions going across his face: he was clearly processing his understanding of his vision. At the end of a session, I was always amazed to see what was on the canvas.

I never thought it looked like me. The portrait was identifiable as a representation of me—the cast of my features, the colors of my jacket and shirt—yet it wasn't truly a likeness. Of course, it didn't look like the artist, either. The painting was another entity, a new reality that this artist had created out of his ideas of me and his manner of representing those ideas.

It is only Citi who can create wholly from her own being—and in her case, she is not only the artist, with ideas and styles of expression, she is also the paint and the brush and the canvas. She is everything.

In one sense, this is obvious on the face of it. If it were not so, Citi would not have free will, for she would be subject to some other power and, as a consequence, she would be neither supreme nor fully conscious. Freedom, you may recall, is one of the attributes of Consciousness. Citi's power of freedom, her *svātantrya-śakti,* gives her total sovereignty over everything she creates, a power that cannot be detached from the splendor that is the one Reality.

Upon this conscious screen, sutra 2 indicates, the universe unfolds *(viśvam unmīlayati).* The verb *unmīlayati* comes from the root *mīl,* which signifies opening the eyes or raising the eyelids, and by implication indicates something that becomes visible or appears. The term *unmeṣa,* which came up in our discussion of sutra 1 to describe the unfolding of creation, derives from the same root. Kshemaraja explains that in this context, *unmīlayati* brings into expression that which already exists within Consciousness in a subtle form—just as that painter expressed on canvas a vision that already existed within his own mind. Even without exercising her full creative capacity, Citiśakti already contains the entire universe within the infinite space of her own luminous womb. And when she does bring the world into being, as we have said, Citi herself is compressed into the entire gamut of her creation's immensely varied forms. So states the Supreme Being in the *Vijñāna-bhairava:*

> Just as waves arise from water, flames from fire, [and] rays from the sun, even so the waves of the universe have arisen in differentiated forms from me.[24]

The Reflection of the Object

In his commentary on sutra 2, Kshemaraja explains the relationship between Citi and the world she creates by invoking the metaphor of the mirror: Citi is the mirror and the reflection is her creation. In this case, we're ignoring the presence of an object that is being reflected; the metaphor deals only with the relationship between the reflection itself and the mirror. The concept is known as *pratibimba,* "the reflection of the object," and it comes up often in the writings of the Śaiva sages of Kashmir. In the *Paramārtha-sāra,* Abhinavagupta employs this image to explain something of significance about the nature of Reality:

> Just as in a mirror's reflection a town or a village or the like appears as an image that is not separate from them, yet it appears as separate, and each is separate from the other as well as from the mirror, similarly, this universe also appears differentiated as one thing is from another and as well is different from the awakened Consciousness of Bhairava, most pure, though that difference too is empty.[25]

If a city were reflected in an enormous mirror, the likeness would show buildings, vehicles, street signs, sidewalk newsstands, and all the other aspects of urban life. This reflection might seem to have a life of its own, just like the city itself does. And yet if we looked closely, we would observe that we could never extract an image from the surface of the mirror. No matter what is reflected in a mirror, the substance of the image is still nothing other than mirror. Just so, the many creations of Citi have no life apart from Bhairava, as Abhinavagupta calls supreme Consciousness. Our perception of differences is "empty" in the sense that differentiation, in and of itself, is not the reality of the most pure

One. Citi's universe, of course, is not the reflection of another reality; it is a projection of her own being. Though Citi's universe is three-dimensional—the various forms breathe and move and interact with each other in a dizzying variety of ways, creating new forms and destroying old ones—yet all this takes place within Consciousness, projected onto a portion of her own being. So, these diverse forms with all their play are not different from Consciousness or from each other.

You might think, *Ah, but this has been said before.* Indeed it has. Yet, having heard in relation to the first sutra that the entire world is Consciousness, are you now living in a state of equality awareness? If you are like most of us and it takes time for you to imbibe these sublime and highly subtle understandings, you could let yourself contemplate this thought once again, from the perspective of *pratibimba.* Allow yourself to sink into the thought, *I am a mirror, and my life is nothing but a reflection on my Consciousness.*

This contemplation has been extremely meaningful for me in *sādhana,* in spiritual practice. Baba Muktananda often spoke about *pratibimba,* which he always referred to as *bimba pratibimba,* meaning, literally, "the object and the reflection of the object." I think Baba used that term not only because he liked the rhyming phrases, which he did enormously, but also in order to emphasize the position of the perceiver. That's you and me—and that's what makes this concept so significant. When I first heard Baba bring it up, I wondered, *What does this have to do with me?* And then I understood that I could view my own awareness as a reflective screen. In other words, I could consider that whatever I saw (or heard or tasted or smelled or even touched) was received on the mirror of my awareness—or, to forge another metaphor implied by the language of this sutra, on "a portion" of consciousness. Almost immediately, I noticed that adopting this perspective freed me from some of my personal entanglement in the dramas of life. Later I learned that this is the natural stance of a yogi. As Baba Muktananda says,

> An enlightened being does not become attached to momentary pain or pleasure. He realizes that these are merely reflections.[26]

Yogis call this perspective "witness-consciousness," which is the ability to view one's experiences from the perspective of the supreme Self. In other words, it's as if the yogi were watching all of life on a mirror, the mirror of his or her awareness.

You might ask, *But what is this mirror of awareness you're talking about?* To consider this more deeply, refer back to our question from the last chapter when you asked yourself, *Is my consciousness in this space? Or is this space in my consciousness?*

My own answer to that question is that both are true. Your consciousness is in this space, because that is the way it appears, and appearances have their own reality. At the same time—and this is a more compelling viewpoint—the space is inside your consciousness because you are the one who is experiencing the space. The space is reflected on your consciousness, and once you understand that, you can see quite clearly that your consciousness is not limited to your body. When I picture my own consciousness, I see it as a vast field of awareness, encompassing all that my mind touches. It is this that is the mirror.

Baba Muktananda makes the point that a mirror is never concerned about what is reflected in it. You can smile at a mirror or frown at it, and the mirror becomes neither ecstatic nor depressed by the appearance of your face. In the same way, pure Consciousness feels neither attracted nor repelled, neither greater nor lesser, neither pleased nor displeased as a result of what is reflected in her. No action or form alters her pure, transparent nature. She remains the witness of everything that happens in the universe. Transparent and clear as the purest crystal, the infinite space of Consciousness is a magnificent reflector.

The Ultimate Experience

Every metaphor has its shortfalls; no comparison is ever a perfect match for what it seeks to describe. As I said earlier, a mirror reflects images that are exterior to it, while Citi, the creative power, is "reflecting" that which exists within her, that which is a part of her. So, in the practice of witness-consciousness, we may have detachment in relation to what we experience, but there is also a sense of connection with it and the joy that accompanies that sense of union. The full experience of *pratibimba* is never one of disaffiliation from life. In his spiritual autobiography, Baba Muktananda writes about his experience of final liberation, as beautiful a description of *pratibimba* as I have ever read:

> The light pervaded everywhere in the form of the universe. I saw the earth being born and expanding from the light of Consciousness, just as one can see smoke rising from a fire. I could actually see the world within this conscious light, and the light within the world, like threads in a piece of cloth, and cloth in the threads. Just as a seed becomes a tree, with branches, leaves, flowers, and fruit, so within her own being Citi becomes animals, birds, germs, insects, gods, demons, men, and women. I could see this

> radiance of Consciousness, resplendent and utterly beautiful, silently pulsing as supreme ecstasy within me, outside me, above me, below me.[27]

When Baba speaks about the light that *pervaded everywhere in the form of the universe,* he is saying that this light is the universe. And when he says, *I saw the earth being born and expanding from the light of Consciousness,* he is pointing out that this pervasive light, which is the universe, continuously gives rise to the universe. Baba is having a vision of this creation, watching the world take form from within the very light that is itself the world. This is the essence of *pratibimba.* Baba says: *So within her own being, Citi becomes*—this is a very significant word, *becomes—animals, birds, germs, insects, gods, demons, men, and women.* Thus, Consciousness is projecting all of these forms out of her own depth. Out of that which is pure and formless come all the forms of the universe. *I could see this radiance of Consciousness, resplendent and utterly beautiful, silently pulsing as supreme ecstasy within me, outside me, above me, below me*—in short, everywhere. This silent pulsing is *spanda,* the pulsation so slight that it is said to be self-contained. It is that very *spanda* that decides, as an act of free will, to expand and move forward, so to speak, into creation.

Once in 1974, there happened to be a toy sitting on the mantelpiece in the living room of the house where Baba was staying. It was a little plastic device, an orange ball suspended before a shiny chrome cup. One day Baba pointed this toy out to me and asked, "How many orange balls do you see?" I could see both the ball and its reflection in the chrome, so speaking from my own perception, I said, "Baba, I can see two balls." He started laughing. He said, "There aren't two. There is only one. The other is a reflection." Still chuckling, he walked away. I knew that I had just received a vivid lesson in nondualistic perception.

The potential of applying this perception in our lives is tremendous. If we think that everything is, in fact, a reflection, then we have the power to take any stance toward this mirror of life, to see it in any way that best suits our practice of yoga. From everything I have seen of Gurumayi, and I have spent a good number of years serving her mission, she clearly lives each moment in the joy of perceiving the highest Reality. I recall that once in a satsang in the Siddha Yoga meditation center in Mexico City, a man from the audience took a very critical look at his own behavior in framing a question for Gurumayi. The man said, "Everyone has a lot of trouble with me. I'm full of negativity, and everything that people do seems terrible to me. Even when I chant I have bad thoughts—even when I meditate or when I'm with you. Since nothing seems to work for me," he added, "what can I do?"

Now, what this man said was true. He *did* give trouble to a lot of people, and there was something about his burly frame and the aggressive tone of voice he used in asking his question that further underscored his point. Gurumayi smiled and told him, "You are a case." She said, "In the court of a king, there has to be every kind of person. In the same way, in the kingdom of God, there has to be a person like you." She added that this man was performing a great service by showing others how they should not be. She said that she liked this man in spite of his faults.

Then, having revised his reality, Gurumayi told the man, "You're just very honest. And your honesty, which allows you to see that you have negativities, will also purify what shouldn't be there." The important thing, she added, was that the man was there, having satsang. "Once you are standing under the sun," Gurumayi said, "you will receive the rays of sunlight. Once you are in this *śakti* laboratory, you will receive treatment. . . .The work of the *śakti* is to cleanse. If there's nothing to clean up, what's the point of having *śakti?* So you are needed."[28]

In my own opinion, what is *most* needed in this world is individuals who can take in the entire range of reflections that appear on the screen of their awareness, individuals who can see another human being from all perspectives, as Gurumayi did this man. There is such power in our perceiving the world as it is. Gurumayi was saying to this man that his own honesty, his clear self-perception, would help him purify the very tendencies he was lamenting. When she spoke of the "*śakti* laboratory," I feel that she was referring to the power of the Siddha Yoga practices—mantra repetition, meditation, selfless service, spending time in the company of a great being. When we perform the practices with an awareness of our own challenges, we are truly offering ourselves to the purifying *śakti.* With such an offering as this, our distortions of understanding are inevitably cleansed.

Transcendence and Immanence

The sacred texts of Śaivism, substantiated by the experience of yogis, state that supreme Reality exists beyond creation while manifesting simultaneously as creation. Reality is beyond form and also it is form; it is unchanging and at the same time it is constantly changing; it is eternal and it is absolutely fleeting. In other words, Reality is simultaneously transcendent and immanent: it is *viśvottīrṇa,* that which is beyond the universe, and at the same time *viśvamaya,* that which contains the universe. Taken together, these two inseparable aspects comprise the totality and fullness of Reality. The difference between these two seemingly contradictory descriptions is a matter of perspective. It all depends on how you look at it.

From our ordinary point of view, Citi is immanent, first of all; Citi takes shape as the entire universe, a cacophony of sound and form. But from the transcendental perspective, Citi has neither form nor content, only an unfathomable boundless depth, which the sages of Śaivism call *mahāśūnya,* the Great Void. The term "void" can be confusing. This is not to say that the Great Void does not exist; *mahāśūnya* exists. It is void, or null, only in the sense that there is no subject to perceive objects, for in the Great Void all manifestation has fused with the light of Consciousness.* Here, one experiences neither happiness nor suffering, knowledge nor ignorance, but a thought-free, steady, peaceful state. Gurumayi describes the attainment of the transcendent state in this way:

> When you sit quietly, everything comes to an end, because that which is transitory must end; that which has begun must also cease to be. Only the beginningless beginning, the Self, which is always new and yet always the same, is unchanging.
>
> When you become quiet, this is the abode that you find within yourself. Different sages have called it by different names. Some have called it the Great Void; some have called it the Great Bliss; some have called it the Eternal Light. Each one has explained it in his or her own words, but it is a true experience.[29]

* Texts on Śaivism distinguish between two voids. One is called, simply, *śūnya,* or void, and is the formless, nescient darkness, a part of the creation that we can witness in ourselves in meditation. We will look into this in greater detail later. What we are speaking of here is *mahāśūnya,* the Great Void, a transcendent state in which the subject has merged with the object (Mark S. G. Dyczkowski, *The Doctrine of Vibration* (1987), pp. 118-22.)

Because our own finite nature is inextricably intertwined with infinite Reality, we are all both transcendent and immanent. The Great Void exists within every aspect of our being. It exists in the body, the mind, and the personality; in every act we perform; and in all the things we know—things whose materiality we take for granted. As Gurumayi suggests, we can sometimes experience this exalted state during meditation. Whenever I enter into this inner silence, I am arrested by its sheer emptiness. There is no thought in this state. There is neither joy nor sadness nor even, it seems, any "I" who could register that there is nothing happening. My consciousness becomes absorbed in a deep, silent serenity, and when I emerge from this state, I invariably feel that I have touched the very foundation of my existence.

After a draft of this soul-drenching silence, we might well ask why Citi bothers to take form. It is a question that has arisen in many variations, one not asked just by philosophers and their students but also by very ordinary people: *Why me? Why this? Why is this happening? Why did God create this universe anyway? Why did the supreme Reality create anything at all?*

Abhinavagupta has a beautiful reply. He says it is the nature of supreme Reality to create, and so to ask why God brings the world into existence is as absurd as asking why wind blows, why fire burns, why water is wet. It is an intrinsic quality of Citi to create a universe, something she cannot avoid doing. I have often thought about this, and it seems to me that if God has any limitation, it is his inability to stop being God. Abhinavagupta puts it this way:

> If the Highest Reality did not manifest in infinite variety but remained cooped up within its solid singleness, it would neither be the Highest Power nor Consciousness but something like a jar.[30]

The creation of the universe is an expression of the *svātantrya-śakti,* the power of freedom—the freedom to do or not to do. If Citi did not express herself in creation, how would she know herself as a conscious, vital, creative power? If God were only the Great Void, isolated in his unity with no worlds or sentient beings, how would he know that he possesses the capacity to create? It is as a natural expression of this capacity that the ultimate Reality manifests the world of things. In Kshemaraja's words:

> Śakti, leaping in delight, lets herself go forth into manifestation.[31]

As an act of divine creative will, the universe appears.

3

The World of Our Experience

Sūtra 3

तन्नाना अनुरूपग्राह्यग्राहकभेदात्

tan nānā anurūpa-grāhya-grāhaka-bhedāt

That [Consciousness becomes] diverse
because of the division
of reciprocally adapted objects and subjects.

tat:	that
nānā:	diverse, in many ways
anurūpa:	reciprocally adapting, mutually corresponding
grāhya:	object, that which is perceivable
grāhaka:	subject, perceiver
bhedāt:	because of division

The first two sutras establish that Citi, by her own free will, is the cause of the emanation, maintenance, and dissolution of the universe and that she unfolds the universe upon a part of herself, which is Citi's own light. But how is manifestation carried out? Why is there such startling variety and texture to this world? In sutra 3, Kshemaraja says that diversity arises through adaptation. This is an idea that has become familiar to the modern world through the theories of biological evolution, though the sages of Kashmir go much deeper.

One image in this varied universe that has always fascinated me is a fish in water. Here is a creature that moves and breathes, eats and breeds, lives and dies in what to me is an alien environment. To the fish, of course, water is not at all foreign or unnatural. The fish has adapted to his world just as you and I have to ours. In fact, there is scientific evidence that all life began in water; that between the fish and me, I am the one who has made the most recent adaptation.

As human beings, we live at particular latitudes, breathe the air, eat the food that is available to us, and beyond becoming accustomed to our physical environment, as social beings, we also become accustomed to each other. When it's necessary, we can adapt to new cultures, new philosophies, new ideologies of all kinds—and our world adapts to us as well. In sutra 3, Kshemaraja speaks about this reciprocity of influence between the subject and the object. In other words, depending on how I relate to the world around me, both that world and I can be altered. Here, Kshemaraja is saying that no one is isolated, that we are surrounded by beings, substances, and situations that affect our experience of life—and that we, in turn, affect them.

In this sutra, the words *tan nānā* imply that Consciousness has become diverse. But why are there suddenly distinctions within Consciousness? The answer is *anurūpa-grāhya-grāhaka-bhedāt.* The diversity comes from a division *(bhedāt)* that arises in the interchange, the mutual give-and-take *(anurūpa)* that naturally occurs between objects *(grāhya)* and subjects *(grāhaka).* Notice that Kshemaraja mentions object before subject. It's not what we are accustomed to. I think that possibly he wanted to emphasize our power to influence the world, particularly with our state of mind.

A woman once told me about her attempts to understand this sutra in the late 1970s, when Baba Muktananda was talking about Śaivism in his evening programs and encouraging his disciples to study the *Pratyabhijñā-hṛdayam.* This woman was pondering sutra 3 late one morning, sitting at a desk in her room in Baba's temporary ashram in Santa Monica, California. She was running over and over in her mind the words "reciprocally adapted objects and subjects." She just couldn't understand what was meant. Sometimes it seems as if the mind is made of concrete, particularly in relation to scriptural topics. One contemporary professor of Asian religions has described the sutras of Kashmir Śaivism as "bits of frozen enlightenment."[32] We put a sutra into our mind and heart, and when it melts and we merge with the meaning, our entire state is expanded. But initially, as the sutra rattles around inside us, the experience can be painful, like being stabbed by the jagged points of a block of ice.

That's what this woman was going through, tapping her pencil on the desk, writing her thoughts down on a pad, crossing them out, tapping the pencil some more. Unbeknownst to her, one of her roommates, a woman who offered her seva in the ashram bakery, was in an upper bunk on the other side of the room, trying to catch a nap after hours of early-morning work. Every time our sutra student sighed and rustled her papers and tapped her pencil, it had an effect on the woman in the bunk—we'll call her the baker. At one point, the baker thought, *I'm going to kill her. If she taps that pencil one more time, I'm going to get up out of bed, walk over there, and wring her neck . . .*

After a few moments of silence, the pencil began to tap again, and the baker rose from her bed. She was a little surprised at the power of her reaction, but true to her own inspiration, she climbed off the bunk, walked over to the desk, put her hands around the sutra student's neck—and began to give her a massage. As the baker's hands deftly worked tension out of her neck and shoulders, the student explained her struggle to understand this sutra. The baker described her experience of that struggle, and, after laughing at the projected scene of her own "murder," the student cried, "But this is it! This is the sutra!" With her words tumbling over themselves, she described how each of them was an object to the other's subject and how in their interaction, they both had been changed by each other. Their states had been elevated; they had become friends—and, on a more mundane note, they both got what they wanted. The baker was able to take a nap as the student happily pondered her new insight into the sutra. It was a good beginning.

In Kshemaraja's commentary on sutra 3, he describes subjects as perceivers or "experients," the *pramātās.* These are beings at seven distinct levels, identifiable stages that exist between our waking, embodied, mind-driven experience *(sakala)* and the ecstasy of the highest state. We look at these seven levels in a little more detail when we discuss sutra 4. For now, it's important to know that these seven experients represent levels of perception that exist within each one of us. All of us have had glimpses of at least some of these stages as well as experiences of moving between them. Contrast, for instance, the way you feel in deep meditation, when you have no awareness of your body or mind, with the way you feel when you are angry. Kshemaraja is saying here that although all of these perceivers exist in the same universe, each has an entirely individual view of it. As he says, the world is different for each of them—they are creating the world differently—and, as he indicates in the sutra, the world responds differently to each.

A Theory of Manifestation

The intricacies of our experience of the world and just how we create that world are, for me, the main point of sutra 3. The sage Utpaladeva takes a compelling approach to manifestation in his *Īśvara-pratyabhijñā-kārikā* with a discussion of *ābhāsa-vāda.*[33] A *vāda* is a doctrine or theory, and an *ābhāsa* is that which flashes, illumines, appears, or manifests, and it also means "splendor." Utpaladeva postulates that everything we experience and perceive is an *ābhāsa,* or a combination of *ābhāsas.* That's like saying that everything in life is a projection, a flashing forth, of Reality. This understanding has been an invaluable tool for me, helping me keep the world in proper perspective.

Shortly after I was introduced to *ābhāsa-vāda,* I was traveling between the Ganeshpuri ashram and Mumbai, past thousands of apartments and housing colonies; some of them were opulent, some austere, and many were achingly meager. After a few moments of contemplating the disparity between the inhabitants' lives, I turned to my companion and said, "Isn't it amazing to think that these are all the *ābhāsas* of Lord Śiva!" She said, "You're joking." I said, "No. There is nothing in this universe but God. It's all God. Only our understanding makes us see it otherwise." This is not to say that every form God takes is good or should be permanent. It just is.

In my position as a swami, I speak with many different people. Some have profound insights and some have serious personal problems; some are articulate and witty and others are very clear and simple with their words; some have lived for many decades and others for just a few years—and all of these individuals are, for me, *ābhāsas.* With each person, I find myself in some way reminding myself, *This is a form of God speaking to me.* This is one way to apply the principle of Baba's experience of Self-realization that we read in sutra 2 when he observed how the world arises from Consciousness, how it is sustained in Consciousness, and how it is pervaded by Consciousness. We could say it's all an *ābhāsa.*

How are *ābhāsas* created? It's like staring at the sky on a winter day: the snow seems to fall from some undefined space. Similarly, all created forms issue forth from the unformed and undifferentiated space of Consciousness. These expressions of God are apparently propelled into existence in an infinite diversity of form, making explicit what lies implicit in the light of *prakāśa.* And just as the snowflakes crystallize from the atmosphere into marvelous delicate designs, so do *ābhāsas* crystallize in an astonishing variety of structures.

If ābhāsas are created things, I've wondered, *why didn't Utpaladeva simply call them "objects"?* By choosing the term *ābhāsa,* he seems to emphasize two significant aspects of the creative act: on the one hand, that objective manifestations are forms of *mahāprakāśa,* the great light of Consciousness, which illumines; and on the other hand, that they are ephemeral flashes, mere projections onto the screen of Citi with no permanent existence. In spite of the flickering and precarious nature of *ābhāsas,* without them, there would be no world to perceive. Without *ābhāsas,* we couldn't understand what it is to be a subject; our existence would be a diffuse spread of light with no form, no limits, no definitions, and no variety.

Let me restate that last point: without objects, we would not be subjects. Which is to say that, from the very outset of manifestation, the reciprocity between an individual and her world is established as the primordial pattern of the entire universe. The basis for reciprocity is the fundamental distinction between subject and object. Why this distinction arises is a question that cannot be answered. It just is. What we're discussing here is the result. This differentiation is the springboard for the entire process of creation. As Utpaladeva writes:

> The Great God [Maheśvara] is, in fact, none other than the real Self of each and every being. He alone endures, having evolved into all phenomenal existence through [his] undiversified Self-awareness, "I am this" *[aham idam].*[34]

The sage is saying that the Lord, who is the experiencing subject (the essential *I am*), has himself created his objective experience *(all of this).* Because of the reciprocal nature of the relationship between subject and object, we can also turn this statement around, acknowledging that it's through the existence of his world that the subject exists.

Let's look at this last point a little more closely. Every time a perception takes birth, the subject also takes birth; the existence of one implies the existence of the other. Every time I see a person or hear a sound or have an idea, I define myself as a subject. Likewise, Śiva is the universal subject only because he chooses to experience his creation; without that creation, he would not be a subject but an abstract entity incapable of manifestation.

Outer and Inner Flashes

Śiva's creation, by the way, is for us a given. The *ābhāsas* (objects of perception) of Śiva are what configure the external circumstances of our world; we experience them as external *ābhāsas.* You may live in Paris as opposed to Rio de Janeiro or Moscow, and, as a result, your experience will take on specific physical dimensions and cultural parameters. People around you will speak particular languages and dress in certain ways; you'll find some kinds of food available and others not; you'll live in distinct atmospheric conditions; and so on. All of these are your external *ābhāsas,* a part of the Lord's creation.

Aha! you might say. *So individuals don't create the world at all; God creates the world!* I would say that both do. Within the Lord's creation, we as individuals create our own world through our inner *ābhāsas.* Baba Muktananda used to speak of this phenomenon in terms of a spider spinning its web in a corner of a room: the Lord creates the whole room, and we limit ourselves to the one tiny portion of it where we have "spun" our own creation. Through our inner *ābhāsas,* we perceive some objects and not others, we make associations with our past experiences, and so we invest our perceptions with our own meanings. This, then, becomes our world, and we do live in it. We have no other.

It's important to remember that no matter how challenging God's universe might appear to us or how contracted our own interpretation of God's world might be, God does exist within it. In his book *Secret of the Siddhas,* Baba writes of *ābhāsas* in this way:

> Our understandings arise from one another. So many of our understandings of different things lie hidden, to be revealed when they are triggered by events or thoughts. We say, "I saw, I heard, I knew," and thus the I-principle always remains one with our experience. It never becomes separate from it. All our understandings branch out with this I-principle as their basis. These different understandings, which come and go, are our *ābhāsas,* our manifestations. But no matter how many thoughts arise, the I-principle does not change. It neither increases nor decreases.[35]

Just as our thoughts emanate from the primordial "I" that Baba refers to—the Self—and just as they very clearly create universes without ever changing the Self, so the manifestations of God never alter his essential and pristine nature.

Hidden Flashes

I find it very interesting that Baba speaks of how the *ābhāsas* arise from one another and how so many are hidden from our view. For me, this quality of "hiddenness" is a highly significant aspect of *ābhāsa-vāda,* one that has helped me come to terms with life's complexity. It's one thing to say, "God creates the universe," but for most of us, our experience of life is so complicated and nuanced that it's difficult for us to comprehend how all these experiences could possibly stem from just one source. One reason it seems so perplexing is that many *ābhāsas* are veiled or unobserved. I received a great lesson on this subject from Gurumayi one day when I happened to see her on the ashram grounds just after I'd given a talk in a satsang.

Gurumayi asked me, "Why did you have fear when you were speaking?" My immediate reaction was defensive: I told her that I hadn't been afraid. Gurumayi said, "When I hear you speak, the words themselves open up . . ." Here, she raised her hand as a closed fist, and then opened it, palm upward with her fingers extending out like petals of some glorious flower in full bloom. ". . .and I can perceive what is underneath them."[36] Her statement—and most particularly her gesture—was very strong. Quite suddenly, I could see that underneath our words, there are always subliminal messages. The words we communicate contain these messages, whether or not we are aware of them ourselves. These hidden communications are also *ābhāsas*. So, we're sending and receiving *ābhāsas* all the time, often without even knowing it.

Let's say you see someone, and that person smiles and says, "Good morning," yet you find that your inner response is very different from what the external situation would suggest—you feel great sadness or you feel anger. Some hidden *ābhāsa* is at play. It could be a covert emotion you are picking up from the person. Or it could be a memory you have of that person, from this lifetime or some other. Or it could be that you are so wrapped up in something in your own mind that you've hardly seen or heard her.

After I'd thought about Gurumayi's observation, I realized I had been experiencing some fear—some sense that I might fail or look foolish—when I gave that talk. At the same time, other *ābhāsas* were at play as well—I had certain understandings about the subject on which I was speaking as well as certain feelings about people in the audience. Also, I noticed people laughing several times at things I said to amuse them, I thought some of them looked bored at times, and it seemed that at one point a woman was moved to tears. All of this was at play for me. And, at the same time, I carried the sense of fear that Gurumayi had pointed out to me. This fear existed as a part of my creation, having its effect on me and on others as well, in spite of the fact that I was completely unaware of it.

Isn't this the way our lives go: we are forever creating realities, and these realities have their own existence and their own effect, regardless of our awareness of what we're doing. In other words, the multiple layers of manifestation happen simultaneously, whether or not we're conscious of them.

It seems to me that the purpose of spiritual practices and, most particularly, of the scriptural study we are doing here is to heighten our awareness—to expand our ability to live consciously.

On All Levels of Creation

Ābhāsas appear at all levels of creation, from the most general to the most particular, from the largest and most concrete right down to the smallest and the most subtle. An *ābhāsa* can be a solar system, a country, a hat, or it can be a molecule or a particle of energy. Anything that streams out of the great light of Consciousness is an *ābhāsa.* Our physical bodies, for instance, are universes of astonishing complexity, comprising countless *ābhāsas.*

I was amazed once watching a microsurgery on my own knee: it was as if I had access to a periscope into another universe, a world of cartilage and muscle, of arterial channels and blood. Look at a section of your own skin the size of a quarter: that one spot contains some three million cells, a hundred glands, fifty nerve endings, three feet of blood vessels, and nearly that volume of lymph vessels. The body's circulatory system is a branching network about sixty thousand miles long—more than twice the distance around the earth. There is so much more to our bodies than we know, more even than we can begin to understand with the intellect. At the subtlest level, our bodies are nothing but shining particles of light, pure energy—and, according to Utpaladeva, each of these particles is an *ābhāsa.*

Thus, the term *ābhāsa* is used in a comprehensive sense to refer to any object. We can conceive of an *ābhāsa* as a basic unit that combines in an infinite number of forms and shapes, creating structures that in turn compose other structures. Subatomic particles form a system around the nucleus of an atom; groups of atoms then combine into molecules; molecules form cells; and these cells in turn form the organic tissue of living bodies. Each of these structures is organized by groups of *ābhāsas.* It is easy to see that even in terms of our own bodies, the possible number of *ābhāsas,* and of combinations of *ābhāsas,* is beyond our imagination. And *ābhāsas* are not, of course, limited to the body, but can be projected in the same way on a universal scale. How could we even conceive of the number of *ābhāsas* that *citiśakti* makes manifest in order to create so many solar systems and galaxies, all the spectacular phenomena that we see in the firmament!

I find that it can be extremely beneficial to contemplate *ābhāsa-vāda* by assuming some of these various perspectives. For instance, if I look at myself in the midst of a crowd of five hundred people—five hundred different *ābhāsas* with all the opinions and prerogatives that human existence entails!—I can feel as if I am fairly insignificant. And if I stand under the night sky, in relation to the galaxy, knowing that there are millions of other galaxies I can't even see with my naked eye, I can feel as if this body and personality, with its likes and dislikes, is so tiny a spot on the face of existence that I might wonder why I even have a name. And yet if I look at myself in relation to the molecules that make up this body, then I am the galaxy, I am the ground of existence for so many organisms that I can't even begin to count them.

You might ask: *Which of these perspectives is correct?* The answer is, of course, all of them. There is no one correct way of seeing this universe; every viewpoint, no matter how odd or oblique, has a foundation in Reality. It is just one more way in which the universe manifests. And we know that it manifests in an immense variety of forms—this diversity is the very question that sutra 3 addresses.

The Fleeting Nature of Life

Ābhāsa-vāda gives us an astoundingly dynamic view of life, because *ābhāsas* are forms of the *spanda*. They're what flashes forth when Citi opens her eyes, the *unmeṣa* we discussed in sutras 1 and 2. These flashes come forth incessantly and at a fantastic speed. Normally, we think in terms of cause and effect: a cell reproduces other cells; a wolf is born of other wolves; earth, water, and fire are combined in a particular manner to produce pottery. Utpaladeva, however, states that this way of understanding creation is restrictive—and not at all descriptive of how things truly come into being:

> The Lord, by virtue of his infinite divine power, manifests these apparent phenomena simply through the power of his divine will (without resorting to the use of any other cause or means); that is what is known as his active nature and his creative aspect.[37]

Objects in themselves do not have conscious, generative power. There is only one cause for each appearance in the entire diverse universe: the unimpeded will of Śiva. When I speak to someone for just a few moments, that person is created and destroyed millions of times right before my eyes. The *ābhāsas* that compose his body, his voice, his feelings, his gestures are appearing and disappearing, vibrating beyond the reach of my senses. Each pulsation of *spanda* creates, maintains, and destroys everything. The reason I can identify the person who appears in one moment as the same person I was speaking with just a moment before is that these *ābhāsas* flash forth in a given pattern, re-creating the person's form and once again animating it. According to Utpaladeva, each moment of our perception is composed of a series of *ābhāsas,* pulsating with tiny consecutive modifications that give us the impression of movement.

In envisioning this phenomenon, it might be helpful to think about a movie, which is made of a series of static takes, each slightly different from the earlier one. When we screen the movie, the succession of images occurs with such speed that it gives the impression of movement—the movement of one form. It is not, however, just one form. At the end of my conversation, the person I walk away from is not the same person I began speaking to just moments earlier. He is a new emanation. This is totally apparent in the instances when we've undergone a shift in mood, or several, in the course of a conversation. The same process is at work when we think, feel, dream, speak, love, meditate, repeat the mantra: all of life, everything in creation is subject to the law of *ābhāsas.*

What, then, about those objects that people maintain are lasting? Consider the Great Pyramid of Giza, which is said to be the oldest structure on the planet and is thought to be between four thousand and five thousand years old. Although on the physical plane we are aware of the stability of the Great Pyramid, on the cosmic level this very structure has vanished and re-emerged billions upon trillions of times. In this sense, even the oldest human construction is only a fleeting appearance, a thing without stability in the infinitude of Consciousness.

It seems to me that the recognition of this perspective is a key to happiness in life. I have long felt that evil, if such a thing exists, stems from an unwillingness to accept change as a natural outcome of the universe. Wars are fought, families dissolved, hearts broken, and lives destroyed because people won't sacrifice their fixed opinions, shift their perspectives, and come to a compromise. And this is often equally true for people on both sides of a dispute. As a result of these observations, at one point in my life I had developed a strong sense of moral indignation at the chaos wreaked on the world by people who rigidly hold on to their opinions.

It came as quite a shock to me when, one day, a friend pointed out that my attitude on this particular subject, which I'd thought of as the proper stance for any right-minded person, was nothing but a rigidly held opinion. What he said was, "Do you realize that you're being intolerant?" I had to answer, yes.

What's at issue, of course, is never the viewpoint itself; it's the egotistical attachment we have to that viewpoint, our feeling that this particular way of seeing the world is the one that's truly correct. I find that in any clash of ideas, it's helpful to remember the fleeting nature of *ābhāsas,* whether they're the external circumstances of a situation or the mental postures I'm taking in response to that circumstance. The recollection that my *ābhāsas* can be turned instantaneously into another form—even into a win-win solution with an adversary—has added immensely to the quality of my life.

Is It Real—or Not?

The question always arises, *Is the universe real or is it unreal?* It's difficult for me to take my world seriously when I know it's ephemeral. And yet I can't really dismiss it as wholly unreal because, after all, in every moment I am experiencing it—or my version of it. Utpaladeva leads us to believe that the world is neither false nor true. What is it then? I've thought about this question for years, and still I don't have a satisfactory answer. All I can say is that holding the view that creation is an expression of multiple systems of *ābhāsas* seems to benefit me greatly. It gives me a sense of detachment, a certain freedom from being caught by the events of my life, and, at the same time, it gives me a sense of reverence and respect for the magnificent power of Consciousness in all her creative expressions. We are, in truth, not any of those particular manifestations.

There are people who tell me that contemplating *ābhāsas* gives them a sense of despair; their life goals suddenly seem meaningless. From my perspective, this seems like a healthy turmoil. The contemplation challenges our self-concepts and self-importance, our to-do lists and personal desires; my own response is, invariably, renewed humility. As

Kshemaraja tells us in this sutra, the objects we perceive, the objects we live with, have their diversity because of the constant interplay between ourselves and those objects. He says that at all levels, the world we perceive is inextricably woven into the fabric of our existence. We have the opportunity to create and re-create—and create again—our experience of that world, and thus, we hold the power to find a direction in our lives that will, ultimately, bring us growth and fulfillment. The question of how we do this is the subject of the next several sutras.

4

The Principles of Manifestation Exist in Our Bodies

Sutra 4

चितिसंकोचात्मा चेतनोऽपि संकुचितविश्वमयः

citi-saṃkocātmā cetano'pi saṃkucita-viśvamayaḥ

Even the individual,
whose nature is Consciousness in a contracted state,
embodies the universe in a contracted form.

citi: Consciousness
saṃkoca: contraction
ātmā: essential nature
cetana: the one who is Consciousness, the individual
api: even
saṃkucita: contracted
viśva: the universe
mayaḥ: embodiment

THE INDIVIDUAL BEING IS a perfect replica of the Lord. Kshemaraja tells us in his commentary on this sutra that the same principles of creation that give shape to the manifest universe also structure the body of a human being:

> As the Lord is universe-bodied *[bhagavān viśva-śarīra]*, so the [individual] experient—because of Consciousness being contracted—has the body of the entire universe in a contracted form, much [as] the *vaṭa* tree resides in a contracted form in its seed.[38]

In the third sutra, we explored the mutual reciprocity between our world and ourselves. In the fourth sutra, we find that this astonishing connection involves absolutely everything in the universe, and that rather than simply being mutually dependent, as the term "reciprocity" implies, the universe and we are one and the same.

This follows from the first sutra, where we learned that the knower, the act of knowing, and that which is known are all the same Consciousness. Not only is everything in the universe made of the same "stuff," but also that stuff contains within itself everything it ever becomes. This means that every particle of Consciousness contains the whole of creation in precisely the same way that every particle of a hologram can re-create the whole. I saw this capacity of a hologram demonstrated once in a museum in Chicago, and for years after that experience I would think, *If a broken piece of glass can do that, why isn't it possible for a fragment of Consciousness like myself!* Recently, while contemplating sutra 4, it occurred to me that not only is this possible for me, but more to the point, I have experienced doing it.

It happened one morning when I was standing with Baba in the courtyard of the Siddha Yoga ashram in Oakland, California. At the time, I was the ashram manager, and my point of view was definitely affected by the weight of my position: I was concerned about the safety of our devotees and the quality of our neighborhood, and as I looked around all I could see were signs that our surroundings were not ideal. I told Baba that I felt the ashram wasn't a pretty place—it wasn't appealing to people—and the main reason for this was that we were located in a seedy and dangerous neighborhood. Baba heard what I had to say, and then he turned away for a moment and looked around the courtyard. After a moment, speaking softly, he said, "Everything is so beautiful." His observation was diametrically opposed to mine, and the only way I could think to reconcile the two points of view was to do what Baba had done. So, I took a deep breath, looked around—and saw a totally different world than the one I had perceived before. The walls of the courtyard were the same warm yellow as the Ganeshpuri ashram, a color I have always loved. There was an enormous rosebush in full bloom behind Baba's chair, and the pink and peach-colored blossoms looked luscious in the sunlight. Baba, with the sun on his beard and his orange silks, was vibrant and beautiful. The dangers of the neighborhood were still there, but instead of being my focus, they were simply a part of a magnificent scene.

What happened to shift my vision? There is an extremely subtle energy, a transformative power that constantly radiates from a Siddha as a result of his or her total mergence with the divine *śakti.* Over the years, I've seen this energy catalyze my intuitive perceptions and expansions of understanding, bringing about all kinds of wonderful internal changes. That day, it opened my inner sight to a deeper dimension. The first reality I saw was projected through my own limited viewpoint, my perspective as a player in the scene. When I paused and took a breath, I was able to see from a higher perspective. I can't say that I saw the world as Baba was seeing it, but at least he and I were now participating in the same conversation. One way of understanding the shift I made is to say that my knowledge of the world was expanded. This capacity for expansion exists within each one of us, and the way that we access it is not by reading books or hearing lectures but by taking hold of the awareness within ourselves, by probing our own consciousness. In this instance, I feel it was Baba's power of grace that enabled me to access a higher perspective: the perspective had been there inside me all along. All perspectives are always there inside each of us—just as they are in the particles of a hologram.

Sutra 4 tells us that everything exists within us. The first phrase of the sutra is *citi-saṃkocatmā cetano'pi,* "even one whose nature is Consciousness in a contracted state"—which is another way of saying, "even an individual." The sutra continues: *saṃkucita viśvamayaḥ,* which is to say that in spite of his contraction, this individual "embodies the universe in a contracted form." Just what is this contracted form of the universe that we embody? Śaivism speaks of thirty-four different categories of existence, *tattvas,* and what the sutra says is that each of these *tattvas* exists within each of us.* In the interest of getting to know ourselves better, let's delineate these thirty-four levels of being.

---

* There are varying views on the total number of *tattvas.* The number is thirty-five if Śiva is considered one of the *tattvas;* it's thirty-six if both Śiva and Śakti are included. In his *Īśvara-pratyabhijñā-kārikā* (3.1-2), Utpaladeva suggests the view we've adopted here: there are thirty-four *tattvas* because Śiva and Śakti are aspects of Paramaśiva rather than the initial levels of creation emanating from that Reality (Translation by B.N. Pandit, *Īśvara-pratyabhijñā-kārikā of Utpaladeva,* publication forthcoming).

The Categories of Existence

The *tattvas* are like a map of the spiritual journey, which I'm sure is why Lakshman Joo, one of the leading exponents of this philosophical system in the twentieth century, said that the entry point to Kashmir Śaivism is through the *tattvas.*[39] Kashmir Śaivism is not aimed at the intellect alone. It is the intellectual arm of a yoga designed to free the practitioner. Its sole purpose is to uplift and redeem the student. The thirty-four *tattvas* are a map of subtle Reality and, thus, a means for us to find out where we are, where we have come from, and how we can get back. The word *tattva* derives from the root *tat,* meaning "that," or "that which is," implying that whatever this term is applied to is as basic a unit as one can find. *Tattva* means "that-ness." What the list of *tattvas* provides is an ontological map, a map of the various states of being assumed by Consciousness as it congeals itself into the universe—and, in reverse, the process by which it then returns to the state of supreme Śiva.

Kshemaraja never explains the *tattvas* as a totality in his own commentary on this text, apparently because he considered a working knowledge of this schema prerequisite to the study of the Trika. He does, and I do, refer to one or another of the *tattvas* in discussing many, if not most, of the sutras. It is necessary, therefore, for the serious student of this text to be familiar with the *tattvas.* There is a list of the thirty-four *tattvas* in Appendix B, and a discussion of both the names and the main precepts associated with them follows here. I strongly recommend that you commit the list and at least some of the attendant concepts to memory. I love the expression "learning by heart" for it implies what memorization allows: taking in information so thoroughly that it can serve one's intuitive center in the search for deeper understanding. It is the traditional means for scriptural study in the Indian tradition, one that every sage undertook as he started the process of mastering this extremely subtle material.

What the *tattvas* chart is the flow of *citiśakti* as it proceeds from its own center, which is both nowhere and everywhere. The map encompasses our life: the beginning point and the ending point and the path in between. Ultimately, we end up exactly where we began. In this sense, the spiritual journey is not unlike other journeys in life: we travel somewhere and, along the way, we see certain landscapes, experience different cultures, meet various people. In the end, we come back home again.

The Pure Creation: Oneness

Home is Paramaśiva, the Supreme Lord. In the discussion of sutra 1, I describe the triad of knowledge: the knower, the means of knowing, and the known. Paramaśiva is the ultimate Knower or Perceiver. He is often identified in reference to his experience—that is, in reference to the awareness Consciousness has of its own existence within the silence of the great heart. This experience is summed up by the term *aham,* "I am." If you think about it, you'll see that this experience is the foundation of your own life—and your *aham* is the foundation of the *tattvas,* of the whole of creation. This word indicates the One, the single Subject that perceives the entire array of "other" to which the Subject has given birth. That other is represented by the term *idam,* or "this." From the perspective of Paramaśiva, however, there is only *aham,* "I am."

In this "I am," there are two distinct qualities: the perception of I-ness, or self, and the understanding of its existence, the verb "am." This relationship was implicit in sutra 1 as *prakāśa,* the illumination or pure being-ness that is associated with Śiva, and *vimarśa,* the awareness of self and power of manifestation that are capacities of Śakti. Although the Āgamas describe Śiva and Śakti as the first two categories of manifestation, Utpaladeva and other main exponents of nondualistic Śaivism prefer the view that they represent the primordial attributes of Paramaśiva. Taking this latter view, the first *tattva*—the first step into creation—is the appearance of the Lord's power of will, his *icchā-śakti,* and his intention to create. This first level is called *sadāśiva-tattva.*

The name Sadāśiva indicates that it is "always Śiva," the eternal subject who creates and experiences his own creation. Throughout the chain of *tattvas,* the primordial subject does not change, only his perception changes according to the self-willed forces that affect him, forces by which he limits himself and imposes on himself the instruments that reduce his all-pervading vision. What emerges at this first level is the phenomenon of *idam,* "this," the ground of all objectivity, that which is counterpart to *aham,* the subject.

Although creation is at its most subtle level here, still the universe has made its appearance in its entirety. The universe has not evolved or developed; it has been created, as a whole, in a flash. As we have noted before, this creation is not a historic event, not something that happened in the olden days of yore, for in the realm of pure creation the principles that generate our experiences of time and space, of cause and effect, do not operate. Here what we experience is that the universe is created anew in every instant. Right now, as you read these words, new worlds are flashing into being and again dissolving into nothingness. Śiva and Śakti do not stop the process of conception at any moment. If they did, everything would instantaneously disappear into the Great Void. The experience of *aham* in *sadāśiva-tattva* is the totality of creation reflected in its own Self.

The next principle that emerges from Consciousness is *īśvara-tattva,* the principle of lordship. Here the balance between *aham* and *idam* leans on the side of the object. It's like an idea, which was seen at first as indefinite and hazy, and then becomes larger-than-life on our mental screen as we invest it with more and more of our awareness. The universe that was previously seen as a blur comes into such sharp focus that our awareness of ourselves as subject pales before it. At this level, perception does not happen with the senses or the mental instruments, for these do not function in the pure creation. Perception occurs through the witnessing capacity of unencumbered Consciousness. As we become absorbed in such a landscape, it seems that we are the lord of all this, which is where this category takes its name. Īśvara is "The Lord," and, like any lord, possesses his own dominion, which in this case is the universe in its entirety. In terms of manifestation, at this level what was something ambiguous is now clear. It naturally follows that the prevailing energy here is *jñāna-śakti,* the power of knowledge.

In the sequential order of the great chain of *tattvas,* the third is *śuddha-vidyā,* which means "pure knowledge." The relation between the subject and his universe, which in the preceding principles leans either toward the subject or toward the object, reaches a perfect balance in *śuddha-vidyā-tattva* and is represented by the awareness of *aham-idam,* "I am this," and *idam-aham,* "this I am." The awareness of the subject and the awareness of the object become equally clear in their real nature. "I am" and "this" rest in perfect balance in the luminous, infinite mirror of Śiva—identical to each other, identical to Śiva. Unity as well as diversity appear as equal expressions of Supreme Consciousness. It is from this stance that the creation can spring into manifestation, and so the prevailing energy of this *tattva* is *kriyā-śakti,* the power of action.

All that has been named so far is known as the pure creation. As Abhinavagupta explains:

> All that is separated from Consciousness is impure, and all that has reached a state of identity with it is pure.[40]

In this pure creation, there is no separation, no differentiation whatsoever between outer and inner. This is why it's called "pure"; at this level only one exists. It is easy, in other words, for God to see that he and his universe are one. In the same way that we would see a connection between our own ideas and ourselves, God is aware that the creation is taking place within the unlimited expanse of his own consciousness. Exercising his own free will, Śiva now takes on the role of *māyā-śakti,* the power of illusion, to create an infinite diversity of objects. These objects may attain concrete expression, yet they shine in full splendor as aspects of the one Reality, as, for instance, they do in the perception of a Siddha, one who dwells in the realization of unity-awareness. What distinguishes the *tattvas* of the pure creation from those of the impure creation is that, in the lower *tattvas,* conscious beings do not experience oneness. Purity and impurity—moral or otherwise—are not qualities inherent in the created objects, but creations of the perception of an individual. The conscious subjects who exist in the highest *tattvas* experience oneness with all that they perceive. In the other *tattvas,* impure creation, we as individuals perceive the world as separate, as different from ourselves, and so our actions are not fully free.

The Impure Creation: Differentiation

This sense of separation is a fundamental impurity, a condition known as *āṇava-mala.* The term *āṇava* is related to the *aṇu,* a particle or point, and *mala* means "impurity, dross, stain." *Āṇava-mala* is the divine force that creates a conscious particle—*cidaṇu*—out of the expansive nature of Paramaśiva. The *cidaṇu* has no body, no mind, no means for negotiating its way through the world; it is pure Consciousness in a contracted state. The experient's *cidaṇu* is the seed that becomes the embodied individual. This *cidaṇu* is not different from Paramaśiva; yet it appears to be different, because it is by way of *āṇava-mala* that the Lord holds the intention *I am separate,* and thus is cut off from his own expansive nature and freedom of will. *Āṇava-mala* is the source of the incompleteness we experience, and yet this does not represent a mistake or a fall from grace; it is necessary in the creation of an individual, arising out of the Lord's volition to enter into the universe he has manifested.

As Abhinavagupta explains in chapter 15 of the *Tantrāloka, mala* is not a substance or an object; it is the continuous act of will on the part of Lord Śiva to contract.[41] As a result of this act of will, the Lord's *svātantrya-śakti* becomes *māyā-śakti*—in other words, the supremely free Śakti becomes the power of illusion—with the express intention of creating differences. The first difference she creates is this very reduction of her own free will, her *svātantrya.* Thus a conscious being, the *cidaṇu,* has, for the sake of bringing about creation, lost his full power. It is because he has lost that power that he can enter into the womb of creation. This fourth level of manifestation is *māyā-tattva,* and its prevailing power, as I have indicated, is *māyā-śakti.* It is this power of illusion that supports the individual's sense of separateness, accompanying him through all the ensuing levels of the contraction of Consciousness, as Paramaśiva enwraps himself in increasingly grosser forms of manifestation.

In one sweep, following *māyā-tattva* come the next five *tattvas,* known as the *pañca-kañcukas,* the five cloaks or coverings. These are the limited powers by which Paramaśiva further obscures his attributes and creates the conditions necessary for limited existence. They function as the Lord's contraction of his omnipotence to limited action *(kalā),* his reduction of his omniscience into a limited knowledge *(vidyā),* his narrowing of his fullness and freedom of will to a desire for one thing or another *(rāga),* his replacement of a sense of eternity and bliss with the passage of time *(kāla),* and his restraint of luminous omnipresence by the natural laws of form, space, and the perception of causes followed by effects *(niyati).* Altogether these six categories (*maya* and the five *kañcukas*) form *prakṛti-tattva,* the principle of nature, a force that provides the material for the remainder of creation.

These six *tattvas* are subtle contractions; we could see them as straightjackets. When the Lord puts on his limited powers, he begins to perceive differences, both between himself and the world around him and also between various objects in the world. This contracted perception is known as *māyīya-mala* (the impurity of illusion), the second of the innate impurities. It is with this perception of differences that the conscious particle that is the *cidaṇu* becomes a limited individual covered by the forces that will give him a body. Now the Lord becomes a limited being, known as *puruṣa-tattva,* the principle of the individual. From our standpoint, the *puruṣa* is the knower, the subject, the in-dweller, the eternal "I am." The term *puruṣa* means "the one who dwells in the castle," and here the term is used to refer to the conscious one who resides in the castle of the body. At this point, there is a sharp, incisive perception of division between subject and object, between us and our world, between our Creator and us.

The Means of Knowing and Doing

Our means of knowing and interacting with the world comes through the next thirteen *tattvas:* the three parts of the psychic instrument and the ten faculties of perception and action.

Most subtle of these *tattvas* is the intellect *(buddhi).* This is the means by which we perceive experiences and determine what they signify. After the intellect comes the ego *(ahaṃkāra),* with which we relate to our experiences in a personal way. Following the ego, comes the faculty by which we make words and imagine *(manas).* The Indian sages have differentiated the mental processes into the three most basic functions to help us gain perspective on the psychic instrument, which we look at more closely in sutra 6, where we deal with the workings of the mind. This psychic instrument, by virtue of its functions—discriminating, relating personally, and thinking—is seen as the commander of the senses of perception and action. All these powers follow from and are under the particular governance of our ego, the *ahaṃkāra.*

First to emerge are the five powers of perception *(jñānendriyas),* which give us the information we need in order to understand the world: hearing, feeling, seeing, tasting, and smelling.

Then we move through the world with our powers of action *(karmendriyas),* which comprise the next five *tattvas:* speaking, handling, locomotion, excretion, and procreation. It is with the individual's assumption of these limited powers of action that the third *mala* arises, *kārma-mala,* the capacity for limited activity as dictated by the five "cloaks" of *māyā.* This *mala* also generates the web of impressions and consequences created by motivated action—*If I do this, then I will get that; if I say this, then that will never happen*—that the scriptures call karma, the force that propels our destiny.

For us the world, the physical object of our knowing, is drawn from the final ten *tattvas,* the five primary forces facilitating sensation *(tanmātras)* and the five gross elements *(bhūtas).*

These primary forces are associated with sound, touch, sight, taste, and smell. Since the *tanmātras* make it possible for us to experience particular sensations coming from the outer world, they arise directly from the ego *(ahaṃkāra)* and work in intimate connection with the senses of perception *(jñānendriyas).* Each of these forces gives rise to a particular element. The sense of sound, for instance, implies the existence of space, since it is in space that sound travels. The sense of touch implies the existence of air, for we are touched by air and can feel its temperature and its movement. Of course, we can also hear air in the movement of wind. The sense of sight gives rise to the element of fire, which can be seen—and, at the same time, also felt and heard. The sensation of taste gives rise to the element of water, which can be tasted and, of course, also seen, felt, and heard. And smell is associated with earth, the element that involves all five sensations. In this way, each of the elements provides a foundation from which its associated sensation can be perceived—and also includes those that have preceded it.

Thus, it is directly from the forces associated with sensation that the five gross elements, the *bhūtas,* take form—space, air, fire, water, and, the most embedded of all the *tattvas,* earth. * It is with these *bhūtas* that the individual's outer garment, the physical body, is created. As the sutra implies, all that has been described to this point is contained in the physical body.

A Word About Numbers

Let us pause for a moment here. A list of thirty-four principles is quite a bit to take in at one go. Before we embark on the next section, I want to say a word about this tradition of symbolic enumeration, practiced in India since the sixth century B.C.E. To someone reared in the Western philosophical tradition, the apparently relentless numbering of the various subtle facets of Kashmir Śaivism might make it appear to be a closed system, with application only within itself. I assert, most emphatically, that this is not the case. The numbers are in service of the student, a claim I'll support with the aid of a contemporary theorist, who compares the study of philosophy to walking in a wood.[42] When you are new to a forest, the branching trails of the terrain can be confusing, particularly when you have no landmarks to help you determine where you are and which of these many paths you should take in order to reach your desired destination. But for someone who lives in the forest—to

* Readers who are drawn to this sequential view of the world may find that my representation of this schema of manifestation is too abbreviated for their taste. For those who may be unfamiliar with, or who may wish to become more familiar with, this elegant cosmology, the list of the *tattvas* appears in Appendix B. For further study, I recommend Mark Dyczkowski's discussion in *The Doctrine of Vibration* (1987) or Jaideva Singh's thorough explanation in the introduction to his translation of Kshemaraja's commentary on this text, *The Doctrine of Recognition* (1990).

the woodcutters and forestkeepers—every tree is a marker, every rock carries its own message: *Oh, yes, now I'm ten minutes from the stream, and from there it will be just a short walk to the top of the hill.* This is the purpose served by these various lists of numbered concepts in Kashmir Śaivism—and in Indian philosophy generally. The sages perceive very specific subtle distinctions between functions, states, and, in the case of the *tattvas,* levels of reality. The most effective way to present these distinctions and, from my perception, by far the most effective way of assimilating them is with these numbered lists. They are simply easier to remember.

That said, we can now turn to a discussion of the next numbered set: the seven perceivers.

The Seven Perceivers

Now that we've surveyed the thirty-four *tattvas,* arriving finally at the stage of materiality, we can return to a question that is so tricky for many of us: Where does our physical world actually come from? Saying that our world comes from our perception seems to imply that the world has no substance. And we know that it does have substance. If you hit your knee with this very book, you will experience pain; the book itself is a concrete entity, derived from the five physical elements. As we indicated in sutra 3, the book is a part of Śiva's manifestation, very much like our own bodies are. Our own world, that reality we create in our own being, is our individual experience of Śiva's world.

In her descent into manifestation, Citi not only creates the universe with its innumerable worlds, she also gives birth to the conscious beings that populate these worlds. The play between *aham* (I am) and *idam* (this) becomes the experiencing subjects with their corresponding circumstances. These conscious subjects are known as *pramātās,* the perceivers or experients, and are identified at seven levels in the creation.[43] This means that there are seven distinct states of awareness through which the creation is experienced, beginning with the *sakalas,* which take the viewpoint of duality, and ending with *śiva-pramātās,* beings in the highest state. (For a complete list of the names of these perceivers, their respective fields of perception, and the *tattvas* associated with each of them, please turn to Appendix C.)

What I find most interesting about the seven experiencers is the certainty that each of these states of awareness is accessible to us as our own. This is the real "proof" of the *tattvas* for me: that these levels of existence are expressed in states that I can experience. My first inkling that this could be true came in my reading of Baba Muktananda's *Play of Consciousness,* in which Baba speaks of traveling to subtle worlds in his meditation. My own sense of adventure was piqued by these accounts; I wanted to see these subtle beings myself, to find out how they live and feel and experience their worlds. So, I began to watch my meditations closely for answers.

My first experience of this sort came during an afternoon nap. I was lying on my cot, and on this day, instead of going to sleep, I entered a state Baba calls *tandrā* in which the witnessing consciousness is alert even though the body and mind are sleepy. In this state, I watched my subtle body, a cloud-like form, rise out of my physical body—and come to sit on top of it. This vaporous "me," translucent and weightless, was so happy to be free from the physical encasement of my body that it began to fly joyfully around the dormitory, going through walls and performing aerial somersaults. Sometimes it hovered over various parts of the room, and then—amazing!—I could see what my roommates were doing: some were sleeping; some were reading or repeating the mantra; several were engaged in a surreptitious chess game, which they seemed to be trying to hide from the rest of us.

I saw that, even without my physical senses, I could perceive what was happening around me. The experience was so vivid that I knew it couldn't be a fantasy. After I came out of this state, I thought about Baba's descriptions of meditation and understood that this was an experience of my subtle body. Much later, after I'd studied Śaivism in greater depth, it dawned on me that this subtle experience must be approximately how the world is experienced by *sakalas* in the subtle worlds of the ancestors and the gods and in the other celestial realms. These are particular *sakalas* who live in the subtle realms below *prakṛti* and *puruṣa tattvas* and yet above the gross elements, the *bhūtas.* (Of course, we're quite familiar with the viewpoint of the other *sakalas,* those that have physical bodies made from the densest aspects of the five gross elements.)

At different times during my *sādhana* I've had experiences that gave me insights into the viewpoint of others of the seven perceivers, and in later sutras I describe some of these. If you are, as I've always been, interested in such exploration, I recommend that you sharpen your understanding of the *tattvas* so that you can recognize these experiences when they come to you. Ultimately, I feel that anyone who couples regular meditation with contemplation and scriptural study will gradually develop a deeper knowledge and appreciation for his or her own being—which, as the sutra indicates, contains the essence of the universe in a contracted form.

Creation Is Nonsequential

The formation of pure Consciousness into matter, as it is envisioned by the Kashmiri Śaivas, seems to be a chain of cause and effect. Consider the *tattvas:* doesn't it appear that they lead into one another, each coming out of the one that precedes it? But that isn't the way it is. According to Abhinavagupta, the *tattvas* appear and disappear in an instant. They are obviously related to one another. As I have described earlier, there is a hierarchy of *tattvas* in which each of the *tattvas* pervades the next *tattva* in succession, all the way down the line. In the same way, each *tattva* that has been pervaded encompasses the *tattvas* that precede it. Here, the words "succession" and "precede" are not entirely accurate, because, as I said, the view is that they all come into existence simultaneously—and dissolve back into their source simultaneously. It is also true that because each *tattva* is, in its essence, pure Consciousness, the whole is contained in every one of them. As Abhinavagupta writes:

> Thus, even though the final element [in the series] is such as it is, it nonetheless contains within itself all the other countless aspects that, step by step, preceded it and are encompassed by it in such a way that they are inseparable from its own nature. [Consciousness] thus illumines and contemplates itself as full and perfect *[pūrṇa]*.[44]

So, at every stage in this process, Consciousness contains the entire sequence within and possesses the capacity both to manifest a universe and to return that manifestation back to the ultimate cause, to pure Consciousness. Understanding this can give us a meaningful context for the spiritual journey. We could say that the exercise in divine awareness we call *sādhana* is nothing more than our own consciousness becoming increasingly subtler, rising through the *tattvas,* as it were. Yet the *tattvas* also illustrate that this inward journey need not happen sequentially or over a span of time. The hopeful implication of this understanding is that the capacity for full Self-realization—knowledge of our fullness and perfection—is within us in this very moment, as the great beings tell us again and again. The most exciting aspect of Śaivism for me is this notion that everything we are to become exists within us and is completely available to us right now—it is only a question of our perception.

A *Śiva-sūtra* that Baba often quoted states this principle very succinctly: *yathā tatra tathānyatra,* "As here, so there."[45] The word "here" refers to the physical body and "there" (or "elsewhere," as it is often translated) means "everything other than the body." What the sutra says is that all of this is essentially the same.

Whoever has realized her own divinity even for a moment learns that her body contains, in a contracted form, all the principles that comprise the universe and also experiences herself as the origin and center of everything that has been created. The *Maitrī Upaniṣad* says:

> Assuredly the Self of one's self is called the leader, [the] immortal, [the] perceiver, [the] thinker, the goer, the evacuator, the delighter, the doer, the speaker, the taster, the smeller, the seer, the hearer, and he [who] touches. He, the all-pervader, has entered the body. . . . This Self, verily, is the Lord, the beneficent, the real, the terrible, the Lord of Creation, the creator of all, the golden germ, truth, life, spirit, the ordainer, the pervader, Nārāyana, the shining vivifier, the upholder, sovereign Indra, [and] the moon. . . . Him, verily, one should desire to know.[46]

Just as the Self is the one energy that assumes all these forms, so the *tattvas*—which are energies that condense according to their particular vibrations—are all, intrinsically, the same energy. That is why it is impossible to define a specific location as the center of the universe, as when we mark the center of a circle. Citi pervades everything equally in all directions: each place is the center of everything. As we recognize the great light that shines in the body, by this very act, we place ourselves within the divine heart and hence in the very center of creation. Startling as it is, this teaching is difficult for our minds to comprehend, for *māyā-śakti* obscures our experience of the Truth. It is easier for us to think that God is "over there," in the heavens, and that we are "here," on earth, but this is a fragmented truth, partial and incomplete. The fourth sutra tells us that the Lord is as much on earth as in heaven—and that he is also in the heart of every human being, pulsating with the awareness "I am."

This understanding has a very beautiful application for *sādhana:* instead of aspiring to reach for knowledge that is far away from us and thus difficult to attain, with regular spiritual practice, we can unravel the knowledge that is hidden within our own being.

5

Universal Consciousness Descends to Become the Mind

Sutra 5

चितिरेव चेतनपदादवरूढा
चेतयसंकोचिनी चित्तम्

citir eva cetana-padād avarūḍhā cetya-saṃkocinī cittam

Consciousness herself, having descended
from the expanded state, becomes the mind,
contracted by the objects of perception.

citiḥ:	Consciousness
eva:	itself
cetana:	expanded Consciousness
padāt:	from the stage or station
avarūḍhā:	descended
cetya:	perceivable; object of perception
saṃkocinī:	contracted
cittam:	individual consciousness, the mind

KSHEMARAJA BEGINS HIS COMMENTARY to sutra 5, saying, "Truly speaking, *citta* [individual consciousness] is the exalted *citi* [universal Consciousness] itself."[47]

What does it mean to us that universal Consciousness is the mind, our mind? Baba Muktananda tells us that this one equivalency is of the highest importance to us as spiritual seekers. He begins his own commentary on this sutra, saying, "This aphorism is the very lifeblood of *sādhana.* It is priceless. If a seeker could understand this aphorism alone and believe in its truth, meditation would come to him by itself, and so would knowledge."[48]

The mind—the very center of our activity as individuals, the instrument that allows us to understand and evaluate our experience of life—is itself a form of universal Consciousness. Think about it: Each feeling, each thought, each image that comes before your mental screen, each apparition from your memory—all the activities of your mind are a form of God. Not just the blissful contemplations or creative flashes, but also the negative thoughts, the painful memories, the nightmarish images that sometimes pursue you; your charitable assessments and also your egotism, pride, and jealousies; your sublime imaginings and exalted understandings and additionally your feelings of unworthiness, your fears, your bursts of rage, and the endless parade of concepts that keep you contracted—all of these are manifestations of the great divine light. Yes, all!

The irony is that this very mental activity, which is so clearly identified here as an expression of divinity, is also what obscures our divine nature from us. I think this is one reason Kshemaraja, after having stated in sutra 2 that all of creation is formed of Consciousness, states here that the mind is also Consciousness. If we, as seekers, can comprehend fully that our mind is God, then, as Baba says, meditation will come to us by itself and so will the highest knowledge.

Holding this awareness is, in itself, an extremely efficacious approach to meditation. Most methods of meditation tell us to focus on some point—a single image, sound, thought, or feeling. We strive to harness the stream of our mental activity in the direction of this focus, and it doesn't take long to discover just how challenging this is to accomplish. All of these meditation techniques attempt to bring the mind to rest on a single point, which stills the mind, thereby allowing the meditator to experience the serenity that lies beyond the mind, in the inner space of Consciousness.

The technique Baba recommends here is to allow the mind to do whatever it will—and, at the same time, to see the mind itself as what it truly is: Consciousness. This so simplifies meditation! Whatever memory or mental image, whatever desire or long-buried emotion, whatsoever at all comes up on our mental screen, we are invited to see that very thing as the goal of our meditation, as Consciousness. This means of meditation—and I can personally attest to its power—is the natural application of all that we're studying in these very sutras: the supposition that Consciousness is all that exists. And that there is, as sutra 5 implies, enormous benefit in turning the mind toward its own divine nature.

The mind is like a chameleon, continually changing its color according to what it perceives. Our happiness, or unhappiness, depends on these mental fluctuations. One moment, the mind is our friend, supporting us and helping us move through our lives effectively; the next moment, it turns against us, spewing onto our lives the venom of wicked thoughts and unkind assessments. The mind that takes the inner posture of understanding its own divinity—of seeing each thought, whether positive or negative, as an expression of the highest Consciousness—becomes strong and stable, setting a solid foundation for meditation and the realization of the Self.

My great-grandfather, who'd never heard of Kashmir Śaivism and certainly never read the *Pratyabhijñā-hṛdayam,* seemed to have imbibed the steadiness that can come with the contemplation of this sutra. There is a story about him that is very well-known among Puerto Ricans of the older generation. Though my great-grandfather was a successful businessman, he came from a simple background and he was always unpretentious. One day, he and his wife were going to the movies, and when he put on his jacket, my great-grandmother said, "Antonio, there's a hole in that jacket. Why don't you wear something else?" He said, "What for? Everyone knows me here." A few months later, they were on a business trip to New York, and as they were getting ready to leave their hotel room, he put on his jacket. My great-grandmother said, "Antonio, you have a hole in your jacket. You can't go out like this!" He said, "What's the problem? Nobody knows me here."

This story has always intrigued and delighted me: this magnificent man knew how to use the mind—the mind by which we can make ourselves unhappy or happy, by which we can create our bondage or our liberation. Once commenting on the significance of maintaining equipoise, Gurumayi said:

> In our life, everything depends on our attitude—the way we think, the way we speak, the way we hear. A good person will hear what you are saying with a good attitude. A negative per-

> son will hear what you are saying with a negative attitude. Man is what he thinks. Whatever you think of all the time, that's what you say and that's what you hear.[49]

When you think of Consciousness, when you even consider the notion that the world and all your thoughts about it are Consciousness, then that is how you see the world. And, as the sutra tells us, the mind itself is that Consciousness.

Creating a Universe

In the sutra at hand, the four most significant words—*citi, cetana, cetya* and *citta*—derive from the same root: *cit,* consciousness. *Cetana,* which in this sutra refers to the most expanded stage, also means "visible, conspicuous, excellent, aware, intelligent." This means that when Citi, the universal Consciousness, is in the state of *cetana,* we say that she is luminous, conspicuously pure, and excellent, by virtue of being free of any conditioning. *Cetya* is "the perceivable," all the things that Consciousness takes within herself as objects of her own perception. Now, for something to be perceived, it must be made concrete; that is, it must appear to be different from the pristine uniformity of pure Consciousness. Thus, *citir eva,* "herself," of her own free will, descends from the state of pure luminosity and becomes contracted, *saṃkocinī,* according to the objects that she perceives, *cetya.* Exactly as a camera imparts the form of a photographic image onto the uniform surface of the film, the uniform light of Consciousness adopts the form of everything she experiences. In this act, a phenomenon of extraordinary importance occurs:

Consciousness turns herself into an experiencing individual. Citi becomes *citta.*

The World of Thought

Kshemaraja defines *citta* in its widest sense as individual consciousness. The main characteristic of this individual consciousness is its capacity to create differentiated perceptions. In Sanskrit, these are known as *vikalpas.* In other words, the one characteristic common to every creature is that we all perceive, we think. This includes dogs and honeybees, as well as human beings and the experiencing subjects known as *mantra maheśvaras* (great lords of mantra), who exist only in a subtle form in the *sadāśiva-tattva* at the very highest level of the pure creation. Each of these orders of beings has a unique set of *vikalpas,* certain perceptions that form its world in a totally specific way.*

Dogs, for instance, whose world is primarily one of scents, determine what to eat, with whom to mate, when to fight, and where to take rest almost entirely with their sense of smell. Imagine trying to do that as a human being! We simply couldn't. We don't have enough olfactory receptors to make it possible. Honeybees, whose perceptions are primarily visual, are directed in their search for pollen by the ultraviolet patterns they perceive on flowers—a range of color invisible to the human eye. In the same way, it's through their own subtle perceptions that the *mantra-maheśvaras* know *I am all this.*

Naturally, we can draw a distinction between these different levels of *vikalpa.* Most of the time, we use this term to designate word-

* For a list of the seven orders of beings known as *pramātās,* or perceivers, please see Appendix C.

formulated thoughts; at other times, we refer to subtler experiences, such as wordless perceptions. In his commentary on the *Spanda-kārikā*, Kshemaraja cites this latter, exalted manifestation of *vikalpa* when he writes the following:

> Śambhu triumphs [over all] by the glory of [his] incomparable and undivided bliss. He, like a newly wedded husband, constantly gazes at his beloved power who, although inwardly undivided, dances in many ways outside [her] own nature, [her] diverse forms and seemingly new aspects conceived in the varied light of *vikalpa*.[50]

As human beings we are likely to perceive our world in less blissful terms, and yet the point of this sutra is to tell us that our perception, like the very world itself, is divine Consciousness. In order to understand what is being said here, let us look more closely at this phenomenon known as *vikalpa*. The prefix *vi* means "separation," implying division and distinction, as when we perceive diversity and differences; *kalpa* comes from the root *kḷp*, meaning "that which partakes of or causes." So, *vikalpa* is a force that creates and partakes of duality. Strictly speaking, *vikalpa* is the conscious activity that separates and distinguishes one thing from another, this from that, as when we make a distinction between Peter and Jane, a city and a town, or ourselves and others. The practical value of *vikalpas* is that they solidify and classify our perceptions, making it possible for us to exist in our world. What we must also understand is that, through our *vikalpas*, we actually create that world. Let me give you an example.

One day while I was shopping, rummaging through a display of sweaters, I happened to look up and catch sight of a man several yards away, looking straight at me. I thought, *That's strange,* and I turned back to the sweaters immediately, not wanting to engage this person. A moment later, I raised my head again and encountered the same man, staring at me, point-blank. I gave him a very definite glare this time, as if to say, *I see what you're doing and I don't like it.* I returned to the sweaters, but I didn't give them my attention. I was remembering that angry face staring at me. I thought, *The nerve of this guy. Such an aggressive stare!* After a few moments, I looked up a third time—and found myself once again eye-to-eye with this angry and intrusive person. *This is too much,* I thought. I started walking toward him, thinking that I would see what he had to say for himself—and found myself approaching a mirror.

I had to laugh at myself. When I thought about it later, however, I saw that this play was more than just an amusing and humbling incident; it was a perfect illustration of how we create our own reality with our thoughts. Remember how we spoke in sutra 2 about *pratibimba,* the world as a reflection in supreme Consciousness? Well, here my world was reflected not just in a store mirror but also in the mirror of my own consciousness. With my thoughts about what I saw, I made a world for myself—I created a hostile being, someone who was staring at me aggressively, possibly even wishing me harm. Once I recognized that I was looking into a mirror, it was an easy matter to see that it was my own mind that had taken form before me—or, from the perspective of the sutra, that my mind had taken the form of what I perceived. What a relief when I saw that the enemy was—me!

Kshemaraja invites us to have this recognition in every instant of our lives: to see that our world reflects back to us our thoughts, our feelings, our interpretations—our *vikalpas,* our *citta*—and that, then, becomes our reality. Notice that the recurrent theme in that thought is the word "our": supreme Consciousness takes the form of our perception.

You might ask, *How does this happen? What does it actually mean that the mind "takes the form of the object of perception"?* Consider what happens when you see an acquaintance. You experience your friend as sensory reality, but how? The image of your friend is within your mind, first of all, even though your friend herself is not within your mind; so when you meet her, you recognize her. Your mind has stored visual impressions of your friend. This power is the mind's capacity to "become" whatever it perceives. This same mental power operates when we smell coffee brewing or hear the phone ring. Further, we add to these purely sensorial impressions our own interpretation of them, based on associations stored in the memory and in the subconscious mind. Also, as we know, these combinations of images, ideas, feelings, and interpretations can occur independently of the senses when we do introspective thinking and visualization, when we fantasize, or when we dream; these are forms our mind has adopted, as it were, for our perception.

And these perceptions manifest at many, many different levels of awareness.

The Levels of Vikalpa

The *Mālinī-vijaya-tantra* describes fifteen conscious states that color a yogi's perceptions, ranging from various levels of *vikalpa* to states beyond *vikalpa.* The basic states range from waking, dream, deep sleep, and *turīya* (awareness of the Self) to the total illumination of *turīyātīta* (universal Self-awareness). Within many of these states, countless additional levels are interpolated, each associated with a specific range of perceptions.[51] When we dream, how many states of mind might we experience, with all their attendant feelings and thoughts and perceptions—perceptions sometimes of extraordinary astral events! And in the waking state, because of the incredibly vast deposit of mental impressions that we carry in our memories, we may go through hundreds of states of consciousness in just one moment. Furthermore, as we have seen, there are thirty-four principles in the universe, and associated with these are seven specific states of being, each encompassing a different level of perception, or degree of attainment, of unity-consciousness.

All of these states are possible for us, all are at our disposal, all are available for our enjoyment, and all are related to perceptions, most of which are governed by *vikalpas.*

When we find ourselves having painful or depressing responses to the world, we may think that our difficulties are evidence that God is unhappy with us, that he is punishing us for some mistake we've made, for something negative we've done or said or thought. Yet, in consideration of the teachings we're examining here, how is it possible to envision God as a wrathful deity, an instrument of vengeful retribution? In sutra 1, we learned that the nature of God is love and light and incomparable bliss. In sutra 2, we saw how God—or the Goddess, if you prefer—witnesses all creation mirrored on his or her own luminous screen. It seems obvious that the Lord neither judges nor punishes us, and yet there is clearly pain involved in at least some of our experiences. How does that pain come to us, and what are we to understand from it? Once when asked about the best ways of dealing with loneliness and depression, Baba Muktananda said:

> These feelings just arise, but you are not necessarily undergoing them. They are the creation of the mind. You should just understand them. Śaivism explains it very beautifully, saying that all these feelings are the creation of limited knowledge. Infinite thoughts arise and subside, arise and subside; infinite creations arise and dissolve, arise and dissolve in the mind.
>
> Sometimes the mind marries somebody, sometimes the mind kills somebody. Should you laugh? Should you cry? A wise person understands that everything is the creation of the mind, and he keeps quiet. Why do you carry somebody else's burden? Why do you carry these feelings on your head? Let them fly away.[52]

We explore further this question of coping with negative thoughts and feelings in sutra 9.

Like supreme Consciousness, the individual consciousness is a creative power. It is through us that God experiences his own wondrous creation. It's because God's own essence operates through our thoughts that those thoughts are strong enough to create a world. The teaching that Consciousness becomes the mind is, as Baba indicates, critical for the practice of yoga. You might ask, as I did once, *If all my thoughts are pure Consciousness, why do I experience them as thoughts?* The answer is simple: because of *māyā's* power to conceal. You might also find, as I did, that this observation is not particularly helpful. In yoga, the question of why something is true is tremendously less significant than the application of that truth in one's life.

Creating a New Universe

The *Maitrī Upaniśad* says:

> One's own thought, indeed, is *saṃsāra* [the cycle of birth and death]. Let a man purify it by effort. What a man thinks, that he becomes. This is the eternal mystery.[53]

We can say the same about the Creator: what God thinks, he becomes. Maheśvara, the Great Lord, is the universal mind, which, with the aid of *vikalpas,* conceives the entire universe. The Great Lord, in his unfading integrity, expresses himself as "I am," the pure and simple *aham.* As it initiates the process of creation, the *aham* emits its expression as *idam,* "this," by which it gives birth to the created objects. In sutras 3 and 4, we read how this play of *aham* and *idam* governs the ways we adapt and relate to our world. *Idam* is the creative *vikalpa.* This is what we do as well.

When I go to a restaurant and say, "I would like some bread," almost inevitably bread appears on the table. When I made the decision, "I will become a monk," that was the first step toward taking vows. This is the power of *vikalpa.* If we were to perceive each *tattva* from this same perspective, we might pick up a glimmer of the cosmic monologue through which Citi actualizes every divine intention in the same manner. "The kingdom of *vikalpas,*" as Baba Muktananda often called it, is wholly embracing and surprising; it includes all levels of existence, all worlds, and, as we said earlier, all conscious creatures dwelling in the cosmos.

The difference between us identified as individuals and us living from the level of Maheśvara is that, in the contracted state, we are limited by our mental activity—we sometimes experience pleasure, sometimes pain. When we experience ourselves as the Great Lord, we are aware of our blissful nature and feel free from the restrictive effect of our *vikalpas.* As an individual, the supreme power offers itself the opportunity to experience the life of a human being, with its dramas and passions, its highs and lows, its ideals and compromises, its victories and defeats. In short, by becoming an individual, the Great Lord lives through the entire dramatic scope of a life. Isn't this phenomenon part of the mystery? The question remains: How do we find our way through this kingdom of thoughts?

It takes consistent effort to conceive, to truly understand that each emotion, each mental image, each idea that arises within you is a form of pure Consciousness. Trying for one or two days will not do it. It takes practice, and practice implies repeated effort, the forging of new habits, truly retraining the mind. I find the following two approaches work quite well for me, as they have for many other people who have tried them.

In the first practice, I let go of a sense of guilt or pride about any of my thoughts or feelings. This is particularly challenging in regard to those thoughts and feelings that I consider unacceptable. If I don't want to experience something that is coming up inside me, I just let it pass, thinking, *This is a temporary configuration of Consciousness.* On the other hand, when I consider the contents of my mind acceptable, pleasurable, or even exalting, I think, *This is another manifestation of Consciousness.* This practice may seem as if it takes quite a bit of energy in the beginning, since it requires effort to maintain the awareness that everything is Consciousness. However, once the habit is entrenched, it saves enormous energy, since all of the various thoughts that one can have about one's thoughts—*vikalpas* playing off *vikalpas*—no longer spin out of control.

The second, and easier, practice that I've adopted involves substituting my mantra for my thoughts. The silent repetition of a mantra, particularly one that is enlivened by the energy of one's spiritual master, can calm the mind and create an inner atmosphere of sweet serenity. As I practice mantra repetition, I find it extremely efficacious to entertain the understanding that the mantra, like the mental activity it replaces, is a form of Consciousness. In this way, it isn't a question of good replacing evil, light replacing darkness, as much as it is one form of Consciousness, something that can free me from my attachment to the world—from my delusions—replacing another form, which is of the world. With this approach, I've found that I've developed increasing tolerance and affection for myself, even when I'm manifesting my least desirable characteristics. As a result, gradually these negative characteristics have been leaving me—and I'm becoming happier and happier.

I'm suggesting that you adopt these practices, and yet I also acknowledge that such a change isn't a simple matter. For those of us who've been educated in a culture that condemns many of the normal manifestations of the mind, it's a challenge to practice the equalizing vision of seeing all mental movement as a form of Consciousness—or, if you wish, a form of God. One of the foundations of my own practice is an experience that I had in meditation shortly after my spiritual awakening. To that point, I'd always believed that my thoughts and emotions were obstacles to a good meditation, and so when I sat for meditation, I'd try to still my mind. On this particular morning, I was having what I might call an "average" meditation, by which I mean that as I repeated my mantra silently, I was observing an endless stream of scenes, faces, tasks, reminiscences, and so on. Then suddenly, as if from nowhere, there was at the center of my mind's screen an exquisite bluish light.

I watched this radiance—it was so beautiful that I was naturally drawn to look at it—and as I watched it, the light became increasingly brighter, until it expanded to fill my entire inner space. Then I began to notice that images were emerging from the light. An image would arise spontaneously from the light. It would hover at the forefront of my mental screen for a while and then, just as suddenly as it had appeared, it would merge back into that splendid light. As I watched the birth of these thought forms, which were made of light and were coming out of light, I was filled with joy. The content of my thoughts didn't affect me at all, and yet I was watching them closely, I was taking a great aesthetic pleasure in seeing them arise and subside. Intuitively, I recognized that the blue radiance was an expression of my own inner being.

After I came out of meditation and contemplated what I'd seen, I was awestruck by what it implied: that everything in my mind—be it pleasurable or painful, exalted or trivial, fantastic or mundane—is a form of blue light. And further, I could feel that it is all an expression of joy. Now I have more words with which to explain the experience. It was the blue light of Consciousness I was seeing, God himself, and the joy that I experienced was his joy—or my own divine joy in watching my creation unfold within me, a creation made of my own thoughts, my own *vikalpas.* These appearances were *ābhāsas,* the playful flashing of manifestation on the impeccable screen of *citi.* What I knew at the time was that I could sit for meditation without passing judgment on the contents of my mind.

In other words, instead of trying to manipulate our thoughts, we can offer each *vikalpa* back to the light of the Self. It's where they all come from; after all, it's what they are! It isn't important that we perceive the inner light in our meditations. Whether or not we perceive it, the Self, as our natural witnessing awareness, is always present. What matters is that we make an effort to remember that the mind is a form of divine Consciousness. The *Vijñāna-bhairava* says:

> Wherever the mind goes, whether toward the exterior or toward the interior, everywhere there is the state of Śiva. Since Śiva is omnipresent, where can the mind go to avoid him?[54]

6

Perception and the Human Condition

Sutra 6

तन्मयो मायाप्रमाता

tanmayo māyā-pramātā

One whose nature is that [the mind] experiences *māyā.*

tat:	that
mayaḥ:	whose nature is
māyā:	power of illusion, limited perception
pramātā:	one who experiences, an individual subject

THE ONE WHO EXPERIENCES MĀYĀ: These words take me back to a time in my youth when I had to stop what I was doing and ask myself, *What is this world all about? Where am I going in my life?* The conclusion I reached was that life made no sense and even death was a riddle. I didn't like this answer, and yet nothing else I found was particularly convincing. My paternal grandmother, who loved me dearly, was worried by this new agnosticism of mine and persuaded a Catholic priest to speak with me.

This priest was a Castilian intellectual with the bearing of an aristocrat, the face of a Velazquez portrait, and a black fringe of hair that formed a natural tonsure. He came to call one day and began by asking me why I wasn't practicing the faith in which I'd been reared.

I knew where he was going with that line of thought, so I cut to the chase: "Look, Father," I said, "we can continue this conversation only if you demonstrate three things to me first. Does God exist? And I don't want to hear theories and suppositions on this; I want evidence as tangible as you and I are in this moment. And then can you prove to me that I have a soul and that this soul is eternal?"

The poor priest, confronted in this brash and unexpected manner, could not, of course, give me what I asked for. He tried for a few minutes and then changed the subject. We spoke quite happily of Spanish art, which we both loved, and in the course of our conversation, we became great friends. My questions, however, remained for the time, unanswered.

Now I see these questions as the expression of a search, a yearning that arises from the depth of a soul frustrated with the emptiness of the world-illusion. This, for me, is the very essence of sutra 6, *tanmayo māyā-pramātā.* The word *tat* means "that," referring to the topic of the previous sutra: *citta,* the individual consciousness and, by extension, its instrument, the mind. The suffix *mayo* is "consists of" or "of the nature of." The word *pramātā* refers to the subject, the one who perceives and experiences. Together, these terms imply that what we are discussing here is the experience of one whose nature is the mind, one who is identified with the mind. That experience is portrayed as *māyā*, which, as we know, is the power of illusion, the generative force of the created universe, and also the appearance of this realm. So, the sutra tells us that it is the nature of the mind to perceive and experience *māyā*.

Māyā is a term so rich with meaning that I prefer not to attempt a full translation. For now let us give it the flavor used by the Śaiva Siddhantins, South Indian dualists who worship Lord Śiva. In this tradition, *māyā* is *pāśa* (the bond) that ensnares *pati* (the Lord) and makes him a *pāśu* (a bound soul). The word *pāśu* also means "beast," which implies that the loss of divine knowledge leaves the human being in a condition no better than that of any other animal. The description is not flattering, but it reminds us that the purpose of our lives is to attain something higher. When the bond of *māyā* is loosened, the bound soul becomes free and returns to its condition as *paśupati*, the Lord of all creatures.

Sutra 5 describes the divine essence of the mind, then sutra 6 identifies what the mind does—the mind perceives *māyā*—and, by implication, what happens in our own lives as a result. In this sutra, Kshemaraja speaks of the human condition. As the Śaiva sage Vasugupta points out in *Spanda-kārikā:*

> Operating in the field of the subtle elements, the arising of mental representation marks the disappearance of the flavor of the supreme nectar of immortality; due to this [a human being] forfeits his freedom.[55]

The experiences born of perceptions *(vikalpas)* picked up by the senses generate innumerable desires in the mind, and these *vikalpas* rule our lives with impetuosity.

It might seem that we said so much about *vikalpas* and the workings of the mind in our discussion of the last sutra that there is nothing left to explore. In truth, we've only just scratched the surface. In sutra 6, Kshemaraja alludes to the mind's act of perception, *pramāṇa,* which in turn introduces the threefold psychic instrument by which most perception takes place, as well as the three qualities, the *guṇas,* that make up both the mind and all in *māyā* that is perceptible. Without understanding all of these, you are under the control of the mind, and, as Baba Muktananda once said in commenting on this sutra, "As long as you are under the control of your mind, you cannot know the Truth, you cannot become supremely happy, you cannot manifest your own divinity."[56]

Perception and Individuality

Of the operations of the mind, the most important is perception, *pramāṇa,* the activity that makes it possible to know and to understand something. *Pramāṇa* is a process initiated by Citi to connect the subject with whatever it experiences. It is the perceptive movement that relates the one with the other. When I have an experience of any sort, I perceive it in my mind; this is how I know I'm having an experience. At the deepest level, *pramāṇa* is the reflection of an object in the light of the inner Self, which adopts the particulars of what it perceives and mirrors them in the screen of its light. This act of knowing makes the projections of

Reality, the *ābhāsas* that we discussed in sutra 3, present themselves afresh in every instant, taking on colors and various forms in accordance with our attitudes and desires. Etymologically, the term *pramāṇa* is associated with measurement. In perceiving objects, we take their measure, finding them different from other objects and different from ourselves. Thus, *pramāṇa,* the act of perceiving and knowing, is at the very root of our existence as individuals. The term "individual" means "a particular being"; here, we are referring to that which distinguishes each of us as a separate, experiencing entity. As sutra 5 indicates, our existence as individual subjects is the result of a decision whereby Consciousness leaves her state as the non-manifest Self and becomes a separate entity in accordance with the objects that entity perceives. That is, my perception of created things—such as my family and my gender, my role and my nationality—brings me, a conscious being, into constant relation with the world. The act of my "knowing" in this way is crucial in giving personal meaning to everything around me. Without this capacity, as I've said before, I wouldn't be an individual at all; I'd be in the Great Void.

In the act of becoming an individual *(pramātā)* and the objects that this individual perceives *(prameya),* Consciousness does not surrender her essential nature. She vibrates unceasingly as that individual, knowing that she is free and blissful. However, having taken the form of an individual, Consciousness chooses to forget, at least partially, her attributes of omnipotence, omniscience, and rapturous fullness; of eternality, freedom, and all-pervasiveness. She now experiences that her creativity becomes confined to specific efforts; her knowledge is limited to measurable portions of information; she becomes dependent on emotions, desires, and her ideas of good and evil; she experiences the passing of time in specific, well-defined intervals; and her will has to live within the sequential spaces of causes and their effects.*

The mind is the instrument that allows us—requires us!—to experience these limited conditions, and our perception is further qualified by our understanding and attitudes. This all involves not only our transactions in the world, but also, and more fundamentally, our *vāsanās,* our deep-seated predispositions to perceive life in one way as opposed to another. Rather than try to explain this further, I'll give you an example from my experience.

One day while I was meditating in the temple of Baba's Guru, Bhagawan Nityananda,** in Shree Muktananda Ashram, I felt my awareness sink to the center of my chest. There, I came across a dark cloud, like a veil of sadness, which seemed to hover at the core of my essential being. I know from speaking to many Siddha Yoga students over the years that it's easy to dismiss a feeling like this. We tend to tell ourselves that it's only our imagination, it's the mind playing tricks on us, it's the ego trying to upset us, or other things of that sort. I've learned, however, not to dismiss or ignore these feelings, but to go even more deeply into them. On this day, I prayed to Bhagawan Nityananda to help me understand why I had this sense of sadness, and I began to direct my attention into the cloud itself. As I went into it, the cloud began to open and disperse. At its core, I found—it surprised me enormously—that this sadness was only the outer froth of a profound and splendid sentiment: a longing for God! This longing pulsated with intensity, and as I

* This is a description of the five *kañcukas* (coverings), the principles that follow *māyā-tattva* in the great chain of being that we discussed in sutra 4.

** For more information about Bhagawan Nityananda (Bade Baba), please see Appendix A.

experienced it, I began to weep and to plead with Bade Baba, *How long is this separation going to last? Can my longing be fulfilled?* Inside myself, I heard a benevolent voice say, *Look into your heart.*

So, cutting right through that sense of longing, I directed my awareness to my heart. Just as my sadness had dissolved, so did my intense yearning. I entered a space of profound silence, a space in which I could see a tender, sparkling blue light. I felt a quiet, tremulous pulsation—and perfect serenity.

Coming out of this experience, I understood that the sadness I'd glimpsed, rooted as it was in my aspiration for God, stretched so deep into my subconscious mind that it affected the way I'd perceived everything in my life—particularly since I wasn't even aware that I had such a feeling. After the disappearance of that sadness, I felt lighter about everything; I was happier than I'd ever been.

A transformation like this works in two ways. One is that as we become conscious of a hitherto unconscious tendency, the very light of our awareness begins to attenuate that tendency; eventually it simply disappears into the light. The second way, which is what happened for me with this feeling of sadness, is that the tendency can simply dissolve on the spot. The point I wish to underscore is that *vāsanās* like the one I experienced are one of the ways *māyā* limits our freedom and promotes, as the *Spanda-kārikā* indicates, the disappearance of *the flavor of the supreme nectar of immortality.* In understanding this phenomenon of limitation, it's helpful to look closely at the way the mind works—just how we create the psychic representations of Reality by which we live. Gurumayi says:

> Going through the scriptures and texts of many different traditions, it is always amazing to see how much emphasis there is on the pure heart and pure mind in all religions and cultures. In fact, if God dwells in the heart, the mind is the gateway to knowledge of Him. When you become aware of the way your mind thinks, the way your intellect judges, the way your ego parades around; when you become aware of how your subconscious mind retains all the impressions of your thoughts and actions, then you come to understand the necessity of spiritual practices. The effort it takes to cleanse the psychic instruments becomes very precious to you.[57]

The Threefold Psychic Instrument

The term "mind" is far too general to cover all of our mental processes. The name I use for these functions is the threefold psychic instrument, the inner apparatus that encompasses the workings of *manas* (thinking faculty), *ahaṃkāra* (ego), and *buddhi* (intellect). Some commentators call these functions the three psychic instruments, but I prefer to think of them as one unit with three facets, each performing distinct functions. In sutra 5, we discussed how Consciousness descends from her expanded state and becomes the mind—our mind—by contracting in accordance with the objects of perception. Now we're going to see just how this process takes place in each of us.*

* The discussion that follows describes the operation of the *tattvas* of perception previously mentioned in sutra 4. In the chain of *tattvas*, the *buddhi* (intellect) is the highest and most subtle aspect of the mind, and the *jñānendriyas* (senses of perception) are several steps lower in the hierarchy. However, the "order" of creation is not necessarily the order in which these functions operate.

First, the psychic instrument gathers perceptions through the senses, the *jñānendriyas,* which bring in impressions of a world that is seemingly "out there"—all of the things we see, hear, smell, and so on. For me, the fascinating part of perception is the way the great Śakti becomes the senses, adopting their capacities, as she works through them. One of the most renowned of the Śaivite sages, Maheshvarananda, describes how the light of Consciousness, our own awareness, emanates from the center of our being and flows in surges of delight through our senses to take hold of impressions of the world. This same awareness then brings these impressions inward and, through the agency of the psychic instrument, leaves them as offerings for the enjoyment of the Self. These impressions are offered on the screen of the *buddhi,* the intellect.[58]

When they first come in, these impressions are simply a sweep of sensation: something we see is nothing more than a shape and a blur of color on the *buddhi.* Then the second form of perception comes in: discursive information pertinent to that blur of color. This the *buddhi* receives from an inner reservoir of memories held in the second aspect of the psychic apparatus, the thinking, word-forming faculty, *manas.* In the West, we most often consider these memories the province of the subconscious mind. Yogis know them as *saṃskāras,* subtle impressions that are left by all of one's experiences from this and every other lifetime.* This vast store of memories is said to be held in an etheric body, which we discuss in the next sutra. The *manas* selects the appropriate information and presents it to the *buddhi,* classifying and explaining what is seen. In this way, the *buddhi* knows, for instance, that the figure

* Our subtle impressions *(saṃskāras)* combine to form our more deeply rooted tendencies *(vāsanās).*

appearing before you is a human being, a woman, and a particular person with such-and-such a name, place of origin, and profession.

Thus, the *buddhi* is a screen, but it isn't inert like a film or television screen; it's a living monitor, made of conscious energy. Remember in sutra 2 when we talked about *pratibimba,* the reflection in which all objects remain distinct and recognizable. Well, in individual beings like us this reflection takes place on the intellect. One of the main functions of the intellect is to discriminate among the various sense impressions that come into us and to recognize what they are. When you walk in the woods, you might hear the singing of crickets and several birds and, at the same time, a plane flies overhead and someone speaks to you. The intellect easily distinguishes between these sounds. Even though they're all coming in simultaneously, through the information provided by the *manas,* the *buddhi* recognizes what is what.

Up to this point, the mental operation is very straightforward, but now the third aspect of our threefold psychic instrument comes into play. This is the *ahaṃkāra,* the ego, which brings us into the picture. The ego is what connects you, the *pramātā,* to the world out there, the *prameya,* through the experience, the *pramāṇa.* It's the ego that says, *This is my experience. This is my friend,* or, the reverse, *This is not a person I know. He is not my friend.* The *ahaṃkāra* is a relational power, and there is something intrinsically beautiful about this: it shows that we aren't indifferent to the world around us, that we are in constant relation to our world in the same way that God is in relation to his creation.

However, this *ahaṃkāra* is significant in other ways. The term literally means "I-maker," a perfect description of the way the ego operates. It creates the notion of "I." It also functions as a surrogate Self, telling us that our own individuality has created these thoughts and feelings and actions and results, when actually the real doer is the pure *aham*, the pure "I am" awareness that is not attached to anything at all.

In the operation of the psychic instrument, the *buddhi* acts as both witness and judge, the one who sees and the one who decides. The *buddhi* is not identified with the images it reflects. It is the *ahaṃkāra* that appropriates experiences as its own. The *ahaṃkāra* says, *That's mine. That's who I am. I don't want that.* The *ahaṃkāra* sends orders to the *manas* to gather more and more specific information. Thus, the thinking faculty, always alert to satisfy the ego's voracious appetite for experience, is constantly selecting and associating sensations to form a coherent picture.

This process of perception also applies to experiences that arise from our inner being without the participation of the senses. Besides the deposit of impressions stored in the memory, we have the system of psychic centers of the subtle body, the *cakras*. From the *cakras* arise energies that enable us to have emotions, flashes of intuition—even phenomena related to powers that we call extrasensorial—and all types of mental tendencies, both positive and negative. For us to be able to feel and express these experiences, they too must be mirrored in the intellect, classified by the mental faculty, and personalized by the ego.

It also takes the entire mental apparatus to understand the discussion we're having right now, to learn and master concepts—to think abstractly, to write poetry, to play the drum. Flashes of artistic inspiration arise as an impulse directly from the Self, and yet it is the psychic instrument that notices these insights and inventions, that remembers them and finds ways to give them expression.

The yogi looks at the complex operation of this threefold psychic instrument in relation to *sādhana*, the spiritual path. In that respect, there is no difficulty with our perception of objects or having thoughts about those perceptions. The difficulty arises only in the way we relate to those thoughts, when we identify with them. Baba Muktananda had this to say to a man, a Hindi poet, who visited the Ganeshpuri ashram in 1964 to seek help with his meditation:

> The mind is as restless as a monkey. Your mind is restless and you are aware of it. This very recognition will help you to make it concentrated. . . . You do not suffer any loss when a horse that is standing near you runs away and then returns; it is the same between you and your mind. Just watch the mind. Become the witness of the mind. I also passed through a state similar to yours. I am advising you to follow the *sādhana* that benefited me.[59]

When we adopt the stance of a witness, we are identifying with the great Witness, the Self. *Vikalpas*, our differentiated perceptions, are a creation of *citiśakti* playing in the mind, and the Self witnesses these *vikalpas* without being affected by them in the slightest. On more than a few occasions, I've meditated while my mind was producing all sorts of events and conversations. In this situation, I find that a moment comes when somehow my attention dips under the maelstrom, and even if the activity doesn't then cease, I am uninvolved in it. I feel myself to be the witness of what is happening.

When we cannot witness our thoughts, the *ahaṃkāra* appropriates the perceptions of the intellect for itself, and a whole web of consequences arises in which we seek supportive information and further sensation and which, ultimately, inspires us to all sorts of motivated actions.

We may tell ourselves that we live in response to challenges of the world, but in truth the operations of our psychic instrument are testimony to something completely different: we create that world. Think about this for a moment. What we perceive as being "out there" is actually a projection appearing on our inner screen, and the understandings we have about that projection come from our own memory. How can we say that we have nothing to do with the world when it's all taking place inside us!

Having said this, we must once again acknowledge that there are horrors—excruciatingly painful circumstances—in the universe. At some time or another every single one of us comes into contact with pain. When this happens, the intellectual understanding that the world is a play of *citiśakti* may not seem relevant, and the equanimity of our more balanced moments may not be immediately available to us, no matter how hard we try to access it. And yet I've seen again and again that, given time and the right kind of contemplation, the medicinal value of even our most painful experiences, either personal or in the world around us, will be revealed to us.

I'll never forget the time I invited a scriptural study group to contemplate and discuss their experiences of the message Gurumayi had given the Siddha Yoga *saṅgham* that particular year: "Everything happens for the best." Several people described how they had come to terms with extremely difficult circumstances in their lives. The last person to speak was an elegant woman in her early forties, who said, "The worst that ever happened to me was when my husband was murdered." This was an event of another order from the ones that had been shared, and the group became very still. The woman went on: "When it happened, I grieved deeply, and the anguish continued for years. In time, however,

I could see that it was this very pain that had brought me to God and to the spiritual path. I'm a much happier person now. So, in that sense, what happened was for the best."

She obviously left much unsaid, but her simple words were voiced with conviction and sincerity, and without a trace of lingering regret or pain. Her state of calm, which was evident in her voice and manner, had its foundation in her understanding. Through contemplation, she had come to the stance exemplified by the great souls who face any challenge with equanimity.

If you think about this woman's response to her life, the implications are tremendous. It seems clear that while we cannot control all the events of our lives, we can take responsibility for what we perceive, how we understand our perceptions, and what kind of behavior that understanding inspires.

I must also acknowledge here that the person who killed this woman's husband is himself the subject in his own universe—and that he is no less Śiva than anyone else. It seems, however, that he was operating from his instinctual needs and desires in such a violent manner that he was apparently, at least for that time, merged in the deepest ignorance.

Having said this, there are some additional factors that can influence what we take in and what we put out to the world in any given moment.

The Three Qualities

The psychic instrument, along with every object it perceives, is configured by three distinct qualities, known as the three *guṇas.* These are purity *(sattva)*, activity *(rajas)*, and inertia *(tamas)*. In the scheme of the *tattvas*, these three *guṇas* come into existence with *prakṛti*, nature. *Prakṛti*, you may recall from sutra 4, is the name given to the creative force that wraps herself, so to speak, around the *puruṣa*, the individual Self. In addition to the five limited powers of *māyā-tattva*, which we also discussed in sutra 4, *prakṛti* also contains these three qualities, and depending on which of them predominates in us, we perceive and relate to creation through that quality.* In culinary terms, if we were preparing a special dish, we could say that the psychic instrument would be the staple foods we put into it and the *guṇas* would be the herbs and spices—the flavoring. Our dish could be sweet or hot or totally indigestible, depending on what seasonings we added.

To begin with the densest, *tamas*, the quality of darkness, gives one the perception of inertia, of sluggishness, and of delusion. *Rajas* gives the perception of activity and dynamism and sometimes agitation and passion. Then there is *sattva*, which grants the perception of clarity and harmony, and is the closest to the truth of the *puruṣa*.

In the scheme of the *tattvas*, immediately after *prakṛti* comes *buddhi*, the intellect. So, even our conscious screen is colored by these three qualities of nature. This is why our perception itself can be deluded. We may be projecting onto a screen that is dismal and dour or, at another time,

* There is an explanation for the sudden appearance of these three forces in the panorama of creation. According to Utpaladeva, the *guṇas* are the condensation of the Lord's main powers: *jñāna-śakti*, the power of knowing, becomes *sattva*; *kriyā-śakti*, the power of action, becomes *rajas*; and *māyā-śakti*, the divine free will turned into the power of illusion, becomes *tamas*. In this way through the *guṇas*, these primordial capacities take form as the qualities through which individuals live as knowers and doers, like the Lord though on a smaller scale. (*Īśvara-pratyabhijñā-kārikā*, 4.1.4-6; trans. B. N. Pandit, *Īśvara Pratyabhijñā Kārikā of Utpaladeva*, publication forthcoming).

a screen that is tinged with passion and attachment. Of course, there are times when our screen is clear, and we easily view what is projected on it with equanimity.

Everything in creation under *prakṛti* is composed of the *guṇas.* These three qualities are also at play in the objects we perceive, and, in the case of other living beings, the *guṇas* are fluctuating in them just as they are in us. As Baba Muktananda points out in his commentary on this sutra, a person manifests whatever quality is predominant in his mind at any given time, and, if you look closely, you can actually see that quality in his face.[60]

What matters most to us, however, is the effect the *guṇas* have on our own mental screen. Gurumayi says that for this we must observe and we must contemplate—truly contemplate:

> To understand the workings of the three *guṇas* in your life, you have to pay very close attention to everything that happens to you. You have to perform true self-examination, self-inquiry. Most people tend to deny whatever they are feeling, good or bad. Also, they usually try to avoid taking responsibility for their feelings and the actions that produce them, either by defending their actions or by justifying their emotions. In this way, people keep themselves from recognizing the influence of these three qualities on their lives. And the cycle repeats, again and again, with no room for change.[61]

This is why the sages of Śaivism speak about the need to purify the intellect. Imagine a mirror that is stained or covered with dust. It doesn't work well: images reflected in it can be distorted. We perform spiritual practice to clean the surface of the *buddhi* so that it becomes a perfect reflector. The *guṇas* still move in the yogi who has purified his mind, but he isn't confused by them—he recognizes them for what they are—and in these fluctuations, *sattva* predominates.

The I-Feeling

If you're wondering how to purify the psychic instrument, you could follow a method offered by Utpaladeva. He calls it *ahaṃbhāva,* the "I-feeling," or awareness of the pure "I am." The sage is referring to the awareness of *pūrno'ham,* "I am complete" or "I am perfect," which is the experience of our highest Self. Kshemaraja, who considers this the most significant technique of the Pratyabhijñā School, threads it through the *Pratyabhijñā-hṛdayam.* It appears repeatedly in the text. The thrust of the method is this: instead of identifying with the limited "I" of the ego, the source of most misconceptions, strive to identify with the supreme "I" of the Great Self. This is the pure "I am" feeling, the unalloyed *aham,* that we associated in sutra 4 with Paramaśiva. The limited "I," the *ahaṃkāra,* or ego, is the same sense of identification, except that it's limited by desires; feelings; notions of personality and character, of social position, and physical appearance—which, of course, are all nothing more than ideas.

What I find so tremendously exciting about *ahaṃbhāva* is that the feeling of I-ness that is its foundation is utterly natural to us all. It's our own ego, expanded and purified to total, ecstatic identification with Śiva. Abhinavagupta, commenting on this practice of Utpaladeva, describes it in this way:

> *Ahaṃbhāva* has been declared to be the merging of the object in the subject. This is the resting-place, the perfect freedom, the

> supreme causal agent, and the supreme creative power, because it involves the dissolution of all desires.[62]

The practice of *ahaṃbhāva* is connected with the exercise we introduced with sutra 5, when we dissolved all mental fluctuations *(vikalpas)* in the serene space of the Witness. This is exactly what I was doing during the meditation in the Bhagawan Nityananda Temple that I described earlier. The way it works in practice is this: Every time a thought or fantasy or desire comes up—*I want this, I hate that; he did this, she did that*—allow the *vikalpa* to merge into your awareness, melt into the mind-stuff from which it came. This is the *merging of the object in the subject.* Continue to offer everything that arises, and as these mental constructs dissolve, watch the feeling of the pure "I am" spontaneously reveal itself. Rest your attention steadily on the perfect "I am." Relish the way the inherent freedom of "I am" liberates you from your slavery to mental turmoil. This is *the resting-place.*

And if you're feeling that this technique is nothing new, then I invite you to let go of that concern as well. It is enormously effective to return again and again to the same contemplation, the same technique of *sādhana.* With repetition, you can refine a practice and truly take it in. People who find repetition boring have not, I think, given themselves fully to it. Try being totally present for this particular repetition, and I think you'll find yourself immersed in the experience of the delight and beauty of the *śakti.*

7

The Many Facets of the One Reality

Sutra 7

स चैको द्विरूपस्त्रिमयश्चतुरात्मा
सप्तपञ्चकस्वभावः

sa caiko dvirūpas trimayaś caturātmā
sapta-pañcaka-svabhāvaḥ

And so he is one,
is of two forms, consists of three, is fourfold,
and is of the nature
of the seven groups of five.

sa: he is
ca: and
ekaḥ: one
dvi: two
rūpaḥ: form
tri: three
mayaḥ: consisting of, made of
catur: four
ātmā: individual self
sapta: seven
pañcakaḥ: group of five
sva: one's own
bhāvaḥ: the nature of, the true condition of

THE UNUSUAL LANGUAGE OF THIS SUTRA is simply a restatement of several major ideas that have been explained earlier in the text. Kshemaraja introduces the sutra in this way:

> Since liberation *[mukti]* is possible only by a correct knowledge of the true nature of the Self, and transmigration *[saṃsāra]* is due to incorrect knowledge, it is therefore appropriate to analyze the true nature of it [the Self], bit by bit.[63]

As a summary of what's been discussed, sutra 7 serves as a pause, allowing us to review what we've gone over so far and supporting our engagement with Kshemaraja's reflections on the condition of the human being, the *māyā-pramātā.* This is why, I believe, the translation begins with the word "and," which could also be read as "and so" or "and therefore," indicating that what's about to be said is a restatement of what has come before. This sort of reiteration is not uncommon in collections of sutras.

This sutra is also an opportunity to test the premise raised in sutra 4 concerning the many sets of numbers used by the sages of Kashmir Śaivism. This numbering is a way to identify, examine, and classify the multifarious facets of the one Reality. It establishes a structure of related names and numbers in the universe so we can meaningfully interact with it and, as Kshemaraja says, analyze its nature *bit by bit.*

The One, the Two, and the Three

And so, the sutra begins, *sa caiko,* "And so he is one," in reference to the oneness of Paramaśiva. By extension, this observation applies to each of us, for we as well can say, *I am the one, indivisible, and all-pervasive Self.* In two words, Kshemaraja has encapsulated the text's primary message.

Then that one becomes *dvi-rūpas,* "two forms." This term can be interpreted in many ways, but fundamentally, it refers to the duality that arises with the initial expression of the creation, the subject and object, Citiśakti and her limited manifestation. We could then say, *The one Self of its own accord has become me, as an individual, and my world with all the related circumstances of my day-to-day life.*

The one also becomes three: *tri-mayaś,* a reference to the three impurities by which the subject becomes separate from her divine nature *(āṇava-mala),* sees objects as different from herself *(māyīya-mala),* and performs actions to acquire some objects and avoid others *(kārma-mala).* These *malas* are called "impurities" because they keep us in a state of ignorance about our identity with God and, therefore, also unaware of our own divine powers to know and do. Yet the *malas* are also the very capacities that enable us to understand, to feel, and to participate actively in a social environment.

He Is Fourfold

The one then becomes four, in this case *caturātmā,* the fourfold self. Kshemaraja is referring here to the individual with his four encasements. These are, beginning with the most subtle, *śūnya,* the void, which is associated with *māyā* and what Śaivites call the causal body; *prāṇa,* the system of energies that animates both of the next two levels; *puryaṣṭaka,* the subtle body, including the psychic instrument; and *sthūla-śarīra,* the physical body. For those who are familiar with Baba Muktananda's *Play of Consciousness,* I want to point out that this is not parallel with the discussion of the four bodies that Baba presents, but it is a different way of organizing what is much the same thing. * Because they are an intrinsic aspect of our individuality and because they map out the trajectory of our inner journey, it's worth spending some time getting to know these four encasements. Once again, they're listed in the following sections by decreasing levels of subtlety.

The Void

Śūnya, the void, is made of *māyā,* and emits a black light that can be seen in meditation. Just as the power of illusion is the cause of the impure creation, the void is the source of the other three bodies. This is why it is known as the "causal" body. It is the storehouse for *saṃskāras,* the karmic impressions established from one's actions in the past, and these are determining factors in the creation of the physical and subtle bodies. Moreover, many of the karmas stored in the causal body are waiting their turn to become active, to "cause" circumstances in the future. To put this in terms of the *tattvas, śūnya* encompasses the principles contained in *prakṛti,* that is, *māyā-tattva* along with its offshoots, the five *kañcukas.*

The experience of *śūnya* in meditation is, I've found, like being enveloped in black velour. There are no thoughts, no images, no sounds,

* Baba Muktananda calls the subtlest of his four bodies the supracausal body, which he describes as the *nīlabindu,* or Blue Pearl, a supremely significant construct of Śaivism that we discuss later. Also, the *prāṇic* and mental functions that Baba ascribes to the subtle body are divided in Kshemaraja's schema between two entities: *prāṇa* and *puryaṣṭaka* (subtle body) (Swami Muktananda, *Play of Consciousness* (2000), pp. 97-98).

no emotions—only a sweet tranquility. Because of the darkness they experience in the void, many people who come to this point in meditation feel that something has gone wrong with their practice. On the contrary, the experience of the void can be compared to *samādhi,* absorption, because of the mind's serenity and focus.

The Vital Energies

Slightly less subtle than the void is *prāṇa,* which is the name given collectively to the five functions of *prāṇa-śakti,* also known as the five *prāṇas.* In the yogic scriptural tradition, these are identified as the vital energies, the forces that give life and movement to the physical and subtle bodies. These vital forces and their physical functions are named *prāṇa,* which regulates the in-breath; *apāna,* which regulates the out-breath; *samāna,* the equalizing force that ensures an even allocation of energy (including the nourishment from food) in all parts of the body; *vyāna,* the pervasive force that distributes the energy; and *udāna,* the power that carries the energy upward, giving strength and radiance to the body and also propelling the soul out of the physical body at the time of death.

If one of these *prāṇic* functions is disturbed for very long, the mind and the physical body will eventually reflect the dysfunction with an ailment or disease. Since it's extremely difficult to pursue spiritual practice when either the body or mind is out of balance, purification of the five *prāṇas* is considered one of the main goals of traditional yogic hygiene.

From the standpoint of meditation, the two most relevant of these energies are *prāṇa* and *apāna,* which not only generate movement of the breath but are also understood to be the support of the mind. If you wish to experience the connection between the breath and the operations of the mind, just watch what happens to your breath when your mind is disturbed by anger, fear, or any other strong emotion. In sutra 18, we discuss the necessity of harmonizing and stilling the *prāṇic* energies so that the mind can more easily enter the highest states of meditation.

The Subtle Body

Śaivism calls the subtle body *puryaṣṭaka,* meaning literally "city of eight," because it is composed of eight *tattvas.* These are the five subtle elements (the *tanmātras*) and the threefold psychic instrument (the thinking faculty, *manas;* the ego, *ahaṃkāra;* and the intellect, *buddhi*). Since, as we learned in sutra 4, the subtle elements provide a foundation for us to perceive external objects and the mental faculties provide the means for that perception, it's easy to see that the main function of this subtle or etheric body is to facilitate our relationship with the world through perception and understanding. It's through the subtle body that the physical senses register sensation, transmit that information to the intellect, and refer it to the mental impressions stored in the memory. The *saṃskāras* that are ready for enactment are held in this body.

Although it carries the instruments through which we perceive, the subtle body itself can be perceived. When I've seen my own subtle body in meditation, it's appeared to have the same shape as my physical body, though it seemed to be made of a vaporous substance, as if it were a cloud cut to my measure.

The Physical Body

The densest of our bodies is the physical body, *sthūla-śarīra*, the perfect instrument for habitation on the planet Earth. Composed of the last fifteen *tattvas*, it includes the five senses of perception (*jñānendriyas*), the five organs of action (*karmendriyas*), and the five gross elements (*bhūtas*). Through the physical body, we enter into contact with the objects surrounding us: we feel the softness of silk, smell the fragrance of perfumes, taste chocolate, hear symphonies, and see the visual forms of an ever ebullient world. With the physical body, we do everything that we do in this world: we travel, do business, meet people, marry, bear or sire children. It's also through the physical body—through the stimulation of external objects perceived with the senses—that we become aware of the array of possibilities for action. And at the time of death, it's only the physical body that decays. It is the other three encasements that come together in transmigration, eventually, to take on another life form.

I like to consider the physical body as the sphere in which I experience the results of my good and bad actions, and also as the vehicle for my *sādhana*. It is, after all, in the physical body that we have the opportunity of reaching ultimate freedom. Speaking along these lines, Abhinavagupta writes:

> Thus one should think of the body as full of all the paths [to enlightenment and cosmic emanation]. Variegated by the workings of time, it is the abode of all the movements of time and space. The body seen in this way is all the gods, and must therefore be the object of contemplation, veneration, and sacrifice. He who penetrates into it finds liberation.[64]

It is possible to intuit the presence of some of these paths to liberation the sage speaks of by undertaking a journey through the various bodies, beginning with the physical body and traversing increasingly subtler inner realms until we arrive at the very heart of our being.

A Pilgrimage through the Bodies

Begin by assuming a good meditation posture. Now, close your eyes and direct your attention inside. Become aware of your physical body, noticing how it feels to be carrying the dense structure of bones and to be encased in flesh, how the liquids affect the various activities such as digestion and the circulation of blood, and what effect it has on you to have senses of perception and locomotion. In this way, examine how you are affected by the fifteen *tattvas* of your physical body. After a while you might observe, as I have, that the connection with the physical body becomes increasingly tenuous. It often seems to me that a vortex of energy swivels my attention gently into the next state.

In a similar way, watch how the subtle body, which is the seat of the mental faculty, creates a different kind of reality than you experienced in the physical body. As mental images arise and subside, notice how the mental faculty associates these experiences with words, how the ego appropriates them, and the intellect seems to hold them together. If you pay attention carefully, you can observe how the eight *tattvas* of the subtle body function.

With your awareness on the workings of the mind, you may also be able to detect the almost imperceptible flow of the *prāṇas* activating the inner movements—not the breath itself, for instance, but the impulse to take a breath, the energy on which the breath comes.

After another slight vortex of energy, you may find that all mental activity disappears, leaving you in what seems to be a state of deep sleep. This is the void in which the power of *māyā* wraps itself around the witnessing Self, restraining its splendid expansiveness. There have been times when, in spite of the awesome dark of the void, I've experienced it as a condensed form of energy, existing within the conscious space of the Self.

Eventually, the energy vortex will bring you out of this meditative deep sleep and place you back in the waking state. On this pilgrimage through the four bodies, it's possible to perceive the presence of the Self as the witness-consciousness that is present in each of them. Thus, it is apparent that it is the One that becomes two, three, and fourfold.

The Seven Groups of Five

In sutra 7, the One then expands into the "seven groups of five," *sapta-pañcaka,* by which Kshemaraja encompasses all of creation. This is in reference to the thirty-five *tattvas* (by some numbering systems) that emanate from Paramaśiva. While there's a great deal more that could be said about the *tattvas* beyond what I mentioned in sutra 4, the point I would like to underscore here is the understanding that emerged in the pilgrimage through the bodies. It's just this: in emanating from the one Reality to form the structure of creation, the *tattvas* also form the structure of the individual being—you and me. If you were to go over the *tattvas* once again keeping this point in mind, you'd be doing much more than just reviewing familiar ground. You'd be plotting connections between these aspects of Reality and yourself.

In the sutra, there is another turn of *sapta-pañcaka,* in which it is translated as "seven and five." By "seven," Kshemaraja is referring to the seven perceivers *(pramātās),* which we also discussed in sutra 4 and which range all the way from the mundane, dualistic awareness of the *sakalas* to the highest level of experience, that of the *śiva-pramātās.* The "five" can be understood from Paramaśiva's point of view as the five *śaktis* (the divine powers of awareness, bliss, will, knowledge, and action) or from the level of manifest creation as the five *kañcukas,* the limited capacities by which the Lord's powers are contracted (limited action, limited knowledge, desire, a sense of time, and the operation of natural laws).

Once again, as we indicated in sutra 4, it is possible to experience for yourself the viewpoint of the various perceivers within yourself in meditation. I'd like to point out to you that when you're perfectly absorbed in your identity as Śiva—in the state of the highest experiencer, the *śiva-pramātā*—you will naturally know his powers of awareness, bliss, will, knowledge, and action. And when you return from deep meditation to the normal level of your daily existence—to, for most of us, the experience of the *sakala*—you will become acutely aware of how the innate expansiveness expressed by those five *śaktis* is restricted by the five *kañcukas* as they enter into full activity through the mind. And you also will know, from within yourself, that the One that has become two, three, and fourfold, has also become the seven and the five.

Order in Diversity

Whatever one's interpretation, it's apparent that with this single terse sentence Kshemaraja has summarized a great many of the seminal doctrines of the Śaiva tradition. The array of lists and groups and connecting principles that he catalogs in this sutra is a form of presentation that often irritates contemporary readers attempting to study Indian philosophy. We're not accustomed to the paradigms so familiar to students of the ancient East, and many of the principles we are familiar with—for instance, the scientific approach that is so admired today—didn't exist at the time this philosophy was written.

Indian philosophy may sound simplistic when stated baldly, as it is in sutra 7, but the purpose of this simplicity is to aid us in remembering what is, ultimately, an incredibly complex schema. When I began my study of Kashmir Śaivism, I tried to streamline what I was learning, but as I continued to study, I found that part of the message was in the complexity of these myriad aspects and the multiple relationships between them. In the same way, the traditional numbering of subtle concepts—so cumbersome to understand for someone with a Western education—became an incredibly useful tool over time.

In engaging the, at times, baroque nature of this philosophy, I find it helpful to consider the exuberance of Indian culture, rich with nuance and subtle, complex relationships. Take, for instance, the Indian *rāga,* a melody out of which other melodies spring in a totally organic and spontaneous manner. According to Western standards, classical Indian music isn't logical or sequential or solidified. The melodies arise and develop and interweave, until it seems that the music has a life of its own. A concert of classical Indian music can go on for hours—literally five, six, seven hours—as the musicians improvise and build on their theme. It's not so much a performance as an experience that the musicians and audience share. The *rāga* is usually familiar to the audience; what absorbs the listener is the nuances the musicians express in their exploration of this very familiar ground.

The same can be said for much of Indian literature, drama, and dance—art forms that are often based on the two epics, the *Rāmāyaṇa* and the *Mahābhārata*, known by all Indians almost from birth. Everyone in India is familiar with the stories, and yet people never tire of watching plays and dances based on them; they read the books as if it were all totally fresh for them. The delight is not in the outcome, but in the way the story is being told. In the nuances, we gain insights about life, about the mind and the emotions, and the strength of desire, and the greatness of God, and the power of a saint. Isn't this the way our lives are! We may know what's going to happen at the end of the day, but there are so many surprises in what unfolds as we walk through it, so many lights and shades and little twists. It's in these that we find the joys and substance of life.

Baba Muktananda shared that taste. He used to tell the same story again and again—and yet, seeing it another way, he never told the same story twice. Gurumayi, who served as Baba's translator for the last years of his life, once said that she used to wonder why he so often repeated stories. She said that on one day when he told the same story several times, as she translated, it became clear to her that each time he told the story, he was emphasizing a different facet of it, much as if he were turning a crystal and looking at it from different angles. Each time Baba approached that story, he would either go deeper into it or bring forward another aspect of the teachings.[65]

The same quality of ever-deepening contemplation is represented beautifully in the very architecture of Indian temples. There is a great deal that we could say about these temples, but what is especially significant for me involves the central section, the inner sanctum where the deity is housed. This is known as the *garbha-gṛha,* the "womb house," a name that implies for me a gestation of the grace that is imparted to worshipers who enter this sacred space. It is usually a square room (the square being the symbol of perfection) with no windows, patterned probably after the caves to which yogis traditionally retire to perform their spiritual practices. It also represents the cave of the heart, the innermost sanctum in each of us—the place where we, too, retire to have the darshan of our deity, our innermost being.

In an Indian temple, a *śikhara,* a crest or tower, is always above the deity. This is one of the most characteristic elements of these temples. Reminiscent of a mountain, where yogis' caves were always found, it also takes our attention up, toward the most sublime, toward the supreme Consciousness.

I remember visiting the famous Kandariya Mahadeva, a temple dedicated to Lord Śiva, in Khajuraho in North India. This eleventh-century structure was built at about the same time Kshemaraja lived. The outer shape of the Khandariya Mahadeva looks like several hills attached to one main mountain, the temple's principal *śikhara,* suggesting a crested Himalayan range. When I first approached the temple, I was struck by the profusion of decorations and sculptures displaying scenes of mythology and ordinary people's lives, as if the temple were a representation of the universe itself. But once I entered the temple, it was a totally different experience. I moved away from this multiplicity through a series of halls into the simplicity and essence of the inner sanctum where the deity resides.

The study of Śaivism isn't an intellectual exercise as much as an organic journey into the heart. As Kshemaraja writes at the conclusion of his commentary to this sutra:

> Thus only when it is recognized that the one Reality, which is only Śiva, becomes thirty-five principles, seven experients, a pentad of five powers consisting of *cit* [and so forth], does it [one's awareness] become a bestower of liberty; otherwise it is the cause of *saṃsāra*.[66]

When we're caught up in the complexity of the world, then we become trapped by it. And when we recognize the one Reality, the Self, at the center of the panorama, then this awareness alone can be the power that frees us.

8

Revelation and Concealment from Different Points of View

Sutra 8

तद्भूमिकाः सर्वदर्शनस्थितयः

tad-bhūmikāḥ sarva-darśana-sthitayaḥ

The positions of all philosophical systems
are stages of that [Consciousness].

tat:	that
bhūmikāḥ:	stages, roles
sarva:	all
darśana:	a system of philosophy
sthitayaḥ:	positions

THE KEY WORD HERE IS DARŚANA. We can describe a *darśana,* a philosophy, as a point of view, a way of understanding ourselves and interpreting our world. The word *darśana* means, literally, "seeing" and "observing," as well as "examining" and "contemplating," implying that one who propounds a philosophy presents his observations and contemplations so that others may see them as well. There are countless philosophical systems, and they have reached just as many differing conclusions! Despite this abundance of opinions, sutra 8 tells us that all *(sarva)* these positions *(sthitayaḥ)* are just stages *(bhūmikāḥ)* in that *(tat),* meaning Consciousness. In other words, the points of view of all the many philosophical systems are nothing but varied phases of *citiśakti.*

At the time this text was written, there were six classical philosophical schools in existence in India—Nyāya, Vaiśeṣika, Sāṅkhya, Yoga, Mīmāṃsā, and Vedānta—as well as the variants of each; in addition to the grammarian school of Vyākaraṇa, Buddhism, Jainism, Islam, and Christianity with all their assorted versions; and the dualist, nondualist, and dualist-nondualist currents of Śaivism, Śaktism, and Vaiṣṇavism. The adherents of many of these schools engaged one another in debate. It was customary for sages to present even their written teachings as argument, including, as Kshemaraja has here, critical analyses of other philosophical positions and incisive defenses against the counterarguments their opponents were likely to proffer.

I find this tradition of philosophical debate enormously invigorating. Today, we're more likely to argue about work or politics than about the nature of God or Reality. And yet debate is an effective way of coming to understand a philosophical point of view. The competitive tone adds rigor to logic. Spurious arguments are discarded, and the explanations and comparisons that naturally come up in the attack and counterattack of debate help make the explication clearer and more precise. Of course, in debate everyone likes to feel that he's right. In Kshemaraja's day, yogis didn't argue for the sake of polemics but to present and emphasize observations they felt to be true and beneficial—more true and of greater benefit than those they were arguing against!

In his commentary to sutra 8, Kshemaraja constructs a concise outline of the teachings of the Trika system of Kashmir Śaivism, of which he was an adherent. He points out the comparative shortcomings of other systems, assigning each of them a position in the *tattvas* according to that philosophy's perspective on the nature of supreme Reality. Beginning with the lower *tattvas,* Kshemaraja moves from one level of subtlety to the next, positioning other philosophies according to their teachings and areas of focus. The Cārvāka system, for instance, which teaches that there is no reality beyond the physical universe and that humanity should take every opportunity to enjoy life, is placed in the *tattvas* of materiality. On the other hand, the Nyāya system (which advocates the study of logic, dialectics, and analytical reasoning) and the Vaiśeṣika system (which deals with physics and metaphysics) regard the Self as practically identical with the void when *buddhi,* the intellect, disappears at the time of liberation. Thus, both Nyāya and Vaiśeṣika are placed on the level of the *buddhi-tattva* (the intellect), along with the followers of Mīmāṃsā, who think that the "I" veiled by the conditions of pain and pleasure is the Self. Kshemaraja situates the Jains in *prakṛti-tattva,* the womb of the three qualities *(guṇas),* because they claim that the Self is an atomic particle that has been modified by the *guṇas,* and he assigns the Mādhyamika school of Buddhism a place in *māyā-tattva,* where the void reigns because that is for them the highest. The followers of Sāṅkhya and the Patañjali system of Yoga, who see the Self as the *puruṣa,* are situated just between the pure and impure creation. Vedāntins, who honor Īśvara as the supreme Reality, are placed in *īśvara-tattva,* and the proponents of the Vyākaraṇa system of grammar, who believe that the *paśyantī* level of speech is the ultimate Truth, do not reach beyond the *sadāśiva-tattva.* Other monist Śaiva and Śakta schools, believing either that the Self is exclusively immanent in the universe or that it is exclusively transcendent, are also shown to be incomplete in their understanding.

One by one, Kshemaraja slots the major Indian philosophies and philosophical currents in an ascending order, each in its proper niche among the thirty-four principles of creation. At the top of the scale, on the level of Śiva and Śakti, stands the Trika School, which Kshemaraja presents as the crown jewel, the purest and most complete expression of a monist point of view, positing both the immanence and transcendence of the supreme Self. As he explains:

> Thus, of the one Divine, whose essence is Consciousness, all these roles are displayed by his absolute will, [and] the differences in the roles are due to the degree to which that absolute free will chooses either to reveal or conceal itself. Therefore, there is only one *ātman* pervading all these [roles].[67]

For Kshemaraja, all these existing points of view are perceptions of the Supreme Lord, who assumes the role of an individual to experience these perspectives as his own, to adopt their beliefs, and perform the corresponding actions. With the utmost care, Kshemaraja asserts that each philosophical position is correct in that it describes perfectly the understanding of a person situated at that particular level in the chain of *tattvas*—or to be precise, of those who *identify* their sense of being with the perception of these aspects of creation. He also argues, however, that all but one of these philosophies fall short in their knowledge of the non-dual Truth, and are therefore inadequate for attaining the experience of the one Reality. In yoga, the veracity of any particular perspective is gauged by the extent to which it reveals or veils the nature of the Great Light. This is not just a demonstration of how differences of opinion arise; it's a highly significant distinction.

Consider the possibility that looking at life from a particular perspective can predispose one toward perceptual error, toward seeing the illusory as real. Baba Muktananda used to illustrate this with a traditional tale of six blind men coming upon an elephant. Each man caught hold of the part of the elephant nearest to him. Later, when they described their experiences, they couldn't come to an agreement. The man who had held the elephant's ear said, "An elephant is like a winnowing basket." The man who had held the tail said, "That's a lie. The elephant is like a broom." The man who had taken hold of a leg stated, "I don't know what either of you are talking about. The elephant is like a stout club." The fourth, having held the elephant's tusk, said, "No it isn't. The elephant is the size of my arm, slightly curved, and quite hard." The fifth fellow had felt the trunk, and he said, "The elephant is like a hose," and the sixth blind man, who had touched the elephant's belly, said, "You're all wrong. The elephant is like the bottom of my washtub." Baba concluded:

> So six blind men, none of whom had seen the elephant, were each defending their particular viewpoint and attacking the others. Those six fellows had not seen the elephant in its entirety; they

> were only describing the different parts of its body. But a man with eyesight, who saw the elephant, knew that these descriptions were just partial. Those blind men are like those who haven't seen God, who are incapable of seeing things in perspective, who haven't been able to grasp the Truth.[68]

For those who experience illusion, the *māyā-pramātās*—which means humanity, including us—there is no other way to see. The scope of our perception is as limited as that of the blind men. Thus, the constant practice of yogic discrimination is crucial. Yogis must always ask themselves, *How complete is my view of Reality?* It is vital for us, as seekers of the Truth, to hold at least an awareness of the whole. This is why I find I must agree with the venerable Kshemaraja in his view that the nondualism espoused by the Trika is the most generous, the most comprehensive viewpoint, the one that encompasses all of Reality.

A Tale of Self-Inquiry

Having told one classic tale, there is another, from the *Chāndogya Upaniṣad,* that reminds me even more specifically—with this sutra's focus, dealing as it does with the nature of different points of view—how these views arise, and what comes from them. The story is this:

Once Indra, lord of the gods, and Virocana, lord of the demons, went to the universal Guru, Prajāpati, whose name means "Lord of the creatures." Prajāpati told his two disciples that they should seek the Self, that only the Self is free from old age and death, free from hunger and thirst. One who understands the Self, Prajāpati said, obtains all worlds and all desires.

Indra and Virocana served their Guru for thirty-two years, and at the end of this time, Prajāpati asked what they wanted from him.

"We want to learn of this Self," the disciples said, and Prajāpati imparted to them the following teaching: "The person who is seen in the eye is the Self. That is the immortal, the fearless. That is Brahman."

Indra and Virocana asked, "But, Venerable Sir, when we see our reflection, who is this?"

The master said, "It's the same one."

The disciples looked at their own reflections in a pool of water and returned to Prajāpati, saying that they had seen the Self with hair and nails, with a face and a body. They had seen the Self wearing gold ornaments.

Prajāpati confirmed their perception. "That is the Self," he said. The disciples started for their homes with their hearts at peace, but as they left, Prajāpati told himself, sadly, "They leave without having known the Self. Whoever follows such a doctrine shall perish." The Guru had given these disciples a clue as to the true nature of the Self—that it is the one who perceives—and yet they could take in only a bit of the teaching. They saw the Self as what they perceived—the body!

Back in his kingdom, Virocana taught the demons that the Self is the physical body, which must be adorned and satisfied, for that is how one attains glory in this world and beyond. This teaching, the Upaniṣad maintains, is a demonic doctrine.

Indra, on the other hand, pondered what his Guru had said, and even before he reached home he thought, *If the Self is well-dressed when the body is well-dressed, then this Self will also be blind when the body is blind, lame when the body is lame, and it will perish when the body perishes.* Indra returned to the Guru and asked for further instruction. Prajāpati told him to perform service for another thirty-two years.

After the time had passed, Prajāpati told Indra, "He who is happy in a dream is the Self. He is the immortal, the fearless. He is Brahman."

Once again, Indra left for home, secure in his new understanding of the Self: that at least in one's dreams the Self cannot be blind or lame, nor can the Self die. Yet, once again, as he traveled, Indra began having doubts about this teaching. After all, the dream world is not free from pain and suffering; it is the province of the mind.

Again, Indra returned to his Guru, ready to serve him for another thirty-two years. This time Prajāpati taught him: "When a man is deeply asleep, composed, serene, and knows no dreams, that is the Self, that is the immortal, the fearless. That is Brahman."

Indra started home again, contemplating the Guru's words. His discrimination was becoming increasingly sharp, and so before very long, he found that there was some defect in his new understanding. He thought, *In truth, the one in deep sleep doesn't know who he is or any of the things of the world. He's annihilated. I see no good in this!* Indra quickly realized that although one feels great peace and no pain in the dreamless state, there is no awareness of objects and the existence of a subject is veiled.

Aware that his knowledge was still incomplete, Indra went once again back to his Guru. Prajāpati noticed that his disciple had matured, so this time he asked him to offer only five years of service. At the end of his apprenticeship, Indra had spent a total of one hundred and one years of disciplined life, dedicated to discovering the Truth within himself. As he received enlightenment by his Guru's divine grace, he realized that beyond physical consciousness, beyond the mind, and surpassing the causal void, while simultaneously pervading the entire universe, is the supreme light of Consciousness, the true eternal Self.[69]

Exercising Yogic Discrimination

Indra's *sādhana* is a classic example of the path of knowledge, guided by grace. Baba Muktananda used to say that everything in the universe is perfect except for one thing: human understanding. This statement has stayed with me throughout my *sādhana* as a great incentive for the exercise of *viveka,* discrimination. What truly matters on the path of knowledge is developing what Baba used to call "right understanding," the comprehension that all this is Consciousness. What I find particularly interesting in this story of *sādhana* is the clear image of the various layers of instruction that Indra receives from his Guru. It might seem as if his Guru misled Indra, so partial were the instructions that Prajāpati gave along the way. And yet Indra's contemplation, which he conducted over the course of many years, could be compared to peeling an onion, one layer at a time: each new level of understanding was based on the one that preceded it; each was necessary to his gaining the ultimate knowledge. Gurumayi says that on the path of knowledge, the instructions we receive are not meant to be understood easily; they're meant to stop the mind and inspire contemplation.

> In Baba's talks there were always contradictions. Particularly if you were a newcomer, you would think, *How can he say that? A moment ago he said the bird is white, and now he says the bird is black.*

> *How can it be?* So, you start contemplating. *How can he say "white" one time and "black" another time?* In this contemplation you experience the Truth.
>
> In reality, the bird is neither white nor black. It is what we think it is. Other than this, there is no color, there is no form, no shape, and no name. We have given the shapes, the forms, the names, and the colors. Deep within, none of these exist. So as you contemplate: *Why black? Why white? Why red? Why yellow? Why green?* you begin to understand what Tukaram Maharaj said in his *abhanga:* "When I perceived the Self, I saw it was beyond all colors."[70]

On the path of knowledge each experience is contemplated, questioned, analyzed to its core. We ask, *Is this my Self, the eternal and unchanging One? Who is having this experience? Who am I?* Step by step, our understanding is disengaged from the limitations of *māyā* until finally we recognize Reality.

Then, recalling the teaching contained in sutra 5—that all our perceptions vibrate with the light of *śakti*—we can apply the other face of discrimination, affirmation: *All this is a creation of Consciousness. All this is the vibration of my own Self. The projections I'm seeing are full of bliss.* In the practice of discrimination, the paths of negation and affirmation lead to the same place—a clear demonstration that, as the sutra implies, all points of view are like beads on the necklace of Consciousness.

Our story from the *Chāndogya Upaniṣad* demonstrates this very process of inner growth, a point that Kshemaraja makes strongly in his commentary on sutra 8 by offering a second interpretation of the sutra. Here, he defines *darśana* not as a philosophical system but as knowledge of various objects of perception, both inner and outer. With this interpretation, *sthiti* is now understood as "inner cessation" rather than "position," and *bhūmikāḥ* becomes "means" instead of "role." The sutra now would be translated as this:

The inner cessation of the *darśanas* [all limited knowledge] is the means for the manifestation of that [Śiva, who is an infinite mass of blissful Consciousness].

Such cessation takes place when all mental activity comes to rest in the inner divine knowledge, "I am." We thereby open ourselves to an unsurpassed peace and, gradually, as Kshemaraja observes:

> This venerable [Śakti] being resorted to more and more makes her devotee her own, step by step.[71]

There is yet another nuance to the term *darśana* that could be drawn from this second interpretation, and this is the connotation that is most familiar throughout India: *darśana* as divine vision. This can refer to the sensory experience of seeing a saint or a deity, but at the heart of the term stands a mystical and devotional experience, an inner vision of the One beneath outer appearances. This mystical vision is the sole purpose of a true *darśana.* As a philosophical point of view, it allows us to dissolve the limited perceptions that stand in the way of divine vision. Here, we would take yet another meaning of *sthitayaḥ,* "standing in" or "abiding in," indicating that to come to rest in the ultimate *darśana* is truly a means of making God manifest. This synthesis of immanence and transcendence is the heart of the sutra.

9

Destiny: The Choice Is Ours

Sutra 9

चिद्वत्तच्छक्तिसंकोचात् मलावृतः संसारी

cidvat tac chakti-saṃkocāt malāvṛtaḥ saṃsārī

That which is full of Consciousness,
due to contraction of its powers,
becomes a transmigratory soul, covered by impurities.

cit:	Consciousness
vat:	full of
tat:	that
śakti:	powers
saṃkocāt:	due to contraction
mala:	impurities
āvṛtaḥ:	covered
saṃsārī:	a transmigratory soul

KSHEMARAJA INTRODUCES SUTRA 9 by posing a question: If the Self described in sutra 8 is so magnificent, how is it possible to say that it's covered with impurities *(malāvṛtaḥ)*, hampered by restricted authorship and the other limitations—a soul that moves from one life to another *(saṃsārī)*?[72] Sutra 9 is his answer: It is through a contraction of Śakti that all this takes place—and, yes, Kshemaraja is saying, it does take place. Of all the themes developed in Śaivism, the chain of our actions and their effects—which is what leads us to transmigration—is arguably the most pertinent to our lives and, thus, the most controversial and also the most often discussed. This is what's known as destiny—or fate or, if you prefer, karma. It's what leads us to ask questions like these: *Why am I so limited in what I can do? Is my life ruled by destiny? How does this thing called karma operate? What can I do to have better karma? Is it possible for me to decide what I'd like to do with my life? Or are all my apparent "decisions" determined by conditions beyond my control?*

Some years ago, when I was in a group studying Kashmir Śaivism, I posed such a question to our tutor, a swami who was extremely well versed in the Indian philosophical tradition. I said, "Considering that God created everything, why do we have to suffer so? Why doesn't God suffer for what he has himself created?" The swami didn't so much as blink before delivering his reply: "And who do you think *you* are?" I was silenced. I was expecting some kind of philosophical discourse concerning our bondage to limitation, and in the moment I heard his words, *And who do you think you are?* my mind came to a halt. In that brief lapse of thought, I had an instantaneous gleam of recognition: *I am God!*

I am the one who creates my world. The question of how I, as Śiva, experience my world as painful or otherwise is something we'll go into later. For now, let us focus on our authorship. As Kshemaraja says, commenting on this sutra:

> When the highest Lord, whose very essence is Consciousness, conceals by his free will [the] pervasion of nonduality and assumes duality all round, then his will and other powers, though essentially unlimited, assume limitation. Then only does this [soul] become a transmigratory being, covered with *mala.*[73]

The sutra begins *cidvat tat,* "that which is full of Consciousness," an image that evokes the plenitude, *pūrṇatva,* of the supreme Power. Śakti is always full. She doesn't need anything in order to feel her love, her complete satisfaction. Then comes *saṃkocāt,* "due to contraction," which implies that Plenitude herself chooses to condense her essence. The result is *malāvṛtaḥ:* she blankets herself "with limitation." We contemplated this in sutra 4, when we charted Śakti's contraction into the thirty-four *tattvas* and an infinite number of objects: Consciousness becoming *apūrṇa,* imperfect, incomplete. We noted then that this process of contraction produces concealment through three states of imperfection, *malas.* We could say that *mala,* or impurity, is how Consciousness feels as she assumes a limited state. Why then does she do it? Kshemaraja tells us that it's to become a *saṃsārī,* an individual who operates in the material world. It is her play, as Gurumayi's name (Chidvilasananda) implies: the bliss of the play of Consciousness.

The term *saṃsārī* derives from *saṃsāra,* which is defined as transmigration and means literally "to wander, to drift, to pass through successive states." A *saṃsārī,* one who lives in *saṃsāra,* is a soul that transmigrates from one body to another in a succession of lives, like someone walking across a vast expanse of land, residing first in one world and then in another. The worlds may be pleasant or painful, delightful or fearsome. It is the soul itself that chooses which world it will visit, as Abhinavagupta explains in *Paramārtha-sāra:*

> A soul who lives within a body may be bound for heaven or hell, and when separated from [one] body is joined to another according to its [the soul's] own proclivities.[74]

Let us take a closer look at what is behind these proclivities, the three *malas.*

The Three Impurities

I Am Separate

The writer Mark Twain once said, "Deep down in his heart, no man much respects himself." This lack of self-esteem is a clear sign of the presence of *āṇava-mala,* the initial, root constraint by which the utter freedom of the divine will *(icchā-śakti)* contracts and becomes our experience of being imperfect, incomplete, unsatisfied, and incapable. *Āṇava-mala* is what divides and separates us from the experience of our own infinite expansiveness. *Āṇava-mala* gives rise to the understanding *I am separate,* the first of the "covers" referred to in this sutra. We no longer have the capacity to be and do everything; we have instead a discrete existence that limits our possibilities.

Now, based on what we have studied so far, is it possible for that which is eternal, infinite, and fully free to be limited? Certainly not. And yet we can't deny the times we've felt inadequate or unworthy, times when we may feel ourselves to be undervalued, unloved, unappreciated, unheard, or unwanted. Even while we're proclaiming our self-importance, there's quite likely to be an insidious and unacknowledged feeling, *Really, I'm not worth that much,* pecking at our soul. This experience is so strong that we take it as the Truth, and a sense of our imperfection then colors everything we perceive.

This sense of imperfection, which stems from our feeling separate from the Perfect, only exists because it's reflected in the mirror of the Perfect. Rather than looking at our feeling of inadequacy directly, we often identify with the negative concepts and emotions that come from it, and so we never see *āṇava-mala* for what it is: the impetus for our desire to merge with the Perfect, an impulse that is itself a function of the Perfect. In sutra 6, I described a meditation in which I went through what felt like a veil of sadness and yet turned out to be, at its core, a longing for God. In that discussion, I described the sadness I encountered as a deeply rooted tendency *(vāsanā)*. This is accurate, for clearly it was associated with some of my karmic tendencies. And yet, ultimately, in that meditation, I went through this predisposition toward sadness and depression into something even more fundamental—into *āṇava-mala,* my innate sense of separation from God. This is truly what I felt: separate from God. And this sense of separation expressed itself as a yearning to merge with the source of my being.

Contemplating this experience, I've been able to trace my every psychological tendency toward feeling incomplete, unfulfilled, and unworthy to this primal identification with a sense of isolation. And I do mean primal. *Āṇava-mala* is not a wrong idea or a dark mood; it is an act of divine will. This sense of being separate from God is truly fundamental to our being.

Kshemaraja implies that the seed of *āṇava-mala* appears precisely at the moment of the conception of the universe, when Śakti begins to draw the creation from the Great Void. This happens in the state known as *anāśrita-śiva,* just before the emergence of *sadāśiva-tattva,* the first created principle. This bears going through in some detail. Immediately before the appearance of the first created principle, the *sadāśiva-tattva* described in sutra 4, a process takes place that marks what we might call the point of conception in the creation. It occurs when Śakti draws the universe from the undifferentiated Śiva. At this precise point, Śakti generates a state that temporarily deprives Śiva of his *vimarśa,* his conscious and creative capacity.

There is a story in the *Śiva Purāṇa* in which the ever playful Goddess Śakti slips behind her beloved Lord Śiva and puts her hands over his eyes.[75] Though he's resplendent with the light of *prakāśa,* pure being, Śiva's knowledge of the universe disappears. This state is called *anāśrita-śiva,* because as the term *anāśrita* (unrelated) indicates, Śiva exists without support from or relationship to any objects. The state is, as Kshemaraja describes it, "more void than the void itself." When Śakti removes her hands and Śiva can see once again, the universe bursts forth. *Āṇava-mala* comes into play now, here in the impure creation. *Āṇava-mala* is no more than a seed, a tenuous presence within the beings of the pure creation. They have conceived of separation but do not identify with it. *Āṇava-mala* begins to manifest fully with the perceivers *(pramātās)* known as *vijñānākalas,* who dwell between the pure and the impure creations, and it then extends itself to all of the beings in the impure creation.[76]

What this means is that the dominion of *āṇava-mala,* the perception of something "other" than one's undivided Self, extends to virtually every conscious being in the universe. Let me say this again: No one who possesses a trace of individuality is free from this feeling of being separate from God. Only the liberated ones we call Siddhas, whose sense of separation has totally dissolved—which is the very meaning of the term "liberated"—are free from the effects of *āṇava-mala.* Otherwise, contraction is the *sine qua non* in the experience of creation, and the fact that we do not remember having chosen to take it on is just a part of the play.

I Am Different

Its divine nature hidden from itself, the soul seeks satisfaction. The second constraint, which is *māyīya-mala,* the veil of differentiation, is established from the divine will's inclination toward experiences, *bhoga-vāsanā.* This undefined and ambiguous propensity is a product of *māyā* and all the principles that emanate from it. The limitation of *māyīya-mala* defines the effect that living in a body has on an individual. Let us remember what is implied in having a body: we are carrying *māyā,* with her five coverings; *puruṣa* and *prakṛti,* along with the threefold psychic instrument, the five senses of perception and the five senses of action; as well as the five subtle elements and the five dense ones—a total of thirty-one binding forces!

How does it feel for the soul, whose essential nature is light and perfect freedom, to carry all that weight? Don't you sometimes feel you'd like to break away from everything? When I have dreams that I'm flying free, like a bird or a celestial creature, I feel indescribably happy. It's in those moments that my soul delights in its diaphanous essence.

Māyīya-mala contracts the supreme power of knowledge *(jñāna-śakti)* so that a person experiences differences through these layers of limitation, which are often compared to veils. Imagine trying to see with five veils over your face! Well, this is what we're all doing. The soul sees itself as different from other individuals, and it also perceives distinctions between one person or object and another—it perceives, in other words, a universe of varied and disparate forms. Here, desire has a perfect stage for its play, giving rise to the third *mala,* which provides the script.

I Am the Doer

The power of action *(kriyā-śakti)* contracts into a third limitation: *kārma-mala,* the veil of doership. The term *karma* means, simply, "action," but it is no longer the free, spontaneous action of divine power; it is now the capacity to do, to perform deeds and have thoughts under the sense of possession that is the province of the ego. *I'm going for a walk. I built this house. I pay my bills. I have strong emotions.* This is how we think and speak, how we lend veracity to the idea that we, as individuals, are performers in the drama of our lives. *Kārma-mala* keeps us ignorant of the one source of all action, and at the same time it enables the soul to fulfill its desire for experiences—to fulfill its intentions.

Karma and Intention

Commenting on sutra 9, Gurumayi says:

> Once these *malas* have covered you up, all you experience is the destiny created by each of them. Because of the first *mala,* you

> experience the destiny of imperfection. Because of the second, you experience the destiny of differentiation. Because of the third, you experience the destiny of your actions. In this way, you become more and more bound. The sutra says, when Consciousness is limited, it is covered by these impurities, and then one is called a transmigrating soul—a worldly person, or, in colloquial terms, an ordinary individual.[77]

And what we, through our power of will, have chosen to experience is now made perceptible in our lives.

Several times, I've stated that an individual is responsible for creating her own universe, and I've also described factors that contribute to this: perception, thought, perspective, and so on. With karma, we come to what we might call the fundamental factor in this creation: one's intention, one's will. In *Tantrāloka,* which is considered by many scholars to be the most thorough expression of Kashmir Śaivism, Abhinavagupta discusses the relationship between intention and destiny. At the most basic level, any act performed under the auspices of the ego—that is, with the sense *I'm the one who's doing this*—becomes the seed for another action for which we're accountable in the future. This is the law of cause and effect that is the heart of the doctrine of karma, and it applies equally to all acts, irrespective of their results, their quality, or their relationship to dharma. Even actions performed for the sake of experiencing the Self can be binding if they are done with ego, with the attitude of, say, *Now I am going to meditate.* One of my fellow monks described how, early in his *sādhana,* he used to be involved in a little unspoken competition with another *sādhaka* to see which of them could be in the meditation hall earliest. The goal was to be seated in a good posture and apparently in meditation before the other person entered the hall. What they were doing may have looked yogic, and it obviously had some beneficial effects on their ability to discipline themselves and quiet their minds, but it was their will to win that would have left the deepest trace—that was the motivating force, the true intention.

You must be getting a sense of how complex this question of karma is. This is why the *Bhagavad-gītā* says, "Mysterious are the ways of karma."[78] These karmic seeds, left within us as a residue, are called *saṃskāras*—"some scars" is the apt word-play employed by Swami Venkatesananda, a teacher who was a friend of Baba Muktananda. The word *saṃskāra,* karmic traces in the subtle system, suggests something that forms, gathers, or accumulates. Every feeling, image, idea, thought, remark, and certainly every deed leaves its imprint as a *saṃskāra,* and the sum of these—which is inconceivably vast—forms one's destiny, what I like to think of as one's "life script." As we said earlier, the idea is that the soul, before it takes birth, chooses a particular "script" for the life to come—certain of its karmas that will be lived out, certain experiences that will be tasted. The star of the play, so to speak, is also the author.

Abhinavagupta uses a vivid metaphor to describe the workings of destiny. When a *saṃskāra* comes to fruition in our life, he calls it *phalonmukhatā,* which means, etymologically speaking, "the fruit has risen to show its face." This is an impression we've begun experiencing and which cannot be obliterated before it's completely lived through. It's karma we must go through. The second type of *saṃskāra* described by Abhinavagupta involves impressions that are latent and which we haven't yet begun to experience. This form of *saṃskāra* he calls *phalānunmukhatā,* the roots of which mean, "the fruit has not risen to show its face." These *saṃskāras* can be eradicated through meditating, repeating one's mantra, chanting the divine Name, and all the other forms of *sādhana* by which we expand inner light. In other words, through *sādhana,* we can eliminate parts of our karma without ever having to experience it.[79]

As for the creation of new *saṃskāras,* that depends entirely on our attitude. Although an act committed with the understanding *I am the doer* leaves traces as inevitably as fingerprints remain on glass, an identical act performed without ego—with the conviction *I'm not the doer; this impulse arises from the Lord*—leaves no binding impression. Whatever memory remains from the action has a liberating effect. According to Abhinavagupta, the yogi who is able to perform actions with a sense of non-doership—that is, without wanting benefit from them—receives a very special benefit: the experience of being aware of *spanda,* the creative vibration of *śakti.*

So it is possible to avoid creating *saṃskāras* and, according to Abhinavagupta, we can ameliorate the effects of *saṃskāras* already created—by sincerely repenting, for instance, for some wrong we have committed. We can also transfer the results of our actions to others. The latter often happens in the form of blessings. If, for instance, we perform a sacred chant for the benefit of someone we care about, we are, through the power of our intention, passing the merit of that action from ourselves to this other person. This is exactly what a blessing is. If the other person finds out about our blessing, he might pray that the merit of our action pass back to us, and, of course, then it would. In this way, saints and great yogis traditionally confer the merit of their good actions as blessings that benefit others and return to others the good wishes that they have sent to the saint.[80]

This transfer of *saṃskāras* can also apply to negative actions. When someone is shouting insults at someone else, if the person being yelled at feels provoked, he becomes a fertile field for the insults to bear their fruit. We have ourselves given our assailant the power to wound us. On the other hand, when negativity is directed toward us, if we could hold the firm conviction that it doesn't define us, there would be no supporting intention, and the insults, no matter how virulent, would not harm us. And, in that case, if the one who is yelling were also totally convinced that his action was divinely inspired, that it was taking place through him rather than being done by him, then the action wouldn't have any effect on him, either. In both cases, the negative action has been neutralized by the power of the conviction *That isn't me* or *I'm not the doer.*

Obviously, there are people who claim they're acting on the Lord's behalf when in fact they're deluded about the nature of their own motivation. Truly selfless action is extraordinarily rare. The nondoership we're describing isn't an intellectual stance. It isn't a matter of deciding, or thinking, or even believing, *I'm doing this for the Lord*—although just to entertain that notion is a very good first step. What we're talking about here are actions that come from a state of genuine alignment with the *spanda* of the Self.

It takes a pure intention to maintain a stance of such profound detachment. I remember the experience of one of my cohorts, who was in an amazingly expanded state once while en route to the Ganeshpuri ashram. On the train from Mumbai, a man walked up to him and shoved a pistol into his face, and my friend was experiencing so much love that he didn't consider this might be a threat. He smiled at the man and said, "Nice gun." The man dropped his menacing pose.

I find it endlessly fascinating to contemplate the connection between my intention (as evidenced by my thoughts, words, and actions) and the events that can seem to be the result. One day, decades ago as I was browsing in a bookstore, I found, seemingly by accident, a collection of essays on yoga by an author who was then unknown to me, Swami Vivekananda. I don't know why the book *The Practical Yogas* caught my attention—I didn't practice yoga at the time—but I bought it, and that night as I began to read, I found one revelation after another. I was fascinated by Vivekananda's lucid explanation of the law of karma: everything that one does leaves mental impressions that must become experiences, and yet, given the number of impressions, several bodies are required just to experience them all. Inexorably, one is bound to a recurrent cycle of lives. I'd never believed in reincarnation before that night, but all of this seemed so reasonable and authentic that it made perfect sense to me. The next day, I enrolled in a yoga school and began to practice *haṭha-yoga* . . . which led me to learn meditation . . . which led me, in about a year's time, to travel to India, where I met my Guru Baba Muktananda. So, reading a book that expanded my perception was the first of a series of steps by which, ultimately, I changed my life forever.

Speaking of intention, do we actually formulate our intentions, or do we come into this life with intentions already made? Who decides? It is the *saṃsārī*, the transmigrating being, who lives her own life script.

The World: Dream or Reality?

In a magnificent explosion of creativity, the supreme Self conceives an infinite galaxy of life dramas, in which the individual Self (or, you could say, "the soul") plays the role of actor and author. In this way we, as the ever-free divine power, choose the roles, the script, the scenarios, all the other participating characters, and the audience. What we wish to live is what God wishes us to experience.

Saṃsāra, the cycles of birth and death, has been pictured as an enormous wheel on which each soul spins, trapped in endless rounds of lives; or as a dense forest, where a traveler is easily lost in the darkness of ignorance; or as a vast ocean, which the soul tries to traverse and in which he almost inevitably drowns. In truth, transmigration is designed not to torture the soul but to promote its evolution. The soul progresses from life to life, not necessarily in linear stages but following the organic growth of a vine, winding its way through a trellis. At each step, he is presented with the opportunity to experience the most expansive concept of himself and also to live out the desires and consequences of actions impressed on his memory. As the soul moves from body to body, undergoing the experiences of each life, he may appear to ascend or descend on the scale of conscious beings, the way the tendrils of a vine may appear to move up or down at any given juncture on the trellis. Yet just as the fundamental movement of the vine is toward light, so the purpose that flows like a hidden current through all of the soul's choices is his intention to recover all of his *śaktis* and to become, once again, as Śiva.

Interestingly, Śaivism says that transmigration originates from the psychic instrument. As one of the Śaiva sages comments:

> All thought is *saṃsāra;* there is no bondage except thought.[81]

Let's say that you imagine something. The stronger your intention and the longer the time you hold onto that thought, the more likely are its chances of manifesting in the physical realm. This is one way we shape our reality through our emotional reactions. With this action, *vikṣepa,* projection, takes place. In the Vedānta text *Yoga-Vāsiṣṭha,* these phenomena are explained through anecdotes that leave us with an almost surrealistic impression of *saṃsāra.* My favorite of these stories, the one about Queen Lila, which is almost as long as life itself, reflects beautifully the tenets of Kashmir Śaivism.

The Story of Queen Lila

In brief, the story begins with Queen Lila's prayer to the goddess of wisdom, Sarasvatī, "O Divine Mother, grant that when my husband departs from his body, his soul shall remain in the palace." When her husband, King Padma, died, the queen was instructed by a celestial voice to cover his body with flowers so it wouldn't decay, and, thus, "he" wouldn't leave the palace. This wasn't what Queen Lila had wanted; she'd hoped for the impossible: that her husband's body would remain alive. Again she prayed to Sarasvatī, "Tell me, where is my husband?"

The goddess appeared to the queen and told her, "There are three types of space: the space of the mind, physical space, and the infinite space of Consciousness. By meditation on the infinite space of Consciousness, you can see and experience the presence of your husband." Queen Lila dedicated herself to spiritual practices and eventually, through Sarasvatī's grace, she attained the highest state.

Then in meditation, Lila was able to see her husband, who had now become an emperor, Viduratha, and sat on a throne surrounded by kings, sages, and soldiers. She recognized many members of her court and wondered if they too were now dead. When she came out of meditation, she was relieved to see these people were still alive. She was puzzled, however, as to how they could exist in two places simultaneously, and she wondered which of her experiences was real.

Sarasvatī told her, "All creation is the effect of the emptiness of Consciousness and therefore the creation is empty too. All this is illusory, the effect of imagination."

Then to illustrate the dreamlike nature of all creation, Sarasvatī told Lila that in a tiny corner of the Supreme Creator's mind, there stood a dilapidated shrine. In that shrine, the fourteen worlds were the rooms, the three divisions of space were holes in the walls, the sun provided light. Inside the shrine were tiny anthills (the cities), piles of earth (mountains), and pools of water (oceans). "This is the universe," Sarasvatī said.

In a very small corner of the shrine, the goddess said, there lived a holy man called Vasishtha and his wife, Arundhati. One day, the holy man saw a splendid royal procession, and a desire arose in him for the life of a king, a life filled with the delight and glory he had seen. Not long after making this prayer, Vasishtha died. His wife prayed to the goddess Sarasvatī that his soul not leave the house, and she was granted this boon. Vasishtha became King Padma, and when Arundhati died, she became Lila, the king's wife.

Seeing Lila's surprise, the goddess explained that the world that the emperor Viduratha lived in was within the world of King Padma, and that the king's world was within the world of the sage Vasishtha, and all these worlds were taking place within Consciousness.

"Birth that arises from a wish," Sarasvatī told Queen Lila, "is no more real than the wish itself. It's like a wave in a mirage! Your palace, you, the king, and I are all pure Consciousness—all exist within the Self. In every atom, there are worlds within worlds. You and your husband have been through many incarnations. Though from the divine standpoint the whole universe is experienced right here, from the physical point of view, millions of miles separate the planes."

In that moment, Queen Lila was able to recall eight hundred of her previous births. She had been a nymph, a vicious woman, a serpent, a forest tribal woman. Then, because of her evil deeds, she became a vine; then, through keeping the company of sages, she became a sage's daughter; then she became a king, and because of evil deeds done during that lifetime, she became a mosquito, a bee, a deer, a bird, and a fish. Later, she once again became a celestial nymph with scores of male celestials falling at her feet.[82]

This is the wheel of *saṃsāra.* The message of *Yoga-Vāsiṣṭha* is that the notions of karma and transmigration, of bondage and freedom, of ignorance and knowledge are all transient distinctions manifesting on the clear mirror of infinite Consciousness. The central theme in all of these illustrations is how Consciousness, the eternal subject, becomes the object of its own perception. What is most interesting to me is that Baba Muktananda used to say that *Yoga-Vāsiṣṭha* is not a collection of metaphors but a replication of reality.

The Complex Mosaic of Past Lives

There is a stage in meditation in which a yogi can perceive his past lives. Usually, this happens after the yogi has a good degree of detachment so that he's able to witness these events without feeling trapped once again in a morass of old emotions. Even though he might have been a powerful *mahārāj* in Rajasthan or an oracular priestess at Delphi, a famous European novelist or a Renaissance beauty, in many other lives he would have undergone hunger and pain, the humiliation of returning to life as an animal, or the guilt of having committed heinous acts against others. Past karma presents a complex mosaic of the pleasant as well as the unpleasant. With detachment, however, we can see all this much as someone who watches a film, fascinated and yet not swept away by the action.

The vision of these past lives may feel like a present-moment experience—but how can it be? And, what about the vision of future events that some people perceive through clairvoyance? If it's possible to "see" the future, then it must have already happened. Does this mean that the present doesn't exist? Certainly, it doesn't mean this in our experience. Remember the observations we made about *ābhāsa-vāda* in the discussion of sutra 3: each object we see is a sudden flash of light that breaks into our perception. What we're seeing is in constant vibrational flux. While our mental instrument is digesting an experience, classifying it, giving it a name, and deciding how to understand it, the object that stimulated the perception has changed many times. This is why we never actually see the present—by the time we perceive it, "it" is past.

Our understanding of past and present—the future we deal with later—depends on the sequence of time and space. In this, the conclusions of modern astronomers have become part of our common lore. When we look at the firmament on a clear night and admire the marvelous mantle of luminaries we see there—stars, planets, constellations—what we are actually seeing is an image of the past emanated from many points in time. These shining bodies are so far distant from us that in many cases it takes thousands of light years for their image to reach our eyes. A light year, by the way, is the distance light travels in an Earth solar year—that is, 5.88 trillion miles. So, the constellations we see do not necessarily correspond to the position these stellar bodies have now, if indeed those stars still exist at the present time. The image we now see is light that emanated from various stars in a mosaic of times, sometimes millions of years ago!

Space and time are like two sides of a coin: inextricably interconnected. Calculations have been made to describe the perspective of an individual observing the planet Earth from a supernova, a giant exploding star whose light travels at a speed of 186,282 miles per second and takes 170,000 years to reach Earth. From the viewpoint of a conscious being who is that distance from this planet and who has the capacity to collect the planet's light into a detailed image, Earth would be inhabited by pre-Neanderthal humans, hunting mammoths in Eurasia during the lower Paleolithic period of the Stone Age. If this observer were at half that distance from Earth, she would instead see Neanderthal man inhabiting various parts of the planet as it was 85,000 years ago. At a position one-tenth the supernova's distance from Earth, she would see Cro-Magnon man of the upper Paleolithic period painting on the walls of the Lascaux and Altamira caves.[83] Meanwhile, all of us would be in the twenty-first century, living in the bustle and noise of some metropolis like New York, Tokyo, Paris, or Delhi, while our observer out there was watching Earth in scenes from its remote past. And whose perception would be correct?

Consciousness is free from the boundaries created by the principles that govern time and the natural order of space and form, cause and effect. For Citi, everything exists. It simply exists. The present is eternal. In other words, the events and living beings of the universe, with the entire gamut of possibilities and variations, are "happening" in Consciousness simultaneously. The universe is an apparition, without a sequence of cause and effect. For those of us conditioned by the notion of time and its companion, space, the universe appears as a sequence of events and moments. Right now, as you read this, you are living the totality of all your "past" and "future" lives! Standing at the most extreme point of a perspective—say, that of Consciousness as a whole—you could see this "I" in many different bodies, living separate incarnations simultaneously, the very condition described in the story of Queen Lila. The intentions of each lifetime, the various arrays of lessons we must master in order to evolve, already exist. If this is reality, then what is it that transmigrates? The mind.

Within this almost inconceivable perspective, one might well ask, *If all my lives have been created simultaneously, who experiences these lives?* The obvious answer would be, the Self as the individual soul. By "soul" we mean the *cidaṇu,* the basic nucleus of individuality created by *āṇava-mala.* Then one might ask, *But how does the soul carry so many different lives at one time?* Accustomed as we are to judging boundaries from the perspective of our physical body, we think that the soul is "inside" the body. According to Kashmir Śaivism, the body exists within the soul, which contains as well as penetrates it. For a soul to contain so many possibilities of life simultaneously, its retaining capacity must include the myriad array of individual bodies, each one with its own intentions and life script. These considerations give us an idea of the potential vastness of *āṇava-mala,* the power that establishes the soul's boundaries.

Let me end our discussion of this sutra with an exercise that has been a powerful contemplation for me: Consider that the saint you will one day become exists in this very moment. Gaining access to your highest potential, you can relish the reality of your own longing fulfilled. It is you. Speak with it. Ask questions about your spiritual journey and how you are dealing with the circumstances of your life. This is a fascinating exploration.

10

The Five Acts of the Lord

Sutra 10

तथापि तद्वत् पञ्चकृत्यानि करोति

tathāpi tadvat pañca-kṛtyāni karoti

Even then, [the transmigratory soul] performs the five acts like [Śiva].

tathā:	then
api:	even
tat:	that; him
vat:	like
pañca:	five
kṛtyāni:	acts, functions
karoti:	he performs

Even though he has taken on all the contractions implicit in individuality, Śiva never stops being Śiva. Like someone behind a mask, the Lord is still recognizable. At a carnival, you can usually figure out who it is in that costume. Something gives her away. The sound of her voice, her manner of walking, a characteristic gesture—there is always some clue to a person's identity, and so it is with the Lord. He may be heavily disguised in his role as ourselves, and yet there is a sign by which we can know that we are he. And what is this sign? Sutra 10 tells us that even in our contracted state, we act exactly as Śiva does: we perform the five cosmic actions.

The five acts, the *pañca-kṛtya,* which are a fundamental concept in the Śaiva tradition, are outlined in a passage from *Svacchanda-tantra* in which the Divine is venerated as the One who brings about emanation *(sṛṣṭi),* dissolution *(saṃhāra),* concealment *(vilaya),* maintenance *(sthiti);* and who dispenses grace *(anugraha),* which destroys the affliction of those who have bowed to him.[84] With these five acts—creation, maintenance, dissolution, concealment, and the bestowal of grace—the Lord carries out everything that happens in the universe. If we pay attention, we can see the *pañca-kṛtya* in the cycles of life that occur all around us: in taking birth, in living, in dying, as well as in the suffering that comes from ignorance of the Self and the delight that follows true knowledge. In the experience of humanity, there is the meeting of cells in reproduction, the maintenance of the tissues and physical functions, and their demise. There is also our lack of awareness that this vital organism we call "the body" is a function of our thoughts, and the grace of experiencing the nature of our innermost being.

Sutra 10 invites us to contemplate that we, too, carry out Śiva's dance, performing the *pañca-kṛtya* just as he does. We can verify this by observing ourselves. Consider what's happening for you right now. The words you are reading at this moment are your creation, *sṛṣṭi.* I might have written them, but they exist for you only through your own perception. In that sense, you are creating them anew in this moment. As these words continue being present in your perception, you maintain them, *sthiti.* They exist and are meaningful to you because you, as a conscious being, make them real. As you continue reading, the words that you perceived earlier disappear; you dissolve them, *saṃhāra.* If you were to close your eyes, the entire book would disappear, together with everything that you might have been seeing up to that moment. These are aspects of everyday life. Now come the two most crucial actions. Do you realize that there is no essential difference between you and what you perceive? In other words, are you experiencing everything as the Self in this moment? If the answer is no, that means that you are engaging in the act of concealment, *vilaya.* However, if you are experiencing the essential identity between your I-consciousness and the objects of your perception, then you have accomplished the act of grace, *anugraha.*

The preceding exercise, which is something you can do at any time with whatever is before you at the moment, is more significant than it might first appear. In his commentary on this sutra, Kshemaraja says:

> If this authorship of the fivefold act, which occurs within one's own personal experience, is pursued steadily with firm understanding, it reveals the Lord's greatness to the devotee.[85]

And what is the *firm understanding* that we are to employ in contemplating the five actions in our lives? Kshemaraja is telling us that these seemingly ordinary observations can *reveal the Lord's greatness* to us—our own greatness!—by leading us to the inner posture *I am Śiva.*

You may think that *I am Śiva* is a pretentious stance to assume, but I assure you that it is not. You're not *pretending* to be Śiva; you *are* Śiva. Whether or not you're in the state of Śiva at any particular moment, you are still Śiva, and the pretense, if you want to call it that, is that you're an individual. I have come to feel that this is true pretentiousness: for me to see myself as a limited individual when I've studied for years, experienced at times, and know very well that, ultimately, *I am Śiva.*

This practice, known as *śiva-bhāvanā,* "identification with the Lord," requires us to use our imagination in order to attain something that we know at first only intellectually or intuitively. The key to success in this *sādhana,* even though it may seem a little strange at first, is to consider you have attained what you think you haven't yet attained. We retrain the mind with language and images that lead us to the Truth. Kshemaraja adds:

> Those who always ponder over this [fivefold act of the Lord], knowing the universe as an unfoldment of the essential nature [of Consciousness], become liberated in this very life. This is what the [sacred] tradition maintains. Those who do not ponder this, seeing all objects of experience as essentially different, remain forever bound.[86]

Peacefully and with the utmost care, you can observe the emergence, maintenance, and the dissolution of your thoughts, memories, and emotions: vibrant waves of *śakti* that emerge and submerge, arise and disappear ceaselessly. For one who does not identify his thoughts with the pulsations of the *śakti,* these forms are like clouds, obscuring the inner light. But for those whose awareness vibrates with *śakti,* these appearances are simply expressions of the eternal principle. This very recognition of one's own actions as the *pañca-kṛtya* is a path that leads to accomplishment in yoga. According to Abhinavagupta:

> Thus Śiva, the agent of the five operations of creation, persistence, destruction, grace, and obscuration, is the conscious nature. Worship, the recitation of mantra, initiation, and yoga are eternally manifest for the yogi who has realized that he himself is, in the fullness of his freedom, the agent of the five operations.[87]

And how does one perform this exalted practice? It happens through the final and most compelling of these five functions: *anugraha.*

The Act of Grace

Concealment is the reason that grace exists: Grace is the solution to concealment. By means of grace, the Lord ends the concealment he has imposed on himself. He comes to the recognition that his own Consciousness penetrates the cycles of the universe. In other words, grace resolves—or dissolves—the illusion of duality inherent in the individual's universe.

The Sanskrit word for grace, *anugraha,* literally means "favor, amiability, bestowing benefits, promoting a good cause." Etymologically, *anu* is a prefix that indicates "following," and *graha* means "grasping, taking hold of." Thus, *anugraha* involves what happens after something has taken hold of us, an image that suits the Western notion of grace: a divine gesture that takes hold of an individual in order to bestow favor on her. I find it fascinating that there is such congruence between the two terms, underscoring for me the position of grace as a universal act, without distinctions of a cultural or temporal nature.

Grace is commonly understood as a gift of God: the elevation of the individual to a state of joy, of ecstasy. For the one who is thus graced, this divine gift permeates her and makes her feel that she is in God's favor. From this influence, virtues are born that confirm the extraordinary blessings one has received. Grace indicates gentility, affability, elegance, ease, benevolence, and beauty. It also signifies merit and friendship. In other contexts, to bestow grace is to pardon or to offer clemency to one who has committed an inappropriate or injurious act. In Spanish, the term conveys a sense of lightness and merriment and is also used to express gratitude: *gracias,* thank you.

These various meanings of the word *grace* are, in my own observation, borne out by experience. I often find myself repeating *gracias, gracias, gracias,* like a mantra, so grateful am I for the abundant blessings conferred by grace.

Moreover, the sages tell us that grace is given by the Lord unconditionally, motivated by his love alone. In the *spanda-śāstra,* when the Lord becomes the bestower of grace, he is called Śaṅkara, a name that means "the doer of auspiciousness." It is grace that is the greatest auspiciousness, the most valued of all possible gifts in this universe. Grace unites the soul with its Creator. Regarding this bestowal of the Lord's compassion, Utpaladeva says:

> Where even agonies transform into pleasure
> And poison into nectar,
> Where the world itself becomes liberation,
> That is the path of Śaṅkara.[88]

The grace of Śaṅkara grants illumination, dispersing the darkness of ignorance concerning the nature of the world and ourselves, and at the same time, that grace facilitates our enjoyment of the world. Utpaladeva says that both spiritual freedom and worldly pleasure, both *mokṣa* and *bhoga,* are available to the soul graced by Śaṅkara.

And how are we to open ourselves to such beneficence? How does grace come into our lives?

In my observation, there is something about grace that is both readily apparent and little understood. It's this: In the life of each of us, there is a point when, arriving at a crossroad, we are given an opportunity to leave the path of darkness and take the path of light. In order to have a choice, of course, we must perceive that choice, and so it is necessary that we receive some sign that this path of light exists.

I had an experience of this in 1969, when I was visiting the ruins of Monte Alban in Oaxaca, Mexico, and because I had no context for it, years passed before the event affected my understanding. The incident was this: I came across the remains of what might have been a temple, from the top of which there was a panoramic view. I was admiring the ruins and the spectacle of the mountain valleys all around, when suddenly, as if by magic, my mind seemed to stop functioning. Abruptly, all my interpretations and imaginings ceased, and I was left perceiving the scene without embellishment. The mountains, the birds, the buildings in ruins, the people walking by—I could see everything so clearly. The colors were vivid, and even the air seemed to have a slight sparkle to it. I was absorbed in the scene, and my experience of this absorption was blissful, utterly tranquil.

It's difficult to convey this experience in words, as it was itself wordless. When I finally came out of it, I hadn't the slightest understanding of what had happened—though I did know that *something* had happened. At that point, I hadn't studied the scriptures, so I'd never heard of *anugraha,* and I hadn't thought very much about grace.

Most people have glimpses of this kind, and yet because they have no context for understanding the experience, they discount it, they tell themselves it was their imagination, and sometimes they forget it altogether. Even if they do hold it in their memory, they have no knowledge of how or why this miracle occurred or what they might do to encourage its happening again. For this reason, it may seem that grace lacks stability: it's experienced in one moment and then seems to disappear in the next. However, the effect of grace has nothing to do with the divine power itself; the effect of grace depends entirely on the degree of preparation of the recipient. We know this because there are times when the aspirant is at a level of such extraordinary spiritual maturity—by virtue of his intense devotion to God, or prayer, or meditation, or merit gained in a previous incarnation—that a single glimpse is enough to change the direction of his life forever. Saul of Tarsus was blinded by a vision of divine light on the road to Damascus, and almost immediately thereafter, he began to serve the very path he had been vilifying. In such instances as this, a flash of divine favor, *anugraha,* has become what the Gurus of the Siddha Yoga lineage call *śaktipāta,* "the descent of divine energy." The difference is that rather than being just an event in one's life, this act of grace also can be a *dīkṣā,* an initiation, which means that it is a beginning, a first step on the spiritual path.

Though there are some texts, especially in the *haṭha-yoga* tradition, that prescribe personal effort as a method to obtain spiritual initiation by grace, this is difficult as there is no subsequent guidance available to one who receives divine favor in this way and no continued infusion of grace. There is an easier and, as Baba Muktananda used to say, safer method of receiving *śaktipāta,* and that is through the intervention of a being who is so wholly identified with God that he or she has taken on the fifth cosmic function. I am referring to the grace-bestowing power of the Guru.

The Guru's Grace

Gurur-upāyaḥ, "The Guru is the means," states the *Śiva-sūtra.*[89] In his commentary on this aphorism, Kshemaraja says:

> [The] Guru may be said to be the power of divine grace. As has been said in the *Mālinī-vijaya:* "That [the power of grace] has been said to be the collective whole of *śaktis,* that has been said to be the Guru's mouth [i.e., the Guru's power of grace]. . . .That power of grace, affording a favorable opportunity to the aspirant, is the means.[90]

In Śaivism, the Guru is viewed not as an individual, male or female, but as a *śakti,* as the very power that bestows *anugraha.* The scriptures state emphatically that the power of grace is not the body or mind or personality of the spiritual master, but is divine will itself, performing the role of spiritual master through that particular vehicle. In other words, grace takes form as the Guru for the sake of the student. In *Kulārṇava-tantra,* one of the clearest scriptural discussions on the nature of the Guru, Lord Śiva tells his disciple, the Goddess Parvati:

> O my Beloved, Śiva is really all-pervading, subtle, above the mind, without features, imperishable, of the form of space, eternal, infinite. How can such a one be worshiped? That is why, out of compassion for his creatures, Śiva takes the form of the Guru, and when worshiped with devotion, O Goddess, he grants liberation and fulfillment.[91]

In the Śaiva tradition, the role of the Guru is seen as crucial on the spiritual path. Baba Muktananda took vows as a monk and practiced yoga assiduously for some twenty-five years with a following of his own—and yet he spent the whole of that time looking for a Guru. He used to say that he always knew that it was only through spiritual initiation, *śaktipāta-dīkṣā,* that his effort could bear fruit. After receiving *śaktipāta-dīkṣā* from Bhagawan Nityananda, Baba said, "My *sādhana* advanced with the speed of a great river in flood."[92] Kshemaraja quotes another Śaiva master on the significance of initiation:

> *Dīkṣā* is that which gives realization and destroys all impurities. Because it imparts the realization that awakens one from the sleep of ignorance, it is called *dīkṣā.* It has the characteristic of both giving *[dī]* and destroying *[kṣa].*[93]

It is understood that through spiritual initiation, the aspirant not only receives the light of grace but he also loses his ties to darkness—to the ego, to the binding forces of the *malas,* and in particular to *āṇava-mala,* the limitation that makes us feel separate from God. By our own spiritual efforts, assisted by the power of grace, we can dissolve the sense of limited doership and the perception of differences. That is not, however, the case with *āṇava-mala.* As I said earlier, this limitation is an act by which the Lord wills himself to remain separate from his plenitude, and so it follows that it can be dissolved only by another act of divine will. This is what happens when we receive *śaktipāta-dīkṣā.* In the *Kulārṇava-tantra,* the movement from spiritual darkness to light is described as the function of initiation by the Guru,* and the connection between the Guru and this initiation is also very strongly drawn:

> It has been laid down by Lord Śiva that there can be no liberation without *dīkṣā,* and this *dīkṣā* cannot be there without a traditional master.[94]

Hearing this, some people think that this initiation leading to liberation can be received only from a particular master, or from the master of a particular path. But that is not the sense in which the scripture interprets *dīkṣā.* The Guru is one with the divine power as it manifests in the form of beings who have attained final illumination and, in addition, have been specifically empowered to bestow initiation through *śaktipāta.* The Āgamas consider the act of grace to be so magnificent that it transcends the embodied form of the spiritual teacher. According to the *Mantriśiro-bhairava-tantra:*

> The Guru's power of grace inherent in the mouth of the Guru is greater than the Guru itself.[95]

The mouth of the Guru is a metaphor for the dispersal of the power of supreme freedom—in this case, through *mantra dīkṣā*—and for the infinity of *śaktis* emanating from that act.

Just as grace is not limited by the body or personality of the one who bestows it, so it is not confined by the actions and events associated with

* "The syllable *gu* signifies darkness; *ru,* that which restrains it. He who restrains the darkness of ignorance is the Guru" (*Kulārṇava-tantra,* 17.7; Ram Kumar Rai, trans. *Kulārṇava Tantra* (1983), p. 328).

its bestowal. Various ways of bestowing *śaktipāta-dīkṣā* are enumerated in the Āgamas: rituals, acts of purification, prayers, mantras, and so on. The purpose of each of these methods is to facilitate the descent of grace, preparing the initiate and awakening his awareness to the significance of the moment. Baba Muktananda explains:

> The different methods are only instruments for transmitting Śakti, and they have no more importance than that.[96]

In other words, a ceremony is not itself the initiation. Baba used to say time and again that *śaktipāta* is the only true spiritual initiation and that when the Indian scriptures refer to initiation, what they are actually talking about is *śaktipāta*.[97]

You might wonder what the difference is between the grace that comes from the Lord and this *śaktipāta* from the spiritual master. For me, the clearest explanation lies in my own experience. When I received grace at Monte Alban, I was intrigued by what had happened and remembered it afterward, and yet nothing really changed in my life. The following year when, as I described in the Introduction, Baba Muktananda sent me into the meditation hall in his ashram to repeat a mantra, what happened in my meditation was actually quite similar. When I came out of meditation, I thought, *Oh, this is exactly what I experienced at Monte Alban!* But there was, in fact, a colossal difference because within a very short time, a sea change had occurred in my own *śakti*, in my energy. Why? Because the descent of grace that came from Baba Muktananda had awakened my *kuṇḍalinī*.

Many of you are probably familiar with *kuṇḍalinī*, at least as a concept. For those who are not, the simplest way of describing this great force is, I think, to say that *kuṇḍalinī* is the power of grace residing within a human being in, as the texts of yoga say, a state of dormancy. As *kuṇḍalinī* becomes activated, it moves through the individual as a sort of beneficial fire, consuming the storeroom of *saṃskāras** as well as negative concepts and feelings. What makes *śaktipāta* an act of initiation is this awakening and unfolding of *kuṇḍalinī*. For the *sādhaka* who follows the path of a *śaktipāta* Guru, there is a continuous outpouring of grace, which not only awakens *kuṇḍalinī* but also sustains the unfoldment and inner transformation that is its natural outcome. Ultimately, *kuṇḍalinī* is the force that fulfills the promise of initiation by dissolving the limitations that come from ignorance of the Self. In sutra 17, we explore further how the inner work of *kuṇḍalinī* is the very essence of the path of yoga.

Śaktipāta-dīkṣā, which is glorious and incomprehensible, is at the same time entirely within one's reach. It is we who attract *anugraha*, through our devotion and our efforts on the spiritual path. Baba Muktananda, who was in a lineage of *śaktipāta* Gurus,** often said:

> It is people themselves who draw my grace, by the power of their service, by the power of their love and devotion, by the force of their own worth. I don't bestow grace on anyone. To me all are equal. To me all are equally dear.[98]

For me, Baba's observation confirms the teaching of this sutra: We ourselves perform the five acts of the Lord, including the bestowal of grace. I say this because it is through an exercise of our own free will—

* As we discussed in sutra 9, the *saṃskāras* that have not yet begun to manifest in our lives can be erased through spiritual practice, particularly meditation.

** For more information on the Siddha Yoga Gurus, please see Appendix A.

through our thoughts, our words, our own actions—that we are drawn toward or propelled away from grace. In order to receive the Lord's grace, we must bestow our grace on the Lord. Time and again Baba would say that the grace of the disciple is much more important than the grace of the Guru. The first time I heard him voice this truth, my mouth dropped open in amazement, but then upon reflection, it made perfect sense to me. Like God himself, a spiritual master is constantly offering grace. If we don't receive that grace, it's because we aren't open to it. For without our explicit permission, neither God nor Guru can enter our soul. As Baba says:

> Everywhere I go, people ask me this question, "Baba, when does a person receive the grace of the Guru?" And I always say: "Only when the disciple bestows his grace on the Guru can the Guru bestow his on the disciple." If the disciple doesn't bestow his favor, how can the Guru give his blessing? If the disciple's grace is there, it will attract the Guru's grace. But if there is no discipleship, the teachings of the Guru cannot take root.[99]

We can confer grace on ourselves through our efforts to pierce the shadow of appearances with the firm understanding *I am Śiva.* When Baba speaks of *disciple's grace,* he is referring to a student's willingness to engage with the teachings, to follow the practices, to take the precepts of a spiritual path into his daily life. Then, as Baba says, these sublime teachings—*I am Śiva; I am the one who performs the five acts of God*—can take root in our awareness and grow. In time, we will see the Lord's divine power expressed in every action of our lives.

11

The Five Acts of the Yogi

Sutra 11

आभासन रक्तिविमर्शन बीजावस्थापन
विलापनतस्तानि

***ābhāsana-rakti-vimarśana-
bījāvasthāpana-vilāpanatas tāni***

These [five acts take place in the form of]
illuminating [the object],
enjoying it, knowing it, planting a seed
[of limiting memories],
and dissolving [those limitations].

ābhāsana:	illuminating, shining
rakti:	enjoyment
vimarśana:	knowing, perceiving
bīja:	seed
avasthāpana:	planting, placing down
vilāpanataḥ:	dissolution, destruction
tāni:	these

IN SUTRA 10, KSHEMARAJA GIVES an external view of the five acts of Śiva; here, he looks deeper, into the experience of yogic absorption, both when the yogi's eyes are open and when his eyes are closed. Sutra 11 reveals an esoteric practice inspired by the *krama-śāstra,* a current of Śaiva thought associated with the sage Abhinavagupta, who was, you may recall, Kshemaraja's Guru. The sutra unveils processes that take place in the innermost recesses of a yogi's mind, with the purpose of offering guidance to those who are advanced in their practice and wish to approach *sādhana* with greater skill.

The steps of this practice can be applied to any experience, exterior or interior. They are equivalent to instructions on how to walk through a minefield without being harmed. How would you accomplish such a feat? Probably you'd be vigilant, you'd keep your senses alert to any sign of peril, and you'd walk on tiptoe because you would know that one misstep could mean disaster. This is a metaphor, of course, but in the life of a yogi, just one obsessive thought, one seductive image, one moment of unbridled passion is enough to shatter the clarity and inner peace of a long and sustained *sādhana.* Sutra 11 shows us a way we can move in the world, knowing it all to be God—and not getting caught by it. Kshemaraja says that it is not a practice for the uninitiated:

> This kind of authorship of the fivefold act, though always within reach of everyone, does not become manifest without the instruction of a good Guru [*sadguru*]. One should, therefore, take to the reverential service of a [*sadguru*] so that this may become manifest to him.[100]

The term *sadguru* is one that Gurumayi uses frequently. The term *sat* means "good, true, venerable, honest, wise," and in reference to a spiritual master, this prefix implies that he has the capability to initiate a disciple and take that person to liberation. The energy that descends as one receives initiation by *śaktipāta* from a *sadguru* kindles the inner process of *pañca-kṛtya,* the five acts, and bestows its benefits on the yogi.

The Five Acts of Perception

From the perspective of the highest goal, a yogi who has been awakened by grace perceives the five acts as an unfolding of power that emanates from his own heart, reproducing the divine functions of Śiva. This is the key to understanding the esoteric meaning of the sutra. Now, walking with Kshemaraja step-by-step through the thorny world of perception, let's explore the significance of our creative powers.

Illumination

We give expression to the creative act of Śiva through the process of *ābhāsana.* Do you remember the *ābhāsas,* those sparkles of conscious light that flash forth all forms in the universe? We spoke of them in sutra 3. In exactly the same manner, through our own senses, we project the objects that we perceive, causing them to appear before us. That may seem like an overstatement, but consider how differently three people will perceive the same object—three universes! Or how when they enter a room, they might all perceive a different selection of the objects present. Consider also the human tendency to remember the one negative statement among hundreds of other remarks made. *Ābhāsana* is the capacity to re-create the world, to make it manifest before us, and this power springs from the heart of Śiva within our bodies.

It is said that when Śiva opens his eyes, the universe comes into being *(sṛṣṭi)*; the same happens with us when we activate our sense of sight, hearing, touch, smell, or taste. Our experience of the appetizing smells of cooking food, or the feel of dewy grass on the bottoms of our feet, or the voice of someone dear to us—these, and so many other of the sensations that fill our days, are *ābhāsas,* reproductions of the divine power creating our own universe. Our senses of perception are beams of *śakti.* Kshemaraja personifies these *śaktis* as goddesses who are fulfilling their divine functions as they manifest our perceptions on the mirror of the mind. The *śaktis* appear from their origin, the Self, faster than physical light, apprehending the objects of the world and projecting them, just as a camera prints images on a film. The act of perception culminates when the experiences are labeled: "toast and coffee," "wet grass," and "so-and-so's voice." The memories that come to our mind concerning these images are also *ābhāsas,* are also perceived on the mental mirror. Behind the screen, the Self—Śiva himself—observes the impressions dancing for his pleasure.

This process of *ābhāsana* is what happens with sense perception, Kshemaraja tells us, and we can employ it as a yogic practice by adopting the inner posture of a witness. That is, you can watch the process of perception without words, knowing but not describing what it is and where it comes from. You simply allow the impressions carried within you by the senses to present themselves on the mirror of your intellect without attempting to interpret them. This is illumination *(ābhāsana),* the first moment of perception.

Enjoyment

As you continue to witness the re-creations of the senses, you are maintaining them. Thus, you maintain within yourself the objects of your universe, performing the act of enjoyment *(rakti)*. This is accomplished with the full engagement of the senses. *Rakti,* as a practice of yoga, occurs when we enjoy the play of the senses being aware that these experiences both arise from and are maintained in the Self. This act of enjoyment is equivalent to the act of maintenance *(sthiti)* performed by Śiva, since the enjoyment of a perception involves maintaining it for a while in the mind.

Inner Knowing

Next comes *vimarśana,* an inner knowing—or, as we have defined it in this sutra, knowledge. Here we disengage the senses, yet the awareness of the object persists within us. This, Kshemaraja tells us, is the yogic equivalent to Śiva's act of dissolution *(saṃhāra),* for when Śiva withdraws the universe, metaphorically closing his eyes, he folds it into his own being. When our attention is directed to a remembered sensation, we can experience a flash of *camatkāra,* the profound, aesthetic delight that is beyond sensual pleasure. I have found that by observing a perception carefully, I can experience a most serene and subtle delight, a feeling that seems to arise as the pulsations of the *śakti* itself. The Śaiva scriptures tell us that all circumstances and objects, even those we might ordinarily consider to be unpleasant, annoying, or threatening, hold the essential and sweet flavor of oneness. Yogis say that, in time and with practice, they learn how to relish each sensation, tasting the ambrosia hidden in the depths of the heart.

How does one apply this principle? Just suppose you're listening to a concert. The music is so captivating that when it ends, a resonance remains within you—with some focus, you can evoke the melodies in your mind and even the feelings these melodies touched in you. As you recall the music, you become aware that this memory is nothing but pulsations of energy—and suddenly the memory, the music, the feelings are all pulsating waves of delight from the heart, from the source of all sounds and all creations. The external experience loses its separate existence; the music becomes one with your own awareness, and you are not just the audience but also the musician, the composer, the music itself.

Vimarśana is the practice of acute attentiveness in which one lifts the veil of separation, glimpsing Consciousness at the moment of perception. Kshemaraja underscores this point in his commentary with the following passage in which a Śaivite master addresses the Lord:

> The mountain of manifoldness that cannot be split by others, even by the thunderbolt of *samādhi,* is experienced as one's Self and thus destroyed by those who are endowed with the power that accrues from devotion to you.[101]

I find it interesting to examine the experiences of union in my own life. For instance, during a visit to Amsterdam a number of years ago, I was walking through the Rijksmuseum when I came upon a painting by Jan Vermeer. It's a small picture, no more than a foot square, depicting a young woman, apparently with child, standing and reading a letter; on the wall behind her is a map of the world. Although it isn't in the picture, there is evidently a window in front of the woman, for from it a tenuous light bathes the entire scene.

Looking at this painting, I could feel the silent joy vibrating in the woman's heart as she reads this letter—which I thought must be from her husband who, from the presence of the map, I thought must be some place faraway. The morning light illumines her face, and I can feel in her soul a numinous and tender love. I had seen reproductions of this painting many times, but never before had I experienced it directly, and the effect it had on me was to stop my mind. My entire body was inundated by delight and wonderment. Even after I walked on, I continued for a while to feel the effect of the picture, recreating for myself my own joy in it.

At this point, my mind was still free of interpretation, but before very many minutes had passed, I began to digress, thinking, *I've just seen a famous Vermeer. What a beautiful painting! Yes, certainly, it's a masterwork* . . . The superfluities of information flooded my mind and buried the feeling of pure joy. How many times in our day do we have experiences of this sort!

To Plant a Seed

In his commentary, Kshemaraja warns us not to make critical connections while the act of *vimarśana* is taking place. If the object of our perception becomes separated from Consciousness, if our observation is that it's something different from ourselves, then that experience becomes the seed of a *saṃskāra.* This seed, buried by its own weight, plants itself in the subtle body. Kshemaraja calls the process *bījāvasthāpana,* the establishment of a seed. Seeds sown eventually germinate and grow, veiling still further the experience of the Self, and the effect of this is equivalent to Śiva's act of concealment, *vilaya.* That is precisely what happened to me after I walked away from the Vermeer: I wasn't able to identify my enjoyment completely with the light of the Self, and so the experience left its impression in my subconscious. Through *bījāvasthāpana* we cover the Truth with ignorance—and create karma.

Dissolution

It should be noted that Kshemaraja does not encourage us to explore our karmas or delve into what we've done in the past. Rather, he directs our attention to the root cause of the attachment—the perception of separation—at the precise juncture in which our perception either creates the seed of attachment or moves us closer toward liberation. And what do we do at this juncture? This is where *vilāpana,* dissolution, comes in.

The five inner acts of a yogi can be performed with one's eyes open or closed. There is a practice known as *haṭha-pāka,* or "forceful digestion," which I've found extremely helpful in dissolving the potential seeds of karma that come up in meditation. Kshemaraja describes *haṭha-pāka* as the best method for dealing with unnecessary thoughts. In sutra 5, we discussed the nature of thoughts, how our thoughts are nothing but Consciousness. The contemplation of this truth is meant to bring us to unity-awareness. Yet there are other means of accomplishing this goal. One of them is to think of our thoughts as something separate, and to then offer those thoughts to the fire of Consciousness.

The Forceful Digestion of Unwanted Thoughts

In meditation, what I do is this: As soon as a thought or mental activity arises, I immediately offer it to the space of the One who is watching, which is another way of describing this fire of Consciousness. I don't fret about that thought, because to worry about a *vikalpa* is to sow a whole harvest of unnecessary seeds. I just let the thought go, and when I cannot do that, when the mental current is just too strong, I withdraw, as it were, offering my own mind to that subtle space where the Self vibrates as "I am." Then I let the mental scenes pass, as one might watch a river flow by without ever dipping into the water. Most of the time in meditation, I perceive light, and it is there that I make my offerings to the Self. Like meteors entering the gravitational field of the Earth, the mental activity that enters this conscious space generates such friction by its very separateness that it burns up on the spot.

This practice of *haṭha-pāka*—offering our mental states to the fire of Consciousness—gives us the experience of *vilāpana* (dissolution) and is equivalent to Śiva's *anugraha* (bestowal of grace). This is a personal act of grace by which the effect of our mental activity is annulled and prevented from settling as karmic seeds. By *vilāpana,* the yogi devours and consumes his thoughts until they become the same as his joyful awareness "I am." Though the yogi performs this action through his own self-effort, what makes the practice efficacious is the grace he has received from a *sadguru.*

In fact, this practice came to me through grace. At one point several years ago, I was bothered by a pattern of negative feelings that kept recurring, like a tape on autoreverse. I started to worry: *Why do I have this tendency? Is it karma? Is it an obsession?* Despairing of being able to handle it myself, I visited Baba Muktananda's *samādhi* shrine at Gurudev Siddha Peeth to ask for his grace in expunging this undesirable tendency from my life. As I was sitting with my prayer, I heard Baba's voice inside me saying, *Just offer these thoughts to the light of Consciousness. Offer them every time they come up, and forget about them.*

The simplicity of this instruction surprised me, but I decided to try it. Each time one of the thoughts connected to that tendency came up, I offered it to the inner space of Consciousness. What I mean by this is that no sooner had the thought sprung up than I used my will to push it into the space of my witnessing awareness, as if I were flinging things into the void. I found that the moment a thought would enter this inner space, it would vanish, just as surely as sugar dissolves in water. As I continued to meditate, this inner space became increasingly luminous, ultimately making it possible for me to offer to it any kind of mental activity, positive or negative, good or bad. Let me add that it's possible to practice this technique even when you're not formally sitting for meditation. You just have to have the intention to offer your thoughts.

In my practice, although this particular negative pattern didn't disappear altogether, its effect on me weakened instantly, and the practice helped me stop judging myself for having negative thoughts. As I continued making my inner offerings, I developed a deeper respect for my mind and gained confidence in the liberating power of grace.

I invite you to try this practice of offering your thoughts to the inner fire of Consciousness. As I have discovered, my thoughts don't always dissolve in the process and, when my eyes are open, neither does the physical appearance of the world dissolve. What does soften for me is the sense of being separate from what I see, hear, touch, smell, or feel.

The diversity of the outer and inner world is threaded through with the unifying awareness of the *spanda.* From this liberating, sublime perspective, I experience my own commission of the five acts of Śiva.

The experience is enormously significant for *sādhana,* according to Kshemaraja, who concludes his commentary on sutra 11 with this warning:

> He . . . who does not acquire complete knowledge [of the authorship of the five acts], owing to the lack of guidance from a *sadguru,* remains deluded by his own powers *[śaktis],* since the real nature of each *[śakti]* is concealed [from him].[102]

12

The Assemblage of Powers Contained in the Alphabet

Sutra 12

तदपरिज्ञाने स्वशक्तिभिर्व्यामोहितता
संसारित्वम्

tad-aparijñāne svaśaktibhir-vyāmohitatā saṃsāritvam

The condition of a transmigratory soul is delusion,
[brought about] by his own powers
when he is not fully aware
of that [his authorship of the five acts].

tat:	that
aparijñāne:	not knowing fully
sva:	one's own
śaktibhiḥ:	by the powers
vyāmohitatā:	delusion
saṃsāritvam:	the condition of a transmigratory soul

ONCE AGAIN, KSHEMARAJA DIRECTS our attention to our performance of the five acts of Śiva. If we don't know we perform these five acts, he says, we become deluded by our own powers and live as a *saṃsārī,* as a transmigratory soul. We may not think of ourselves as beings that transmigrate, but we should, because when we don't, that's exactly what we become: souls caught in a cycle of death and rebirth. In sutra 12, Kshemaraja gives us hints about how to extricate ourselves from this trap of *saṃsāra.* The sutra tells us that ignorance, *aparijñāna*—which means, literally, "lack of full knowledge"—comes about because we are deceived by our own powers. This is a form of deception well worth contemplating.

The core of the term *vyāmohitatā,* "delusion," is *moha,* which has a wealth of associations, none of them promising. *Moha* implies lack of awareness, lack of discrimination, distraction, disorientation, perplexity, infatuation, error, deception, and even madness. Under the spell of *moha,* the soul acts like Don Quixote, waging war against imaginary foes—confused, deluded, and, to the observer, possibly insane. Sutra 9 tells us how Citiśakti assumes limitation of her own free will to become a *saṃsārī.* Here, the same theme is continued from a different angle: we are deluded *svaśaktibhiḥ,* by our own powers. In contrast with sutra 9, Kshemaraja now points out in sutra 12 that these powers—various *śaktis* residing in us—can be turned around to dispel the grip of delusion and to grant the Lord's liberated state even while we are living in our physical body. In a characteristically terse commentary, Kshemaraja paints a complex picture that would require more space than we have to explain fully. So, I have chosen for discussion what I consider the most relevant of these explanations, the one referring to the assemblage of powers inherent in the sounds of the alphabet.

Mātṛkā-Śakti

In sutra 12, Kshemaraja speaks of how the supreme power of Speech, who is identical with the consciousness of the perfect I-ness and who contains within herself the whole collection of powers of the sounds of the alphabet, brings the sphere of the empirical subject into being through the successive stages of the manifestation of sound.[103] This exploration of delusion in reference to the power of the alphabet, *mātṛkā-śakti,* is one of the most fascinating aspects of Śaivism for me, and it is a topic to which Baba Muktananda gives great emphasis.

Baba once presented six consecutive lectures on this sutra, and most of what he said dealt with the power of letters—specifically, the fifty phonemes of the Sanskrit alphabet. Baba says:

> There are fifty letters. The *śakti* has taken on the forms of fifty deities, and they exist in these fifty letters. By assuming the form of these letters, the *śakti* deceives everyone.[104]

Baba goes on to say that once an individual understands the power of the letters, then these very letters can liberate him. To comprehend the full power of *mātṛkā,* we must begin once again at the beginning, with the creation of the universe. In sutra 4, we explore the creation from an ontological perspective, that is, how each of the *tattvas* is the basis for a specific state of being. Now, we're going to look at how the creation manifests vibrationally—through the power of sound, known as supreme speech, *parā-vāc.* This new perspective is not contradictory to what we've already considered; it's parallel and complementary. It's also extremely esoteric, positing the way in which the luminous Citiśakti casts herself into creation, manifesting first on the levels of vibration and sound.

From this viewpoint, the fifty phonemes of the Sanskrit alphabet each symbolize an extremely subtle vibratory level. Taken together, these vibrations create, support, and transform the universe.

As Baba points out, each of these vibratory levels is a power, a *śakti,* depicted in Śaivism as a goddess. According to the traditions of Sanskrit grammar, the fifty *śaktis* are arranged in an order and divided into eight groups, and each of these groups, known as *varga,* is presided over by a deity: Yogīśvarī, Brāhmī, Māheśvarī, and others.* Each of these *śaktis* is a *mātṛkā,* a term translated as "mother," because out of the womb of *mātṛkā* springs the created universe. Other meanings are "little mother," referring to our view of the insignificance of the letters, and "uncomprehended mother," an allusion to our failure to understand the power *mātṛkā* has in our lives—the way we get lost in the meanings of the words we hear, both from others and from inside ourselves. There is a whole constellation of meanings around words; these meanings bring forth responses from us; and these responses tether us to the illusion of the world more effectively than any rope.

I burned the toast . . . This traffic is backed up for two miles. I'm late for work—again! All of this, Baba Muktananda says, comes from the letters:

> From letters, a word is formed with its own meaning. From words, a sentence is formed with its own meaning. That meaning carries an image. Once an image is formed, you begin to feel good or bad. When you feel good or bad, you begin to experience the fruits of these feelings.

---

* These goddesses have different names in various Tantras. Anyone interested in a detailed, technical description of *mātṛkā-śakti* should turn to Andre Padoux, *Vāc: The Concept of the Word in Selected Hindu Tantras* (Albany: SUNY Press, 1990).

> If you divide the letters of a particular word, those letters have no meaning in themselves. For example, take the word *fool.* Now, if you just say these letters—F-O-O-L—one at a time, in themselves they don't carry any meaning. But when you combine these letters and say "Fool!" it really has its own power. It has meaning and it bears fruit too. The fruit of words is either painful or pleasurable; sometimes it is sweet, sometimes bitter, sometimes sour. This is a brief explanation of *mātṛkā śakti.*[105]

Mātṛkā-śakti has the power to liberate as well, by giving *parijñāna,* full knowledge. We'll discuss this further, but first let's look more closely at the way the universe manifests from sound.

The Four Levels of Speech

The creation of matter from sound is described by a number of India's philosophers, including the grammarian Bhartrihari and the Śaivite sages Somananda, his disciple Utpaladeva, and, most especially, Abhinavagupta.[106] In this doctrine, as we have said, the fundamental reality is viewed as pulsating Citiśakti who projects the universe of forms from her own exquisite vibration. This perspective is not unique to Śaivism. The Gospel of St. John, in the Bible's New Testament, begins with a well-known description:

> In the beginning was the Word: the Word was with God and the Word was God.[107]

There is a parallel statement in one of India's most venerated texts, the *Sāma-veda:*

> This, [in the beginning], was only the Lord of the universe. His Word was with him. This Word was his second. He contemplated. He said, "I will deliver this Word so that she will produce and bring into being all this world."[108]

In the same vein, the Bible's Book of Genesis states that when the Lord said, "Let there be light," light appeared; when he said, "Let dry land appear," it did; and when he said, "Let the earth produce vegetation: trees bearing fruit with their seed inside, each corresponding to its species," then this too was so.[109] Divine intention moves into words, and the words give rise to concrete objects. This biblical image is a metaphor for the creative process that Śaivism describes in four stages, beginning with the pure and unconditional *parā-vāc.*

Supreme Speech

Parā-vāc is the most exalted level of divine speech. The term means, literally, "supreme speech," the voice of God. Utpaladeva describes it in this way:

> *Parā-vāc* is Consciousness. It is self-awareness spontaneously arisen, the highest freedom and sovereignty of the Supreme Lord. The pulsing radiance is pure Being, unqualified by time and space. As the essence [of all things] it is said to be the heart of the Supreme Lord.[110]

Parā-vāc contains all letters, all words, all objects, all beings—everything that is to compose the created universe. *Parā-vāc,* immersed in delight, vibrates subtly as *aham,* "I am," the very pulsation of the Self. This is equivalent to saying that at this highest level, speech and the objects named by speech are undivided and indivisible, coexisting as a vibrating power that Abhinavagupta identifies as *śabda-rāśi,* "the totality of sound," and also as *śabda-rāśi-bhairava,* "the totality of sound as Bhairava."* This power rests in the womb of *parā-vāc,* like a seed waiting to germinate. The totality of sound is the source of everything and is simultaneously contained in everything. Of course, this vibration cannot be perceived, as there is nothing at this level either to hear or to be heard. All of creation, and the vibrational sounds associated with it, exist in the vast silence of *mahāśūnya,* the Great Void. It is from this silence that they will emerge into boisterous activity.

Visionary Speech

Then, from the depth of the silence of *parā-vāc* comes the first creative impulse, which is called *paśyantī-vāc.* The name means "visionary speech." Consciousness manifests as a desire to perceive objects as separate and distinct from itself—that is, duality. The supreme will begins to leave behind its transcendental state to turn itself into the manifest universe. The realm of differentiated sounds and forms can be seen as germinating seeds in the womb of Consciousness. It is at this point in the creation that Bhairava experiences the impulse to manifest, and what was resting in him as pure potential unfolds as the subtle *paśyantī-vāc,* reflected in his own being. Acting like a conscious mirror, this second level of speech reflects the mass of fifty Sanskrit phonemes—from the first letter *"a"* to the last one *"kṣa"*—perfectly aligned with all the

* Bhairava is a name often given in the *Trika-śāstra* (the scriptures of this Śaiva school) to Śiva when he's involved in the emergence, sustenance, and dissolution of the universe.

tattvas, the principles of creation. Though the letters and the *tattvas* are somewhat separate, they are still intricately associated. This is a significant arrangement, and the implication is that the *tattvas,* with their corresponding states of being, are truly vibratory levels represented by the letters. For us this means that, at the deepest level, our speech is divine, and so is our world.

Paśyantī-vāc is the cosmic memory in which all forms are reabsorbed and retained during the dissolution of the universe, and from whence these "remembered" expressions emanate as the universe is re-created.* At the time of the dissolution, all created forms and their constituent vibratory sounds are reduced once again into the fifty letters, which wait in the womb of Consciousness, like seeds, until the next creative cycle—the opportunity to re-form the universe of words with their designated objects. To understand this phenomenon, it helps to know that in human beings this second level of speech holds our own deposit of *saṃskāras,* the sum of past impressions. We don't know what these are, and they produce no sound that we can hear with our ears. We can't see or hear *saṃskāras* as we can our thoughts—and yet, more than anything else, it is these *saṃskāras* that determine our experience of life.

We can verify the existence of this phenomenon by observing our own inner experience. Baba Muktananda says:

> If no letters arise in the mind, it remains still. We know this from experience. When we wake up in the morning there's a moment or two when the mind is serene and free of thought, in the state of the pure "I." Then the *mātṛkā-śakti* starts to work.[III]

---

* The Indian tradition describes cycles of time in which the universe dissolves and re-emerges in continous cycles for a period so vast that we could almost call it infinite. At the beginning of each new cycle, the universe is re-created from the seeds of memory that are stored in *paśyantī-vāc.*

It is the unmanifest sound, the initial stirrings of the mind, that Abhinavagupta identifies as *mātṛkā-śakti.* In other words, the extremely subtle vibration that was *śabda-rāśī* at the *parā* level becomes denser at the *paśyantī* level, where it is known as *mātṛkā-śakti. Mātṛkā* emanates from the serene space of Consciousness to assume complete control of everything we do, and don't do, for the rest of the day—and this brings us to the next level of manifestation.

Intermediary Speech

The third level of speech is *madhyamā-vāc,* a name that comes from the term *madhya,* meaning "intermediary" or "middle." This is a way to describe an intermediary experience in which the world is perceived as distinctly separate from the words that describe it, although everything is still bathed in the unifying light of Consciousness. *Madhyamā* is in the "middle" between unity and diversity, and is evident as a mental experience, an activity reflected on the *buddhi,* the intellect.

For those who are familiar with the four bodies that Baba Muktananda speaks of in *Play of Consciousness,* the first level of speech occurs in the supracausal body, the seat of the *ātman* and of the deepest meditation; the second arises in the causal body, which holds the *saṃskāras;* and the third is in the subtle body, seat of the psychic instrument.

At this third level of sound, we experience vibrations that are perceptible. Though we "hear" and even "see" these mental images, ideas, and feelings embodied in words, they are happening on the conscious screen of our intellect and are not yet "out there" as when we perceive objects with the help of our senses. Seeing your pet dog with your eyes is not the same as seeing the dog in your mind with your eyes closed. These vibrations, which are denser than *mātṛkā*, are identified by Abhinavagupta as *mālinī*, which means "garland," referring to the garland of letters that has been created by Citiśakti.

Using a suggestive metaphor, Abhinavagupta describes the appearance of the phonemes and the principles in *madhyamā-vāc.* A creative friction occurs between Bhairava incarnated as the *śabda-rāśi* who merges with his beloved Śakti embodied as *mātṛkā;* the effect is a fusion in which the vowels and the consonants mix with each other and manifest in an apparent disorder, ignoring their original, grammatical arrangement. The child of this divine union is called *mālinī. Mātṛkā* is in the order of Sanskrit grammar; *mālinī* is reordered so that the sounds can be used in words. In *madhyamā-vāc,* the letters form and reform in different orders and combinations, just as one might string an assortment of flowers to create various garlands. We could say that *mālinī,* which also personifies this energy as "the one who holds or makes a garland," is the power by which the letters of the alphabet are strung together in linguistic garlands of various sorts, forming different words and sentences and vastly different meanings from the same alphabet.

The objects we perceive have some demonstrable concurrence, but the names and ideas that we have of them can vary from person to person, according to language. For those who speak English the liquid in a lake is *water,* for those whose language is Spanish it is *agua,* in Hindi it is *pāni,* and so on. Within the varied occurrence of *mālinī,* the names—the very sounds employed—are different while the object is the same and the same power is invoked.

The *śaktis* of the letters function as a matrix of energies, forming a vast vibratory web. These powers weave and interweave, acting together to generate all the various levels and manifestations of the cosmos. This is the source of our thoughts and of the discursive mind itself—and along with the thoughts come the objects designated, and vice versa. I may see an object with four legs, but unless I label it, I don't know that object as a member of the category we know as "table." I may have a sense of largesse, but if I didn't know what to call it, I'd never associate that particular feeling with what we happen to call "generosity." By making these identifications and associations, we begin to structure the way we understand the world and ourselves.

'Quite Solid' Speech

Now we arrive at the fourth and final level of speech, *vaikharī-vāc.* The word *vaikharī* means "quite solid." *Vaikharī-vāc* is the level of speech that pertains to the physical body: the spoken word. Communication now occurs through the vocal cords, the organs of articulation, and the breath. The most telling characteristic of *vaikharī-vāc* is the drawing of a distinction between name and form, between the spoken expression and what it designates. When we're operating on the level of thought, both the name and the image exist together within our mental apparatus. When we begin to articulate our thoughts, the name and the object exist separately, in the frame of time and space, or cause and effect. At the physical level, it's difficult not to perceive differences. As the levels of speech move toward physical manifestation and the divine powers contract, they become increasingly less powerful. Our *saṃskāras* are more significant in determining our experience than our thoughts, and what we think has much more power over our lives than what we say.

Vaikharī-vāc is the power underlying the great variety of languages, of how these languages are pronounced, and of the sacred and secular expressions spoken and written by human beings. Speech is less an acquired skill than a faculty innate to all human beings. What this means is that the mental structures with which we organize letters, words, and sentences into meaningful communication are inherent in us like archetypal forces. Abhinavagupta points to this extraordinary characteristic of humans when he explains that children are able to learn languages because of their innate capacity to associate sounds with objects.[112] This capacity is particularly evident at the level of *madhyamā-vāc,* where the forces of words are superimposed on and blended with the objects they express. Since the *madhyamā,* or intermediary level, is the background for solid speech, we naturally can expand this capacity to associate our perceptions with words into an ability to articulate meaningfully—to speak.

Underlying all the levels of speech is the great light of Consciousness, origin of both the words and the objects they name. Thus all the forms of speech carry weight, for every level is penetrated by the highest, by *parā-vāc.* For this reason, even though they may be less powerful than the more subtle levels of speech, the words we speak have tremendous impact, both on ourselves and on others.

Another Look at the Tattvas

We said earlier that the view of creation we've just been through, creation according to the levels of speech, is both parallel and complementary to the creation theory we presented in sutra 4 in our discussion of the thirty-four *tattvas,* the principles of existence. In common with creation theories from most Indian scriptures, the universal perspective is brought into clear relationship with the individual in both of these schemas. They are both maps that differentiate between levels of subtlety, and there is a clear correspondence between each "terrain" these different systems cover.

For example, *parā-vāc,* supreme speech, is beyond the *tattvas,* at the level where Paramaśiva, the Supreme Lord, exists as Śiva and Śakti, vibrating subtly as *aham,* "I am," the blissful pulsation of the Self.

Paśyantī-vāc, visionary speech, appears at the level of *sadāśiva-tattva,* the first created principle, where *aham-idam,* "I am this," establishes the pattern of the subject relating to object. Here the letters, as well as the *tattvas,* are like seeds in the womb of Consciousness; at universal dissolution everything is again reduced to these basic units.

Madhyamā-vāc, intermediate speech, manifests at the level of *īśvara-tattva,* the principle of lordship, where the Lord's view of creation takes clear form and the words stand distinctly separate from the created objects they designate, even though the objects are still bathed in the light of unity. Intermediate speech also manifests at the level of *śuddha-vidyā,* the principle of pure knowledge, where the Lord comes into a perfectly balanced relationship between word and object—the ground from which creation can physically manifest. And, as we discussed earlier, in a human being, it also manifests as thoughts through the psychic instrument, which is at the level of *māyā-tattva,* the principle of illusion, and includes its progeny, the *tattvas* of limitation that create the individual. At the densest level of *madhyamā-vāc* duality completely separates words from their objects.

Vaikharī-vāc, quite solid speech, is also influenced by *māyā-tattva,* and includes all of the remaining *tattvas,* all the way to gross manifestation.

As we said in sutra 4, the point of drawing a map that charts creation from the subtlest to the densest stages is to enable us to reverse the course and travel back to our origin. In regard to the levels of speech, this begins, quite naturally, with the way we speak.

Discipline in Speaking

Just becoming aware of the power of words in our lives is, in itself, a step forward in *sādhana.* Describing the goddess of speech, Vāc, as the mother of all words, Gurumayi puts great emphasis on the importance of using yogic discrimination in controlling how we invoke her. Gurumayi says that it is vital on the spiritual path to think before you speak.

> First of all, it takes great concentration to discover what you really think. That is the basic issue. Often you don't even know what your mind contains. Before you speak, you have to sort through everything the mind has collected to get to what is really meaningful. Secondly, it takes great contemplation to discriminate between what must be said and what is better left unsaid. It is like walking on the sharp edge of a sword. How do you know what should be said and what should not?[113]

It's a highly significant question, because the words we use have an effect—they have their own power of meaning and they also have the power we give them through our intent. I always used to think that as soon as I'd given voice to words, they dissolved in the air overhead. This may be true in terms of the sound itself, but some aspect of the vibration of those words doesn't disappear. It leaves its mark on the environment—and, as we know, what we think matters even more than what we say.

I was introduced to this notion one morning in the autumn of 1974, when Baba Muktananda was staying in a temporary ashram in New York City. He was receiving people that morning, and I happened to be in the room. At one point, I glanced out the window and saw that the sky was completely overcast. Everything looked very gray and sad to me. There was a moment of silence in the room, and I took that opportunity to call the weather to Baba's attention. I said, "No wonder people in New York get depressed. The sky is so gray."

From his seat, Baba looked outside. He was quiet for a moment, and then he turned to me and said, "It is not like that. The sky doesn't affect people. It's people's thoughts that affect the sky."[114]

At the time, this seemed to me to be quite a startling statement. I'd never even considered the possibility that words going through my mind might affect the environment. Over the years, however, I've observed the truth of Baba's observation many times. I've had the opportunity to accompany Gurumayi on several of her teaching tours. Often some public hall or hotel ballroom is rented for her programs, and in the beginning, the vibrational atmosphere of these places can be dense with agitation and negativity. Devotees will clean the space, but more important than scrubbing the walls or vacuuming the rugs, they'll chant in the room, they'll play tapes of the mantra. Then when Gurumayi arrives, crowds of people will meet in the space for chanting and meditation, and, in no time at all, that ballroom is transformed into a temple, into a sacred environment.

The effect is so powerful that the hotel staff notices it. I remember on one occasion a few years ago, a hotel manager in Houston watched how, day by day, the atmosphere in his ballroom was becoming more peaceful and pure. At the end of our stay, this man came up to Gurumayi with a special request. He said, "The vibrations in the ballroom are beautiful. But you know, our hotel has some business trouble. The board of directors meets every week, they have terrible arguments, and when they vote, they make bad decisions. I'm thinking, the vibrations in the meeting room must be so bad that they are causing these problems. So, could you have the Siddha Yoga people chant in the meeting room? I'm sure this would change what happens in there." I think it must have, because that is the power of a sublime word.

Reflection on Mantra

One way we intentionally invoke the power of *mātṛkā-śakti*—and address the very issue that is raised in sutra 12—is through mantra. The repetition of mantra, or *mantra-japa,* is one of my very favorite practices. Repeating a mantra doesn't control or counteract *mātṛkā-śakti;* it uses the power of *mātṛkā* for our benefit. Every spiritual tradition in India venerates mantra. Even in the West, mantra, if not widely practiced, is at least widely known—so much so that the word is in our common speech and found in all English dictionaries.

The term "mantra," loosely defined, means a sacred word or formula that is repeated, either aloud or silently, as an incantation. In the *mantra-śāstra,* the scriptures that teach the science of mantra, the word means that and much more. Popular etymology connects the syllable *man* to *manas,* "mind," and also *manana,* "to reflect" or "to contemplate." *Tra* is seen as a reference to *trayate,* which means "to protect" or "to save." In this sense, the person who gives his mind a mantra to reflect upon can find that doing so saves and protects him. Protects and saves him from what? From his own deluding and binding thoughts. Or, more carefully considered, from the deluding and binding power of *moha* that is contained in the letters he thinks and speaks, through the contraction of the divine powers.

You may wonder how mantras differ from other words. The distinction doesn't have much to do with meaning. *Rāma,* which is a mantra, is a name of God; and yet the word "God" isn't a mantra. It's not that "God" isn't a sacred word—clearly, the term "God" has a sacred meaning. It's that there are other levels of power besides meaning to consider with a mantra. The whole of the Vedas is said to be mantra in that these prayers were "heard," were divinely inspired, transmitted directly from the level of *parā-vāc* instead of issuing from any one person's mind. This is one way of determining what constitutes a mantra. But looking at mantra in terms of yoga, which is our interest here, what makes a particular combination of Sanskrit phonemes a mantra is the intention with which it is repeated: a mantra is something that we repeat as a means to achieve the goal of yoga, union with God. This is why a yogic mantra is used and how we judge its efficacy.

The efficacy or potency of a mantra, *mantra-vīrya,* is described in this way in the *Śiva-sūtra:*

> The luminous being of the perfect I-consciousness inherent in the multitude of words, whose essence consists of the highest nondualism, is the secret of mantra.[115]

This power of mantra is secret because it's hidden within the letters themselves. In other words, the letters of a mantra encapsulate and hide the *mantra-vīrya.* In order to take any redemptive or protective benefit from a mantra, we must discover and unlock the power, the great light of Consciousness that is hidden in the letters. This is the most basic level of mantric power, and it pulsates with *pūrṇo'ham-vimarśa,* the awareness of the perfect "I am," which can awaken for one who repeats a mantra. As we learned in sutra 1, *vimarśa* is that aspect of reality that reflects upon itself in order to know itself. Through reflection, *vimarśa* affirms again and again its own existence, full of bliss. This is the reflective nature of mantra, the very nature that protects and saves, and it's something that one must discover for oneself.

It's a matter of experience. Everyone knows the difference between hearing a person make an avowal of love as an empty exercise and hearing someone say, perhaps, the same words but with genuine feeling. There is a special power that's conveyed when a speaker is truly connected to the meaning of the words he utters. *Mantra-vīrya* is like this; it's the mantra's potency brought to life.

This brings us to the second level of a mantra's power. It's recognized in the Śaivite tradition that the simplest way to experience *mantra-vīrya* is to receive a mantra from someone who has himself or herself realized the full potency of that mantra. In other words, the mantra has received an infusion of *śakti* through the grace of an enlightened master. A mantra that has been so strengthened is said to be *caitanya,* which means it is conscious, or alive with divine vibration. Such a mantra is brimming with *mantra-vīrya.* Kshemaraja writes in his commentary on the *Śiva-sūtra:*

> The Guru is one who teaches the essential Truth. So he is the means for leading one to the attainment of *mantra-vīrya.*[116]

The mantra *Oṃ Namaḥ Śivāya* that I received from Baba is a *caitanya-mantra.* It was the same mantra Baba's Guru had given to him, the mantra that Gurumayi continues giving, and to this day, many people, including myself, have revelations of inner Truth through the potency of that very mantra. The syllables of a mantra enlivened by the Guru's own practice transmute mundane perception into a vision infused by the grace of Śiva.

So, a mantra has its own potency; it also has the potency given it by a spiritual master, and there is a third source of power as well—our own understanding of the mantra. We've said that the power of mantra is hidden and that we must discover it through reflection. Now, we may reflect upon the sound of the syllables that compose a mantra or on its meaning or on the symbology of the words and letters, and these practices can be helpful. However, the higher approach to reflecting on a mantra is to contemplate its essential power, its potency, knowing that this power is also our own power and that it is the goal of our reflection. Baba Muktananda says:

> Is mantra an ordinary combination of letters or something more? It has been said that the mantra is the Lord, the highest being. To understand this, you must also understand the secret of mantra realization, which is that the mantra, the one who repeats the mantra, and the deity toward whom the mantra is directed are not separate from one another. They are one. Unless we experience this truth, the full power of mantra will elude us.[117]

In the years of my own practice, I have confirmed the power of mantra as a vehicle of inner growth many times.

In one meditation in Gurudev Siddha Peeth, I sat with my eyes closed, repeating in silence the mantra *Oṃ Namaḥ Śivāya,* which means "I offer reverence to Śiva." Whenever I repeat the mantra, I try to be conscious of what I'm doing. I connect not so much with the words' meaning but with the mantra's vibration—the energy itself, and the way that energy feels inside me. I usually begin by combining the mantra repetition with my breath: one repetition on the inhalation and another on the exhalation. Since I am repeating an enlivened mantra, after only a few repetitions, I can usually feel the letters melting into conscious energy and blending with my *prāṇa,* my inner vital energy, and then spreading throughout my body. Soon, quite spontaneously, I feel as if I were in a warm, tranquil cave. Then I know that the mantra has, once again, opened its secret power.

On this particular day, I found that after a while I was no longer repeating the mantra. I was hearing it, and the sound had descended to the base of my throat. The mantra was repeating itself at a velocity that would have been impossible for me to duplicate with my mind, much less with my tongue. The mantra was actually humming. I noticed that I was very happy.

Then that same energy descended to the vicinity of my physical heart. The mantra was humming even faster then, so much so that the syllables themselves seemed to disappear; I could just barely distinguish them. I felt an even greater joy in the heart than I'd experienced at the level of my throat.

After a while, the energy of the mantra descended once again, this time to the area of my navel. There the mantra lost its form altogether. I could hear neither the syllables nor any hum; the only sound was a very fine vibration. Listening to this pulsating energy, I entered a state without thought or images. I no longer perceived the vibration of the mantra in a particular place—it literally penetrated my entire body. All I was aware of was the act of perception itself. It seemed that I was truly immersed in witnessing Self-consciousness.

When I came out of meditation, I recalled that I'd read an essay on the subject of mantra in Baba's book *Light on the Path.* I went back to the book and found that he spoke about portions of the experience I'd just had. In brief, he said that mantra, propelled by *citiśakti,* resounds in the levels of the four bodies, being experienced in the mouth, throat, heart, and navel, respectively, as it goes through the four levels of speech, beginning with *vaikharī* and moving all the way to *parā-vāc.*[118] By reflecting on this experience I was able to grasp that in the process of dissolving its verbal encasement, the mantra had released its true essence, *pūrṇo'ham vimarśa,* the awareness of the perfect "I am."

When I first read that mantra repetition begins as a group of letters and turns into the delightful vibration of Consciousness, I barely remembered the statement. Once I was given the experience, this miraculous transformation was impressed forever on my understanding.

Therefore, I strongly recommend the practice of *mantra-japa.* The *bhāvanā,* the creative awareness, that I cultivate in repeating the mantra is an understanding that I'm carrying on an intimate conversation with my Lord, with my chosen deity. Sometimes I imagine that I'm lovingly saying the mantra to Gurumayi, or I may feel that the vibration of the mantra is her presence in me. This connects me with the *mantra-vīrya,* which, as I've said, is the method that works for me to begin unlocking this divine potency, the power contained in the letters.

13

Paths of Inward-Facing Contemplation

Sutra 13

तत्परिज्ञाने चित्तमेव अन्तर्मुखीभावेन
चेतनपदाध्यारोहात् चितिः

tat-parijñāne cittam-eva
antarmukhī-bhāvena cetana-padādhyārohāt citiḥ

[However,] when one is fully aware of that
[authorship of the five acts],
the mind itself becomes Consciousness,
by rising to the state of full expansion
through inward-facing contemplation.

tat:	that
parijñāne:	knowing fully
cittam:	individual consciousness, the mind
eva:	itself
antar:	inside, inward
mukhī:	face, turning toward
bhāvena:	through contemplation
cetana:	expanded Consciousness
pada:	level, state, station
adhyārohāt:	because of the ascent
citiḥ:	Consciousness

TO THIS POINT IN THE *Pratyabhijñā-hṛdayam,* we have focused on the initial creative movement of Consciousness, descent. This is the thrust of sutra 5, where we discussed how supreme Consciousness plummets from the state of the pure Self to become the mind, contracting to conform with the objects of perception. The present sutra, which is the counterpart of sutra 5, says that once we've obtained knowledge of the five acts of Śiva—once we have the discernment necessary to observe ourselves creating, sustaining, dissolving, concealing, and giving grace to our world—then our own mind turns toward itself in contemplation and ascends to its natural state. The mind *(citta)* changes the direction of its gaze and become supreme Consciousness *(citi)* once again. As Gurumayi says:

> Like plants that bend toward the sun, the mind is naturally attracted to the Truth. It wants to know God. It wants to experience God's love. It wants to rest in its own nature. The mind wants to relish its own nectar. That is its organic inclination.[119]

This has been my experience, and for this reason I consider that the key phrase in sutra 13 is *antarmukhī-bhāvena,* "by inward-facing contemplation."

I like to observe the direction of my own attention. I like to see how easily my attention is drawn inside and how, when I look inward, my mind becomes calm. Then this serene mind allows me to enter a state that feels like a hospitable cave, a place where I'm in intimate contact with the inner me, the silent resonance of *aham,* "I am." Of course, before very long, my mind is drawn outward again, and I get involved in some aspect of my life, forgetting that inner cave. But the pull to go inside always returns. I believe that something like this happens for anyone with a long-standing meditation practice. If one is truly eager to experience *pratyabhijñā,* to recognize one's wonderful heart, it's important to acknowledge and to follow this natural inclination inward. Turning within is the essential gesture of all spiritual practice. You might ask, *What does the mind look at when it goes inside? Inside what?* The mind recognizes its own nature as *citi,* as pure Consciousness. Baba Muktananda explains:

> If while meditating calmly you can regard the countless vibrations of the mind as the movements of *citi,* if you can keep your attention focused on *citi,* if you could remain full of that, then instead of your mind causing you misery and suffering, it would flood you with bliss and happiness.[120]

We discussed the nature of the mind in sutra 5: the mind is made of *citi,* and everything that moves in the mind is *citi.* It's because of this creative power that the mind has the capacity to take the form of whatever it perceives. When the mind expands to its original state, we could say the mind "perceives" *citi,* but more accurately, at that level nothing but *citi* exists. The mind loses its "mindness." In other words, the mind stops identifying with the thoughts and feelings—formed of the words it produces incessantly—and loses any consequent attachment for these *vikalpas.* Blissful and divinely happy, the mind returns to its true nature, *citi.* This is purification of the mind.

The Four Paths

The interiorization, and associated purification, of our awareness is a process that Śaivism describes in terms of four paths, known as the four *upāyas.** The term *upāya* means "to approach, to arrive," or "that by which one reaches his goal." So, the *upāyas* are the approaches we take to *sādhana,* to spiritual practice. Because the *upāyas* are so significant to us as yogis, I want to delineate them in some detail here.

Like virtually everything else we've discussed in these commentaries, the four *upāyas* are arranged in levels of vibrational subtlety. Which of these paths is appropriate for a particular person depends on how he understands himself and the world—and this depends, largely, on his degree of spiritual evolution. For instance, think of the different ways you could perceive a friend. You might describe her physical attributes: she's tall, brown-eyed, freckled, and so on. Then you could take a more subtle view and describe her character, her qualities of mind: she's generous, excitable, courageous. Finally, you could take your perception even higher and appreciate this person for what she truly is, the light of God. With this, your perception of her changes completely, and you become accepting of her just the way she is, seeing her strengths and weaknesses as an expression of divine Reality.

The *upāyas* are arrayed in much the same way: from the objects of the physical world, to the power of mental perception, to the great energy of the Self—in other words, from the mundane to the sublime. And yet in another respect, the example of the four perspectives is a little misleading: Śaivism does view the *upāyas* as progressive, one proceeding to the next. Each, however, is also a valid path, leading directly to the one Totality. The *upāyas* are descriptions of the diverse ways in

* The *upāyas* first appear in the *Mālinī-vijaya-tantra,* which describes three. Abhinavagupta builds on these three categories and adds a fourth *upāya* in his *Tantrāloka* and *Tantra-sāra.* Briefly, Abhinavagupta presents the *upāyas* as a means to classify the numerous yogic practices described in the Āgamas and the various Śaivite schools.

which yogis embark on *sādhana* after receiving *śaktipāta*—and the particular levels of the *śakti* at which they are working. In time, one may move between the *upāyas,* but that isn't the point, for, as Baba Muktananda writes in *Secret of the Siddhas,* each *upāya* leads directly to liberation:

> There is only one Self in all human beings. However, the *upāyas,* or means of reaching that Self, are different. This is due to the three *guṇas,* or qualities—*sattva* (purity), *rajas* (activity), and *tamas* (inertia)—as well as to the fact that people have different temperaments, mental impurities, karmic impressions from countless lifetimes, and various kinds of understanding. In reality, all the *upāyas* are one. Their techniques vary to suit the needs of different individuals, but they do not depart from their original purpose.[121]

In our discussion of the *upāyas,* we'll identify the understanding of the world that is the *ālambana,* "the support," of one's spiritual journey on each of these paths. One's *ālambana* is where his attention naturally goes, and because it is the focus of one's awareness, it is also the foundation for any progress on his spiritual quest. The *ālambana* is as significant a factor on the spiritual journey as the point of departure is in any other journey. This concept of the *ālambana* helps to explain how spiritual practice actually works. In each of the *upāyas,* as we mentioned earlier, one's understanding of the world is different.

The Path of the Individual

When I began spiritual practice, I was focused almost entirely on the physical and mental aspects of what I was doing. I considered following the discipline of ashram life to be very important, with its regular practice of chants, meditation, mantra repetition, selfless service, and so on. At the same time, I was dealing with my mind, trying to clean up and straighten out my thoughts. All of this describes the approach to *sādhana* that Śaivism calls *āṇavopāya,* the primary and most basic path, the path of the individual. *Āṇavopāya* is the approach for the yogi who thinks of himself in the most circumscribed terms—*āṇava* derives from *aṇu,* or "small." In other words, *āṇavopāya* is for someone who identifies with the *aṇu,* with his awareness of being an individual with a body, whether physical, subtle, or causal. Experiencing the dualism of the subject-object relationship, the *āṇava-yogī* focuses on—takes the support of—the three bodies in his spiritual practice, employing the very perspective that binds him as an instrument to free himself.

So *āṇavopāya* uses as instruments for practice external objects: the physical body, the senses, the psychic instrument, and the movements of *prāṇa* activated by *kuṇḍalinī* along with the subtle experiences they inspire (such as the vibrations of inner sounds and visions of inner light). These are all "external" in that they constitute the field of objects *(prameya)* we perceive as being separate from ourselves, the subject. Subject and object: this is what Śaivism calls dualistic perception.

One outcome of having a dualist viewpoint is a sense of being limited in our capacities. This is the incomplete power of action that is experienced by the individual, which we consider in sutra 4 in the discussion of the *tattvas.* As individuals, most of us identify with the good and the not-so-good things we do, taking personal credit for their authorship. In doing this we remain oblivious to the deeper truth that all actions arise from the divine power of manifestation, from *kriyāśakti.* Through the practices of *āṇavopāya,* we can cleanse this distorted notion of individual doership and return to an awareness of the Lord's *kriyā-śakti* as the true source of all action.

Āṇavopāya practices are vast in number and range, as we have said, from the most elementary forms of physical or mental activity to extremely subtle exercises that view the intellect itself as the object of perception.

The Path of Divine Energy

Śāktopāya, which means "path of divine energy," takes its support from the *buddhi,* the intellect. In contrast to the previous path, which required an external focus and which took the support of the three bodies, *śāktopāya* requires an exclusively internal focus and involves an awareness of concepts, feelings, intuitions, images, memories—the dance that is reflected on the screen of the intellect, independent of any sensory activity. In other words, this is not what you see and hear; *śāktopāya* involves thoughts—thoughts that direct you toward an awareness of Consciousness. In brief, the core of *śāktopāya* involves the cultivation of *śuddha-vikalpa,* those pure thoughts, feelings, memories and mental images intent on bringing about the experience of divine unity. Related to this approach are practices such as scriptural study and spiritual contemplation, creative meditation, which we identified earlier as *bhāvanā,* and using the inner movements of *śakti* to expand one's center of divinity.

For me, the essence of *śāktopāya* is thoughts about how the world is God—or, perhaps, not completely God. You might be confronted with the thought that everything is Consciousness, and find that one side of your understanding says, *Yes, that's true; I know that,* while the other side says, *But I don't actually experience it.* Contemplating the dichotomy between these two responses to a fundamental teaching is an example of a *śāktopāya* practice. This path, therefore, deals with *pramāṇa,* what we have described as our capacity to know and understand. The main thrust of our efforts is in correct knowing and allowing our mind to be purified by the grace of Śiva's *jñāna-śakti,* his power of knowledge, that sweeps away the impure thoughts that keep us deluded with ignorance and limitation, that is, *aśuddha-vikalpa.*

Everything that's projected onto the intellect has a double character. On one hand, our perceptions are external to the Self because they're projections, and on the other hand, they're perceived by the Self, so they're at least partially assimilated by Consciousness. In other words, we know they're separate, and we also know we're one with them. Focusing on that oneness in the midst of any aspect of diversity is *śāktopāya.* Let me give you an example from my own experience.

Early in my meditation practice, I began to have experiences of pleasant vibrations, quite subtle, all over my body. I enjoyed the sensation: it was like an energy coursing through my body, and it felt delicious, like a tickle. I knew it was the effect of the awakened *kuṇḍalinī,* and that's really all I knew. Then I began to read books by Baba Muktananda on meditation and Kashmir Śaivism that described this phenomenon in traditional yogic terms. At that point, for me these were no longer "vibrations" but an experience of Śakti, the great power of Śiva. With this change of conception, my relationship with this experience became more sublime, and the experience itself deepened. I continued to study, and my capacity to understand became even more refined. From seeing the vibration as an experience that "I" have, I began to appreciate that it was not different from me. I'd think, *I am that Śakti.*

So, because of the understanding I was able to bring to this experience, my meditations passed from *āṇava* to the field of *śāktopāya.*

The Path of Spontaneous Delight

Sādhana, generally speaking, is a corrective for whatever area of perception deceives us and leads us to identify with what we perceive. In *āṇavopāya,* spiritual practice is meant to correct the wrong identification with our body, mind, and karma. In *śāktopāya,* we rectify our identification with certain concepts and images we hold. In the third path, *śāmbhavopāya,* which I define as "the path of spontaneous delight," we deal not with thoughts themselves but with the very tendency to think. The main effort on this path is to let go of all traces of *vikalpa,* "mental activity," and to enter again and again into the vast space that is *avikalpa,* "free from thought."

With this movement, we dissolve the binding effect of *mātṛkā-śakti* at its very source, the profound silence of the unuttered divine speech, *parā-vāc,* and gain full control of the entire cluster of creative sounds. Ultimately, our awareness is permanently established in the ecstasy of Śiva where thoughts can have their play without affecting our supreme freedom and splendor.

Śambhu, from whom this path gets its name, is the form of Śiva that exists in joy, the benevolent and loving Lord who bestows happiness. The yogis who are able to embark on the path of Śambhu have accumulated enormous merit from having done *sādhana* in previous lifetimes. They dispense with the basic practices that characterize the previous *upāyas* with relative ease and, in a short time, attain their true nature. Bubbling with spontaneous delight in the hearts of these yogis, Śambhu makes their practices full of astonishing joy.

The distinctive characteristic of *śāmbhavopāya* is that the yogi takes hold of the power of divine will to propel his practice. This is not personal will, which is based on ego-awareness and a forceful and persistent effort to attain the effects of practice. Rather, this is an intention the yogi holds, an intention to allow himself to be impelled by *icchā-śakti,* Śambhu's unimpeded will. *Śāmbhavopāya* takes place in the state of meditation *(turīya)*—the state of awareness of one's essential nature. The yogi in this *upāya* truly knows, *I am the Self.* He feels total union with *icchā-śakti.* It follows then that the *ālambana,* the support, here is the *pramātā,* the inner knower and source of the Lord's will.

The effort exerted in *śāmbhavopāya* is one of intention, a willingness to let ourselves be drawn by the Lord. Giving instructions for *śāmbhavopāya,* Abhinavagupta says:

> Neither accept anything nor reject [anything]; abide in your essential Self, which is an eternal presence.[122]

This kind of "effort," if it can be truly called that, is not something we opt to do. Such a yogi has already attained the Self. Several of the meditations I've described in these commentaries are examples of how, through the grace of a *sadguru,* it is possible to catch a glimpse of this magnificent path of Śambhu. What makes a particular meditation an example of *śāmbhavopāya* is one's opening to the flood of luminosity that penetrates all levels of manifest reality. Like a skilled mariner who allows the wind to catch his sail and propel his momentum, adjusting the trajectory of the vessel with just the slightest movement of the keel, the *śāmbhava-yogī* need make only the gentlest shift of awareness.

The Pathless Path

The fourth and most elevated path was conceived by Abhinavagupta. He called it *anupāya.* In this case the prefix *an* indicates negation, so it means literally "no path." This pathless path is propelled entirely by the spontaneity of *ānanda-śakti.* Śiva's blissful energy acts as bestower of grace. A beautiful expression of *anupāya* is this verse from the *Vijñāna-bhairava:*

> The reality of Bhairava is apparent everywhere—even among common folk. One who knows thus, *There's nothing else than he,* attains the nondual state.[123]

What kind of effort does one put forward to gain this sublime knowledge? Truly none is needed. In *anupāya,* the existence of Śiva is apparent everywhere and in every moment, even for *common folk,* for people who are poorly educated in the scriptures and have no special knowledge of yoga. Rather than a path with its own set of practices, *anupāya* describes the final state, the state of a Siddha. If we consider it as a path of "very little effort," as the commentator has called it in *Tantrāloka,*[124] then it is the concluding movement of ecstasy that grants ultimate Self-realization, for *anupāya* also applies to yogis who are on the edge of liberation and who need only *śaktipāta* to complete their attainment. For these advanced souls, just one teaching, one gesture from the Guru is enough to establish in them the full state of Bhairava. Abhinavagupta describes the attainment in this way:

> When the master utters [his instructions] with words intent on the thoughtless, [the disciple] is liberated there and then, and all that remains [of his former state] is the machine [of the body].[125]

Then the reality of Bhairava is apparent everywhere. Such is the awareness of the *anupāya-yogī,* one who has transcended both Śiva and Śakti to enter the state of Anuttara, "the most excellent one." This is the name Abhinavagupta gives to the Absolute. Anuttara encompasses within its own being the entire scope of transcendence and immanence.

In this way with no methods, it's not necessary to meditate, repeat a mantra, study scripture, or purify oneself, body or mind; it's not necessary to employ any yogic method whatsoever. Nor does *anupāya* have a support, an *ālambana.* Unlike the other three *upāyas, anupāya* is *nirālamba,* "supportless." The only effort required of a yogi on this path is to know that no effort is needed. This is why it's called the pathless path! The *anupāya-yogī* depends exclusively on the descent of divine grace. It's difficult to even imagine the extraordinary merit held by a person as fortunate as this—and the Herculean effort this person must have put forward in past lifetimes to so nearly eradicate the three *malas.* Such a yogi is tremendously pure, his mind shining with its own divine nature.

If you wonder whether you could follow *anupāya,* the question itself indicates that it's an unlikely path for you, as it's open only to those who have already transcended individuality. Most of us are, however, at least familiar with examples of *anupāya-yogīs,* one of them being Baba Muktananda's own Guru, Bhagawan Nityananda. I put him in this category because Baba always spoke of his Guru as one who took birth in the state of Śiva-consciousness. Also, in the scores of interviews conducted with people who knew Bhagawan Nityananda in his childhood, none spoke of seeing him in any state other than total expansion. Anyone who has ever entered a temple dedicated to Bhagawan Nityananda, anyone who has ever prayed to him or invoked his grace, has come into contact with this most sublime of beings, an *anupāya-yogī.*

The Interior Journey

As we can see, the inward-facing contemplation, the *antarmukhībhāvena,* introduced in sutra 13, represents an astounding array of experiences, processes, challenges, insights—all existing for the sake of one fundamental goal: the final attainment. There are innumerable different ways of naming and describing the highest state: *anuttara, turīyātīta* (beyond the fourth state), *kaivalya* (aloneness), the Self, the state of Paramaśiva, becoming established in the heart of Śiva, and so many, many more. What I would like to emphasize here is the purification of the mind, which Baba Muktananda used to say is the true purpose of *sādhana.* For once the mind is pure, we do indeed live in the awareness that all our perceptions and actions are expressions of the five cosmic acts of Śiva. In this sense, it doesn't matter at all into which *upāya* a particular practice falls. One *upāya* is not superior to another. Often the practices of one *upāya* will flow imperceptibly into the practices of another, more subtle *upāya.* It is also quite common that while practicing one *upāya,* you may "try out" the practices of the other two. Or you may be able to sustain a subtle *upāya* for some period of time, and then, later, your mind may be imbedded in circumstantial dramas and the only *sādhana* you can perform is the most basic. What's important in spiritual practice is not which *upāya* it represents; what matters is performing the practice. Just do it.

We study this range of approaches to *sādhana* so that we may perform spiritual practices with greater skill and so that we may understand why we might be suited, by our temperament or our prior effort, to one path as opposed to another. It is a question of recognizing what is. Since all of these paths may begin with *śaktipāta,* they are each imbued with grace. Since all end with the realization of God, each is a high road, so to speak. Embarking on any of the *upāyas* implies a commitment to spiritual life. It's this commitment, this intention to take responsibility for one's personal growth, that is most important for a *sādhaka.* The term *sādhaka* means "one who fulfills, one who practices and completes." This implies a willingness to persevere both in our peak experiences, where we feel light and expansive, and at our nadir, where it may seem sunshine never falls. Of these phases of *sādhana,* Gurumayi says:

> You must learn to accept everything—the plain experiences and the peak experiences, the pits and the highest. When you see everything is for your own growth, for your own expansion, then you won't feel contracted. This is right effort.
>
> Those who perform [physical] exercise are very much aware of this. You stretch your muscles and you let them contract; you stretch your muscles, you expand them, and you let them contract. In this way, you allow them to get stronger and stronger. . . . *Sādhana* is like that.[126]

Gurumayi adds that a person may feel at times that he's being beaten and at other times that he's being anointed with cooling water.

In either instance, the true *sādhaka* says, *This is happening for the best.* For it is—and to acknowledge this and to be open to our experiences of *sādhana,* whatever they may be, is the right kind of effort to make, no matter what path is taken. What contemplation of the *upāyas* can give is a perspective on the inner journey and the way it unfolds. Such understanding, I have found, offers encouragement and the patience to carry on.

14

The Self Is Always Apparent

Sutra 14

चितिवह्निरवरोहपदे छन्नोऽपि मात्रया
मेयेन्धनं प्लुष्यति

citivahnir avarohapade channo'pi
mātrayā meyendhanaṃ pluṣyati

The fire of Consciousness, even though [it is] hidden
when it has descended to the [lower] stage,
partly burns the fuel of that which is knowable.

citi: Consciousness
vahniḥ: fire
avaroha: descent
pade: stage, station
channaḥ: covered, hidden
api: even
mātrayā: partly, in stages
meya: that which is knowable
indhanam: fuel, wood, ritual fire sticks
pluṣyati: burns, consumes

FOR CENTURIES FIREWOOD has been used for cooking, a practice we can see to this day in the Indian countryside. In any household with a kitchen fire, at the end of the day the burning logs are banked with ash so the fire can subside without going out entirely. That way the embers stay hot through the night and can be rekindled the next morning. Even though they're covered with ash, the logs continue burning—continue being partly consumed by glowing cinders. This is the metaphor Kshemaraja chooses for sutra 14, where he tells us that even though the light of the Self has descended to the lower stage of creation and is covered with the dross of our thoughts, feelings, and *saṃskāras,* that light continues to make itself felt because it is fueled, at least in part, by the act of perception—by "that which is knowable."

His observation leads to a highly significant conclusion: No matter how contracted, depressed, and insignificant we may feel—or, on the other hand, how expansive, happy, and self-confident—we can always know our deepest Self. No state of mind can completely obscure the fact that we are conscious beings. This is true for all creatures, from celestials inhabiting the highest heaven to the denizens of the lowest hell, from the most brilliant sages to animals that swim or fly or slither across the face of the Earth. We all possess the fire of *citi,* and this fire always remains capable of devouring the perception of difference and separation, however partial that consumption may be. Sutra 14 describes an experience that happens in every moment of our lives.

Right now, I'm writing this commentary. It might seem as if I were projecting the written words onto the screen of my computer, but since the act of writing this occurs within my own experience, it is also happening on the screen of my mind. The written words that appear in my perception are *meya,* "the knowable," the object. What is most significant here is that the object is not something outside of me; what I perceive is always within my own awareness. In this sense, we could say that I've "burned" what I'm perceiving—I've taken it in, in the same way that a fire consumes its fuel. The written words are, through my act of awareness of them, being consumed by—becoming one with—my consciousness.

Isn't it true that we're having this experience at every moment! Our minds are clouded by ignorance, and yet the very act of perception demonstrates beyond a doubt who is having the experience. We are Śiva, the only one who possibly can take in what he himself has created. This is why we are such great devourers of experience. To Kshemaraja, contemplating the nature of our own perception is the key to recognizing ourselves as one with everything.

The sutra says that when Consciousness operates through an individual, it doesn't consume the object of perception completely. It's only "partly" consumed because there is still some sense of separation between subject and object. By taking the object into his own awareness, the subject has made it at least partly his own—and yet, at the same time, the object continues to exist in a seemingly separate objective reality. And when that objective reality ceases, we can cause that object to reappear by remembering it. The image of the object has been deposited as a *saṃskāra,* as an impression in our memory. When these impressions resurface, we perceive them as thoughts, as *vikalpas,* and they create their own reality for us. For instance, when I remember writing these lines, I might feel they're my creation, and I might believe that this act of creation is a part of my identity. So, as ashes obscure the glow of living embers, these mental impressions conceal the Self. Fortunately, as the sutra tells us, the Self never ceases to shine.

Commenting on sutra 14, Gurumayi says:

> Even when Consciousness is limited, the fire is still there. It partly burns the fuel of known objects. It isn't that Consciousness has totally forgotten itself, with no way back home. No! It is still burning. It's just that there are ashes on the coals. Still, the coals of knowledge are bright, they're fiery. [127]

In this way, the creation confirms that in every moment the Self is always apparent. This is something that one begins to observe in meditation when one experiences the inner energy pulsating with all its purity. We have called this by many names: *śakti* (power), *spanda* (vibrating energy), *citi* (Consciousness), *aham* (I am), as well as the Witness and the Great Void. Whatever you might call it, as you have this most subtle and energetic experience, you know instinctively that it has always been with you. Obscured though it may have been, the inner Truth is always present, always vibrating.

Just as banked coals can be rekindled, through his practices the yogi can make the fire of his inner *śakti* grow to a great blaze, until it consumes all differentiation. This is what is meant by the *Śiva-sūtra: jñānam annam*— "Knowledge is food."[128] *Jñāna*, knowledge, can be understood as the limited knowledge that conceals the Truth, which the yogi devours with pleasure in the light of his own Self. And *jñāna* is also understood to be the highest knowledge, knowledge of the Self, which feeds the yogi with bliss to his full satisfaction. As he gets closer to his goal, the flames of Consciousness grow higher and glow with greater intensity, forming what appears like a *cakra* of fire, a circle of luminosity that envelops the triad of perception—knower, knowledge, and known. The yogi then perceives the entire universe as that luminosity. Mystics of various traditions have spoken of this conflagration as the burning ardor of love, that which immerses one's existence in the very heart of God. They exult in the realization that love is intimately connected with knowledge.

Obviously speaking from his own experience, Abhinavagupta describes burning the objects of perception in the great fire of Consciousness:

> All the things flung with great force into the fire burning within our own Consciousness lose their differentiation while feeding its flames with their own energy. As soon as the nature of things has dissolved in this speedy burning process, the powers of Consciousness—the *śaktis* that rule over the sense organs—delight in the universe now turned to nectar. Now satisfied, they identify Śiva to themselves, Śiva the sky of Consciousness, Śiva the God dwelling in the heart, Śiva the perfect plenitude.[129]

This passage—and, indeed, the sutra itself—is reminiscent of a *yajña,* the ritual of fire that is characteristic of Indian religious life. In fact, Kshemaraja's "banked coals" in his commentary to sutra 14 are a reference to a sacred fire ceremony. For him, the application of this sutra is, like a fire ritual, an active practice. In a *yajña,* Brahmins offer to the fire various foods, seeds, flowers, fragrant woods, even at times gemstones that have been ground to a fine powder.

When I sit to meditate, I often call this image to mind, visualizing my body as a fire pit and my Consciousness as a munificent fire, blazing with great freedom. The fire that I create on the screen of my mind soon acquires a life of its own, surging vibrant as a knowing energy, the fire of knowledge. As I engage my attention with this living energy, it begins to release an astounding *rasa:* the sensation of pure love. It is like being pervaded by a warm energy, by an embrace. No wonder mystics and yogis find inner knowledge so appealing! As I continue to meditate, various objects—that is, thoughts, feelings, and images—float into my mind, and I purposefully offer them to the fire, just as a priest would.

You can try this yourself. One way is through the classic Śaiva technique known as *bhāvanā,* which uses the imagination. *Bhāvanā* means, literally, "to bring into existence," and that is what you do in this practice: create something within your mind. Just imagine that you are the officiating priest of a *yajña.* Picture yourself sitting before a sacred fire, offering to the flames the *vikalpas,* the thoughts, that sprout in your mind. These can be good or bad, beautiful or ugly; it makes no difference. As we know, all forms and thoughts are nothing but Consciousness. The fire is the light of your own Self. Consider this fire to be the supreme deity of your ritual. Worship the fire with offerings of devotion, invoke it with ardor, repeating, "Śiva, the sky of Consciousness; Śiva, the God dwelling in the heart; Śiva, the perfect plenitude—you are my very own Self!"

This exercise is a variant of *ahaṃ-bhāva,* the sweet and natural feeling of "I am" that affirms who we are and naturally dissolves the perceptions that stand in the way of our immersion in the love of the great heart. This is a valuable exercise for meditation, and it can be useful also on other occasions, whenever you have the freedom to employ your imagination. Gurumayi once said of the process:

> Whatever comes up, offer it to the fire of love, the fire of yoga. This is how we should establish our life in our own being, so that no matter what flies at us, no matter what comes up from within—from the *saṃskāras,* the impressions that are imbedded in the *suṣumṇā nāḍī*—it all gets burnt in the fire of yoga.[130]

I've noticed that this practice is tremendously emancipating; it makes my meditation continually more free and trains my mind to let go of unnecessary thoughts on matters that it—the mind—deems important or entertaining or even repellent. As my inner fire blazes, this great light consumes all manifoldness, all binding thoughts, in the same way the flames of the *yajña* reduce all the offerings to one mass of ashes. Most significantly, this practice can restore my deep connection with the flames of pure love.

Truly, it doesn't matter whether we see something as positive or negative; we can train ourselves to offer everything unneeded to the effervescent inner light, which is always present, always caressing us with its joy. And just as the Lord bestows grace, with this inner sacrifice we also bestow grace on ourselves.

15

Within Us, the Entire Universe

Sutra 15

बललाभे विश्वमात्मसात्करोति

balalābhe viśvam ātmasāt karoti

On attaining strength,
one makes the universe one's own.

bala:	strength, force
lābhe:	on attaining, on acquiring
viśvam:	the universe
ātmasāt:	one's own
karoti:	one makes

In the previous sutra, Kshemaraja described a banked fire, dimly glowing, unperceived. Now, in sutra 15, he discusses what happens with its natural expansion: acquiring divine strength, *balalābhe,* the yogi brings about the assimilation of the entire universe—he becomes one with it!—*viśvam ātmasāt karoti.* The very nature of yoga is inner expansion. As we go within, our own consciousness begins to extend beyond the body and the mind and to take into itself all that it encounters. When this assimilation is complete, each of the *tattvas*—from earth to *sadāśiva*—appears exactly the same as the Self. Then the yogi's senses, having been purified by the fire of Citi, experience that his existence is full of light and love. Thus by his own power, he manifests unity and causes the disappearance of that which once had made him believe there was difference.

There is another way of examining this process. As we explored in sutras 6 and 9, once the innate impurities of the yogi are dissolved, he attains knowledge of his own Self, of his true and unchanging nature. This knowledge, known as *ātma-vyāpti,* is vast but not all-encompassing. In sutra 15, Kshemaraja implies that the continuation of the practice that results in *ātma-vyāpti* ultimately leads to an even greater attainment—*śiva-vyāpti,* the state in which the whole universe is seen as the light of Bhairava, another name for Śiva. This is true assimilation. The term *ātmasāt* means "to make one's own, to absorb into the system, to take into the mind and thoroughly comprehend"—and, in this instance, "to hold the awareness that all one perceives is, in totality, one's own being."

As esoteric as this state may sound, it is possible to receive a glimpse of *śiva-vyāpti* through the grace of an enlightened master. I've spoken with many, many Siddha Yoga practitioners who have experienced this sublime state. It can be something as simple as coming out of meditation and finding that some veil has been lifted: in that moment you see your world—your own friends and relatives, your own home, your work—bathed in the light of God. These magnificent flashes into a dimension beyond the senses are the result of *śaktipāta-dīkṣā,* divine initiation from the Guru.

I remember hearing about a woman who had a profound experience of *śiva-vyāpti* during a weekend workshop known as a Meditation Intensive, which was being held in a Siddha Yoga meditation center in Canada. As this woman sat in the first meditation session, her mind became quiet and she could feel her awareness expanding beyond the limits of her body. With this expansion came a sense of ownership: she felt that she encompassed the entire hall as well as every one of the several score of people who were sitting in meditation there at that time. There was no feeling of "I" and "other"; she experienced one indistinguishable mass of conscious bliss. Her awareness expanded further: she felt that she was the entire building in which the Intensive was being held; she encompassed the streets outside and the cars and pedestrians on those streets; she took in ever larger portions of the city, then all of Canada, and then the entire North American continent. When this woman's awareness had expanded to the point where she experienced that the Earth in its entirety was contained within her own Self, she noticed that the planet seemed quite small to her and that it was nothing for her to place it into her own heart.

Her consciousness continued expanding through the galaxies toward an astonishingly infinite universe. Everything seemed minute, and finally, she held the whole of the universe in her heart. At that point a question crossed her mind: *If all the universe exists within my heart, who am I?* The answer came immediately, with the same eloquence that one reads in the Āgamas: *I am Śiva, the Lord, the true Self. I am infinite, eternal, and unlimited. I am pure Consciousness. Only I exist. The universe is a play of light and shadow within my Self. I am the only Truth.*[131]

Sometimes in courses and workshops, I lead participants through the levels of identification this woman experienced, expanding the awareness further and further, step by step, until it encompasses everything. This is a much more specific version of the contemplation we do at the beginning of this book, where we ask ourselves, *Is my awareness in this space or is the space in my awareness?* Either side of this question is a richly rewarding *bhāvanā* to take into one's meditation. In this sutra, Kshemaraja tells us that by allowing the universal view of our true nature to emerge, our identification with the body will be subsumed and our false sense of limitation eradicated.

The understanding is this: The resonance of the I-consciousness (the awareness "I am") emanates from the heart in an awesome splendor, encompassing all aspects of manifestation, including every one of our individual acts. When we align our attention with these spontaneous movements of Citiśakti, she leads us into *cidānanda,* the conscious bliss that assimilates creation, the love that brings everything in existence into the heart. This feat is possible through our own conviction, the profound and unshakable conviction that develops by dint of practice and through the grace of an illumined master. In the words of Abhinavagupta:

> *I make the universe manifest within myself in the Sky of Consciousness. I, who am the universe, am its creator!*—this awareness is the way in which one becomes Bhairava. *All of manifest creation is reflected within me, I cause it to persist*—this awareness is the way in which one becomes the universe. *The universe dissolves within me. I who am the flame of the [one] great and eternal fire of Consciousness*—seeing thus one achieves peace.[132]

As it increases strength and power, our conviction awakens us to our own beauty.

Sutra 15 marks a threshold in the text. From this point on, Kshemaraja accelerates the pace, taking us swiftly into the states that arise as the full fruition of *sādhana.* And yet he does not stop here. Enlightenment, he makes clear, is not just an end but a new beginning. The designation encompasses states that are various and distinct, and in his discussions of these states, Kshemaraja is no less explicit in his descriptions, no less scrupulous in his definitions than he was earlier in the text. The sage has as much to say about the highest states of Consciousness as most of the rest of us have to say about contraction.

At this point, too, you may notice that I begin to quote the writings of both my Siddha Gurus with even greater frequency. We are coming into subjects for which I must turn to my authorities. And yet, these highest states are also ones that most disciples experience here and there, during all the varying phases of spiritual practice. Such is the grace of these Gurus.

16

The Bliss of a Liberated Yogi

Sutra 16

चिदानन्दलाभे देहादिषु चेत्यमानेष्वपि चिदैकात्म्य
प्रतिपत्तिदार्ढ्यं जीवन्मुक्तिः

cidānanda-lābhe dehādiṣu cetyamāneṣv api
cidaikātmya-pratipatti-dārḍhyaṃ jīvanmuktiḥ

The state of liberation while living
is the unwavering experience of oneness with Consciousness,
even while one perceives the body and so on,
[a state that ensues] on the attainment of the
bliss of Consciousness.

cit:	Consciousness
ānanda:	bliss
lābhe:	on the attainment or acquisition
deha:	the body
ādiṣu:	and so on
cetyamāneṣu:	when being perceived
api:	even
cit:	Consciousness
aikātmya:	oneness, identity with
pratipatti:	experience, attainment
dārḍhyam:	firmness, steadiness
jīvanmuktiḥ:	liberation while living [in a body]

"THIS IS WHY WE LIVE," Baba Muktananda says, "to experience supreme bliss, the highest enthusiasm, the highest ecstasy. A human life is mysterious and significant; it is sublime and ideal. In this human body, in this human life, we can see the Creator within, we can meet him and talk to him, and we can also become him."[133] In sutra 16, Kshemaraja speaks of this ultimate spiritual freedom, the astounding state of a liberated yogi, a Siddha. Both Baba and Kshemaraja indicated that the most prominent characteristic of the highest attainment is the unalterable experience of *cidānanda,* the bliss of Consciousness.

This bliss of Consciousness is not to be confused with the passing joy and satisfaction we can derive from moments of pleasure or peace in our lives. It's not "blissfulness" that we're speaking of here, but *cidānanda,* a state that is beyond what is pleasurable, enjoyable, delightful, wonderful, or any other qualifying term we might think of. It's the state in which the yogi rests permanently in what is.

Sutra 16 says that when the bliss of supreme Consciousness is attained *(cidānanda-lābhe),* even while one perceives *(cetyamāneṣv api)* one's body and so on *(dehādiṣu),* one is identified with Consciousness *(cidaikātmya)* as a firm experience *(pratipatti-dārḍhyam)*—which is the state of liberation while alive *(jīvanmuktiḥ).* In speaking of "the body and so on," Kshemaraja is referring to the three bodies of the human being—physical, subtle, and causal—with their respective states of consciousness and the experiences that one undergoes in each. One of the *Śiva-sūtra* says: *jāgrat-svapna-suṣupta-bhede turyā-bhoga-sambhavaḥ,* "Even during the three states of consciousness in waking, dreaming, and deep sleep, the rapturous experience of I-consciousness of the fourth state *(turīya)* abides."[134] The state of *turīya,* which is the state of connection to one's deepest identity, flows uninterruptedly, like a deep oceanic current, illuminating the other three states of individual consciousness. Regardless of what a liberated yogi does—whether he is thinking or experiencing emotions or sleeping—he never at any time loses sight of the ecstatic state of *turīya.* For him, even in the midst of his concerns or hesitations, his highs or lows, the experience of bliss has established itself, unalterably, in his mind. Abhinavagupta describes this unique condition:

> It is Śiva himself, of unimpeded will and transparent consciousness, who is ever sparkling in my heart. It is his highest Śakti herself who is ever playing at the edge of my senses. The entire world glows, at one with the bliss of I-consciousness. Indeed, I know not what the word *saṃsāra* refers to.[135]

Liberation While Living

The state of being established in the bliss of Consciousness is known by the term *jīvanmukti. Jīvan* means "living," and *mukti* is "liberation." *Jīvanmukti* thus refers to the state of liberation while still living in one's physical body. Śiva's grace reveals to the liberated being the nectar that permeates all things: *ekarasa,* literally "the flavor of oneness" or "the one flavor" that is the ambrosial and unique taste of love.[136] Having understood the five acts of Śiva as his own, the yogi lives in the awareness of the delight inherent in all his perceptions and states of mind. This nectarean *ekarasa* makes the permanent experience of union with the manifestations of Śiva palpable. According to the *Spanda-kārikā:*

> He who knows that the universe is identical with the Self and regards the whole world as a play of the Divine, being ever united with universal Consciousness, is without doubt liberated even while alive.[137]

One of my very favorite descriptions of liberation is from Gurumayi, who describes this sublime state as true freedom from attachment:

> As you free yourself from everything and everyone, every place and every time, every moment and every year, every planet and every star, you feel this incredible rush of ecstasy. In fact, you enter into another realm, an expanded realm, a realm of light, a realm of understanding. It is inside. Even though we feel it is an out-of-the-body experience, it is within this body. When you have this experience, you become aware of how this body is not a barrier, not an obstacle. In this body, there is honey. In this body, there are gold coins. In this body, there is a ruby. Kabir describes his Beloved as a ruby, so brilliant, so beautiful. This ruby represents the Self within. This is why it is said, the wealth is inside. By detaching ourselves from everything and everyone, we get in touch with our own Self, and the Self within everybody and everything. This is called love. It is for this that you meditate. It is for this you live—to taste this beautiful life inside.[138]

To phrase this in terms that are by now familiar to us, the onset of the state of *jīvanmukti* consumes the impressions of diversity that make the yogi feel limited and disconnected from his essence. The three innate impurities of the human being—*kārma-mala, māyīya-mala,* and *āṇava-mala*—disappear, and the yogi feels that his actions are inspired by the *śakti,* perceives the entire universe to be suffused with the light of the Self, and lives in the awareness of his own identity with the vastness of God. In this state, the yogi's thoughts and actions create no worldly *saṃskāras,* only impressions that affirm his sense of oneness with Paramaśiva. These pure thoughts *(śuddha-vikalpas)* settle indelibly in the mind as indications of the conviction, *All this is Śiva.* As the previous sutra stated, such a one assimilates the universe into himself, seeing it as the manifestation of his Self. Abhinavagupta describes his state in this way:

> The Knower of the Self experiences no estrangement in any way, for the All is his very form, nor does he grieve because ultimately there is no death nor is there annihilation. What is misfortune and for whom when the collection of jewels that is Ultimate Truth has become a full treasury of the heart's deepest secret? When the reality of the Great Lord is truly "I"?[139]

I particularly love the image of jewels that is associated with the highest attainment. Many people have visions of jewels in their meditation, and it's clear that this is not a random sort of experience. I see the gems as symbols in a special language that Consciousness adopts to convey the nature of the inner world. The ruby, for instance, that Gurumayi quotes Kabir speaking of, reminds us in its warm red luster of the heart. The milky sheen of the pearl is like moonlight, which is itself a symbol of the light of knowledge. Then there is the Blue Pearl *(nīlabindu)* that Baba Muktananda spoke of so often, which to my eye always has looked like a sparkling diamond—a perfect symbol for the brilliance and incorruptibility of true inner attainment.

An Illumined Perception

Let's take a closer look at the mental processes of a *jīvanmukta,* one who is liberated while in the body. Maheshvarananda, who lived in Kashmir in the late thirteenth or early fourteenth century and was one of the eminent masters of Śaivism, had this to say about the functions of the threefold psychic instrument—*buddhi, ahaṃkāra,* and *manas*—after Self-realization:

> The three internal organs [of the psychic instrument] endlessly undulate in the waves of the ocean of the heart. Sometimes, they draw to themselves the object; at other times, they attract the subject to the object.[140]

Maheshvarananda explains that in the act of perception, the Great Light *(mahāprakāśa)* pours its luminosity through the psychic instruments. These organs of the mind are floating in the undulating ocean of Consciousness, impressing the vibrations of *aham,* the pure "I am," onto the objects of perception, and making them shine with vitality. Then the Great Light carries the perception of external objects toward itself in order to impress in the Self the vibrations of the *idam,* the "this" of objectivity, as it condenses its light into a discrete experience. The ceaseless movement of our awareness, from subject to object and back again, is like the eternal movement of waves that advance on the shore and then recede back into the ocean, their source.

From the perspective of the *jīvanmukta,* Maheshvarananda continues:

> There is no obstacle to the perception of the external domain, which is illumined by the lamps of the organs of consciousness, always attached to the highest point of their specific spheres.[141]

Instead of producing a sense of separation, the purified senses of an enlightened yogi perceive the Great Light shining within all created objects. Each perception vibrates with the ecstasy of the Self, enjoying the world of its own creation. What is experienced in the mind and what is perceived outside are no longer two different realities. *Citta,* the mind, has become *citi,* Consciousness.

In his description of a *jīvanmukta's* act of perception, Maheshvarananda implies that realization preserves intact a person's ordinary mental apparatus, which is an integral component of the human body. Purified of the tendency to create differences, the mind of the *jīvanmukta* enables that person to enjoy the divine beauty that permeates all forms and names in the universe. The world-embracing state of one whose mind has fully grasped its divinity is described in the following passage from Utpaladeva:

> A person who feels like this—*[So'ham], "I Am He," All this is my own exuberant luxury, my own splendor*—goes on feeling himself as none other than the Almighty God, even while a multitude of thoughts are still going on [in his mind].[142]

I heard Baba Muktananda quote this passage many times when he was explaining that union with Consciousness neither eliminates our natural feelings and thoughts nor rejects the world that we experience with our senses. Once when he was asked, "Does Self-realization mean that you have no ego at all, or that you are not affected by whatever ego you do have?" Baba replied:

> Even when you realize the Self, the ego doesn't leave you; it stays. But the quality of the ego changes. Before you realize the Self, you identify with whatever you have and whatever you are. You think, *I am a woman, I have children, I have a husband, I am a writer.* Once you realize the Self, you experience, *I am the Truth, I am the Self, I am happiness, I have merged into God.* So the quality of ego changes once you have realized the Self.[143]

An Illumined Life

The personality of a *jīvanmukta* mirrors his or her particular destiny. Baba Muktananda loved to describe the immense freedom and personal idiosyncrasies of these liberated souls. In his book *Secrets of the Siddhas,* Baba writes:

> Siddhas are supremely independent. They are totally immersed in God at all times. Their state and behavior are strange. Some look outwardly foolish although they are inwardly intelligent. Others are scholarly and give birth to the literature of Truth. Some appear to be crazy. This is the way of the Siddhas.
>
> Even though some live like kings, they are flawless in renunciation, discrimination, and detachment. They are free of expectations. Although they live like kings, their Siddhahood is perfect. Their position is due to fortune and destiny. It is given by God.[144]

In Maharashtra, the region of India where Bhagawan Nityananda settled in his later years and where Gurudev Siddha Peeth, the mother ashram of Siddha Yoga practice, is located, there is a long-standing tradition of householder saints. For some four hundred years, beginning in the thirteenth century, there were scores of people who worked as barbers and gardeners, as housewives and potters, servants and scholars—virtually the entire gamut of occupations of that day—at the same time they were fully liberated knowers of God. The writings of both Baba and Gurumayi are peppered with anecdotes and songs from these *jīvanmuktas* who led "ordinary" lives while acting wholly for the benefit and enlightenment of others.

When Baba claims that some great souls look outwardly foolish or appear to be crazy, he is referring to another Indian spiritual tradition, that of the *avadhūta,* a term whose root means "shaking off." An *avadhūta* is one who has shaken off his limitations and ignorance as well as the shackles of conventional mores. Baba's own Guru was a renowned *avadhūta* who wore only a loincloth—and that only through the ministrations of his devotees. A number of the other Siddhas who guided Baba in his *sādhana* were even more eccentric in their behavior: Zipruanna was a naked sage who often sat on a heap of garbage, and Harigiri Baba wore multiple coats, one upon the other, and walked along the riverbank collecting pebbles, which he would distribute as *prasad,* holy gifts. And yet Baba often would say that Zipruanna's body smelled of roses and that Harigiri's pebbles brought people fortunes or healed them, body and soul. It's my observation that passing judgment on the behavior or appearance of a *jīvanmukta*—or anyone else, for that matter—is a risky exercise, for how are we to know the aims of the *svātantrya-śakti,* the power of freedom, that operates through that being! In an essay on Siddhas in the book *Meditation Revolution: A History and Theology of the Siddha Yoga Lineage,* the scholar Paul E. Muller-Ortega writes:

> Abiding as the living and absolute consciousness, the siddha is the *jīvanmukta,* the "one who is liberated while still alive." The siddha has successfully carried out the ascent across the many "stages of yoga" *(yogabhūmikās)* to reach total enlightenment. The siddha has reached what is called *sahajasamādhi,* the "spontaneous, natural absorption" of total freedom. Here, the intrinsic "freedom" *(svātantrya)* of consciousness—which is the principal quality of the *śakti,* "divine power," according to Śaivism—has reached its supreme expression within human life.
>
> Thus, the so-called "eccentricity" of the siddha can be understood quite differently. It is not merely the adoption of a particular mode of external behavior that makes one a siddha.

> The siddha abides and acts from a stance that is expressive of the viewpoint of the *jñāni*, the "one of knowledge," whose vision is profoundly nondual. In truth, it is the ordinary person who might be seen as truly "eccentric," that is to say, absent from the center of things.[145]

For a total of thirty years now, I've been serving the work of two Siddha Gurus, first Baba Muktananda and at present Gurumayi Chidvilasananda. In this time, I've heard their teachings, watched their interactions with thousands of people, and deeply contemplated their ways. What most impresses me is that a Siddha's behavior is governed only by love—love for God, love for the Self, love for everything that God has created. This might sound like ersatz logic, but I would say that if a *jīvanmukta* follows societal norms, it's because selfless compassion has inspired him or her to teach us respect for the behavioral and ethical principles that can serve as instruments for our inner growth. And I would also say that if a Siddha breaks those concepts and patterns, it's because compassion has inspired him or her to help us transcend the conditionings that thwart our freedom.

There is another sense in which the behavior of a saint cannot be predicted: The discipline that a spiritual seeker must follow to reach his goal is not necessary for one who has achieved the goal of all discipline. Abhinavagupta gives eloquent expression to the Siddha's relation to spiritual practice:

> Dissolved by the fire of Bhairava, where there is neither pain, nor pleasure, nor doubt, nothing is left in all these beings but the vision of the Supreme undifferentiated Consciousness in which they have penetrated. For them, there is no mantra, no meditation, no adoration, no imagination, none of those wanderings

> that go from the stage of student to the one of master. Armed with sword, they have cut off the net of all restrictions and, from this initiation to the end of their lives, the only rules they have to observe are the ones whose aim is to please others.[146]

The saints *please others* by teaching the path that leads to supreme bliss. Thus, while a *jīvanmukta* may choose to remain in bliss, without engaging in practice of any sort, many liberated beings lead others by continuing to meditate, repeat mantras, sing God's name, perform rituals of worship, or give to the needy. Baba Muktananda used to say that the saints perform these laudatory actions both because doing so gives them immense pleasure and because it serves as an example for those who are still walking the path.

Ultimately, whatever a saint does is an expression of free will. This is the meaning of the aphorism from the *Śiva-sūtra: siddhaḥ svatantra-bhāvaḥ:* "Freedom is achieved," which we can also read as "A Siddha is completely free," or "A Siddha lives in total freedom."[147]

The Path of Liberation

As seekers, of course, it is not our task to fathom all the mysteries of the *jīvanmukta.* Rather, we must act on the opportunities that present themselves for our own growth. Some of the questions that have always come up for me are, *How can I know the state of an enlightened being? What does it feel like to be "liberated"?* That much, I feel, we must strive to find out for ourselves, each one of us.

I've discovered that the best way to understand how an enlightened master experiences life is through the insights of my meditation. There is one experience that stands out in my mind. On one particular morning several years ago, as I was meditating, I saw an image of Gurumayi in my mind. After a few seconds of enjoying this vision, I felt myself become one with it. I mean that literally. Rather than an "I" who was "seeing" Gurumayi, there was only Gurumayi. I felt deeply peaceful. I wanted for nothing.

Then, before my inner eye, there appeared scenes and people, and suddenly I found myself looking at the world through Gurumayi's eyes. I saw people, leafy trees, buildings of some sort—everything was threaded through with an intricate web of delicate, conscious vibrations. These vibrations seemed to be the basic material, the fabric from which everything was fashioned, and since I could see those vibrations as well as the forms they took, it appeared that the world was there and, at the same time, not there. Each form appeared to be made of frosted glass, a faint luminosity that was a reflection of my own inner light. My heart was filled with love, and through that love, I felt a connection with the whole of creation. It seemed as if everything was a part of me.

In fact, I seemed to "pervade"—with my awareness, with my own inner light—everything that I perceived. In this experience, a person's image came up on my mental screen, and without any need for words, I found that I could "read" this man. Suddenly, everything about his body—his footfalls, posture, gestures, facial expressions—was an obvious, easily understood statement about him. I sensed his thoughts, his feelings, and, it seemed, the innermost crevices of his soul. It was as if a language without words impressed messages upon my body of light, communicating to me everything that I could possibly know about this person. There were other people as well, who came up before me, and I found myself "reading" them just as easily as I had the first man.

To me, the most surprising discovery was that this knowledge didn't affect my inner state: I was able to both witness and experience what I was perceiving. Furthermore, I passed no critical judgment whatsoever on these people I was observing so deeply. My only feeling for them was love. It seemed to me that I was given this knowledge for the sole purpose of helping each person I encountered. In other words, the only possible expression of this expanded knowledge was through acts of compassion.

When the experience came to an end and I began to emerge from the state of meditation, an inner voice told me: *This is only a fraction of your Guru's state. There is more, much more, that you haven't seen yet.* Even now, I am awed by the magnitude of what I experienced that day—and of what it tells me of the greatness of the state of liberation. Also, it's clear to me from this experience that the vision of love and delight in a liberated being is wholly in the service of humanity. In the words of Gurumayi:

> The mind of a great being is free from worldly desires. He wants nothing. Therefore, he no longer lives for himself alone. His one desire is that others might also be free, that others might find their way out of suffering and into joy. It is a rapturous experience to celebrate the life of a great being when you recognize one and are blessed by their teachings. For such beings are rare, like a plant in the desert that blooms only once every hundred years.[148]

17

Expanding the Center: Kuṇḍalinī Unfolds

Sutra 17

मध्यविकासाच्चिदानन्दलाभः

madhya-vikāsāc cidānanda-lābhaḥ

The bliss of Consciousness
is attained through expansion of the center.

madhya:	center, middle
vikāsāt:	through expansion, development
cit:	Consciousness
ānanda:	bliss
lābhaḥ:	attainment, acquisition

IN INDIA IT IS UNDERSTOOD that yogis may spend years engaged in meditation, mantra repetition, and scriptural study; they may memorize a collection of sutras or an entire Upaniṣad; they may master the eighty-four classic *āsanas* of *haṭha-yoga;* and, with all of this, still they can fail to attain an experience of inner ecstasy. Sutra 17 explains why. The sutra says that "the bliss of Consciousness is attained, *cidānanda-lābhaḥ* through expansion of the center, *madhya-vikāsa.*"

What is this magical *madhya,* this center, that must be developed? Kshemaraja initially defines it as *saṃvit,* which is another name for universal Consciousness.* Clearly, *saṃvit* is the true center, the fundamental reality of all things. And this sutra is an opportunity to explore that which is central to our experiencing *saṃvit;* that which allows us to center ourselves in bliss; and that which, once awakened, travels primarily along the central channel of an intricate arterial system within the subtle body. In other words, what is for me most central in sutra 17 is the miraculous and fascinating unfoldment of *kuṇḍalinī-śakti.*

The term *kuṇḍalinī* will by now be familiar to the reader. I will not attempt to offer an exhaustive introduction to the subject here, as there are many brilliant discussions currently in print.** It would be interesting, however, in the context of our understanding of the *Pratyabhijñā-hṛdayam,* to consider how *kuṇḍalinī* comes into being and where this *śakti* fits into the universal schema.

---

* In his commentary on sutra 17, Kshemaraja writes, "The exalted *saṃvit* [universal Consciousness] is itself the center, as it is present as the innermost [reality] of all." (Jaideva Singh, trans. *The Doctrine of Recognition* (1990), p. 80).

** My recommendations include Swami Muktananda's *Play of Consciousness* and *Kundalini: The Secret of Life,* and Swami Kripananda's *The Sacred Power: A Seeker's Guide to Kundalini,* all published by SYDA Foundation.

The Domain of Kuṇḍalinī

As we've heard before, during the act of creation, by virtue of its irrepressible will, universal Consciousness *(saṃvit)* chooses to hide its essential nature, which is perfect freedom. Through the power of *māyā*, *saṃvit* assumes the role of *prāṇa-śakti*, the energy that gives form and life to all created things. This *prāṇa-śakti* descends through successive levels, giving shape to the various principles that compose the three bodies of the human being. When it reaches the subtle body, *prāṇa-śakti* creates a complex network of subtle conduits, called *nāḍīs*, through which the *prāṇa* then flows, sustaining the activities of both the subtle and physical bodies.

The *nāḍīs*, which are vital to an understanding of *kuṇḍalinī*, are extremely numerous. In his commentary on sutra 17, Kshemaraja refers to "the thousand *nāḍīs*."[149] Baba Muktananda was fond of quoting from the *Praśna Upaniṣad*, which states that there are 720 million *nāḍīs* in the subtle body of every human being,[150] but this number is not undisputed. Where all texts agree is that one *nāḍī* is of supreme importance. As Baba writes:

> Among all these *nāḍīs*, 72 thousand are important. Of these, one hundred are principal. And of these, three are particularly significant. Of these three, the most important is the *suṣumṇā*, which extends from the base of the spine to the crown of the head.[151]

Kshemaraja likens the system of *nāḍīs* to the intricate filaments in the palasha leaf, whose veins all connect to a single main spine.[152] This is exactly how the *suṣumṇā* is placed in a human being, extending through the physical spine along its full length and connecting to all the other *nāḍīs* throughout the entire system. Gurumayi refers to the *suṣumṇā* most often as a column of light. Also known as the *madhya-nāḍī,* or the central channel, the *suṣumṇā* is the main conduit for *prāṇa-śakti* in the subtle body.

Prāṇa-śaktī, the power that supports spiritual transformation, remains latent in a human being until it has been activated or awakened. This dormant force, which lies at the lower extremity of the central channel, is what we call *kuṇḍalinī.* The name *kuṇḍalinī,* "coiled one," comes from the *śakti's* placement at the base of the *suṣumṇā-nāḍī,* where it is coiled, like a serpent at rest. Innumerable yogic texts present techniques with which a seeker can awaken the *kuṇḍalinī-śakti,* and such an awakening is, obviously, possible. According to the Siddha Yoga Gurus, however, a self-induced awakening is rare and not especially safe. As we discussed at some length in sutra 10, the easiest means of awakening the *kuṇḍalinī* is through *śaktipāta-dīkṣā,* the divine initiation bestowed by a Self-realized master.

I think of *kuṇḍalinī* awakening as the most significant event in a yogi's life, for it is from this initial movement of the *śakti* that all transformation naturally flows. As Gurumayi has said:

> When you receive *śaktipāta,* divine initiation from the Guru, your *kuṇḍalinī* energy is awakened within. Your eyes are opened to an inner world that you never knew existed. You see familiar things in a new way. You see new sights with the innocence and wonder of a child. Sometimes this can be very subtle. Still the miraculous begins to envelop your existence; and you cannot tell if all this beauty is coming from the inside out, or the outside in.[153]

This shift in perception comes about through yogic purification on all levels, both physical and subtle. As the vital energy moves through the *nāḍīs* in the subtle body, it removes inner blocks in the same way that light, by its very presence, "removes" darkness.

In this system, there are centers of heightened energetic activity. These occur at intersections where groups of *nāḍīs* converge. The intersections are called *cakras,* "wheels," because those who have had visionary experience of the inner workings of *kuṇḍalinī* say that the *cakras* have the appearance of whirling wheels of light, with the *nāḍīs* issuing from them like so many vibrant spokes. According to a number of yogic texts, each *cakra* is the focal point of a cluster of energies that align the human body with cosmic forces. Countless *cakras* exist in the subtle body, but six are of particular importance, and these are arrayed along the central conduit, each corresponding to a particular area of the physical body: the *mūlādhāra* at the base of the spine (where *kuṇḍalinī* rests in its dormant state), *svādhiṣṭhāna* at the root of the reproductive organ, *maṇipūra* at the navel, *anāhata* in the heart, *viśuddha* in the throat, and *ājñā* in the space between the eyebrows.*

The six primary *cakras* are the seat of the basic tendencies of a person's character. These tendencies are associated with, though not identical to, *saṃskāras,* the impressions of specific past actions and thoughts, which are stored primarily within the *suṣumṇā-nāḍī.* With respect to *saṃskāras* and the qualities imbedded in the *cakras,* our human system functions a little like a living computer, its programs installed at the

* This classification of the six *cakras* is the one followed by Swami Muktananda and corresponds to Śaivite texts such as the *Ṣaṭ-cakra-nirūpana,* the *Yoga Upaniṣads,* some *Purāṇas,* and some texts of *haṭha-yoga.* In the *Tantrāloka* (chapters 4 and 5) Abhinavagupta uses a variant classification, enumerating five main *cakras: mūlādhāra* or *mūlābhūmi* (the base of the spine), *nābhi* (the navel), *hṛdaya* or *hṛt* (the heart), *kaṇṭha* (the throat), and *bhrūmadhya* (the space between the eyebrows). All these traditions recognize the *sahasrāra* as an independent space located at the crown of the head, from which the *brahmarandhra,* the "orifice of Brahman," arises near the fontanelle.

center of its major operational system. At the three lower *cakras,* the programs contain tendencies such as greed, cruelty, anger, fear, sensuality, and deceit. As the *prāṇa-śakti* expands—or becomes subtler, if you prefer to think of it that way—it moves into the heart and the higher *cakras,* where our experience of such qualities as compassion, love, devotion, eloquence, and poetic inspiration also expands. When the *śakti* moves in the *cakras,* it naturally purifies them, removing energy blocks and revealing what has been hidden from our own awareness.

You might notice that I've only spoken of the *kuṇḍalinī-śakti's* moving through the subtle system in one direction, upward. This is the most traditional way of charting *kuṇḍalinī's* path, and yet it doesn't necessarily describe what individual yogis experience. My own recollection is that my earliest experiences involved the heart; it was some time later that my energy was perceptibly active in the *mūlādhāra*—which is the spot where everything presumably should have begun! However, the path the *kuṇḍalinī* takes through a particular set of *saṃskāras* (which is one way of viewing our own subtle system) is highly individual. When people speak of the movement of *kuṇḍalinī,* they are usually describing the inner kingdom itself and not the order in which its terrain will necessarily be revealed to us.

Kuṇḍalinī's Expansion

In one of the wordplays that so delight Sanskrit scholars, Kshemaraja equates the expansion of *kuṇḍalinī-śakti* with the spread of *viṣa,* poison.*

* In his commentary on sutra 18, Kshemaraja likens *vikāsa,* the expansion of the *madhya,* to the pervasion of *viṣa,* poison; Jaideva Singh, trans. *The Doctrine of Recognition* (1990), p. 85.

Startling as it might seem, this metaphor has veracity and, for me, a great deal of power. The idea is that *śakti* spreads through the body much as venom does from a snakebite. This was precisely my experience when my own *kuṇḍalinī-śakti* was awakened. As I described earlier, I could feel the energy moving up my spine and spreading its nectar through me. The word *viṣa* also means "to fill, to spread out, to invade" as well as "to eat" or "to consume." You could say that *kuṇḍalinī-śakti* consumes negativities, and, again, that is just what I felt happened as the nectar of *kuṇḍalinī* pervaded my mind and replaced my thoughts with the experience of bliss.

Kshemaraja's metaphor also evokes the image of the serpent used by the Āgamas, the revealed scriptures of Śaivism, to represent *kuṇḍalinī,* given the curled form that the energy takes in the *mūlādhāra* when dormant and how it straightens and gracefully glides along the central conduit once awakened. Some of my early experiences of *kuṇḍalinī* involve the piercing of the *cakras,* something that I could actually perceive; these felt almost like punctures or bites.

Kshemaraja also makes another, opposite application of this image of *viṣa,* one I find particularly apt: the "poison" is ignorance, which has a numbing effect on the unawakened soul. While *kuṇḍalinī* sleeps, our own energy is almost benumbed, like the consciousness of someone who's been poisoned. It could be said that a person whose divine energy hasn't been awakened is filled with the poison of duality and that worldly values are spread through all aspects of his life. Once *kuṇḍalinī* is awakened, the energy rises to the *brahmarandhra* and consumes all sense of duality, penetrating the entire body with its "venom" of immense bliss. In the ascending movement of the divine energy, the original poison of duality becomes the all-pervading nectar of liberating Consciousness.

The Path of Kuṇḍalinī

In the early days in Ganeshpuri, groups of us who lived in Baba's ashram would get together each morning at the *chai* shop next door and talk about what was happening in our *sādhana*. That morning's meditation was always a hot topic of conversation. We kept trying to infer conclusions—about our own attainment, about the nature of the universe—from a phenomenon that's far too subtle to be the basis for solid conclusions. Our *kuṇḍalinī* experiences were partial pictures only.

It wasn't until Baba's third world tour, toward the end of his teaching mission, that he began to speak about the unfoldment of *kuṇḍalinī* in terms that were more specific and comprehensive. It was then that he introduced to the Siddha Yoga *saṅgham* the concept of the three "levels" of *kuṇḍalinī*—three stages in the ever-ascending movement toward the ultimate expansion. These forms of the one divine energy are *prāṇa-kuṇḍalinī, cit-kuṇḍalinī,* and *parā-kuṇḍalinī.* This is how Baba describes them:

> *Prāṇa-kuṇḍalinī* dwells at the base of the spine, in the *mūlādhāra.* You experience that place when your *kuṇḍalinī* is awakened, because you feel pain there. When the *prāṇa-kuṇḍalinī* is awakened, you get violent movements of the bodies. *Cit-kuṇḍalinī* exists in the heart, and when it [this level] is awakened you feel an incredible love for God. When in meditation, *parā-kuṇḍalinī* is awakened, you become aware that you are God; that God dwells everywhere, that you are perfect. Thus, nobody has to teach you that you are perfect and that God is everywhere.[154]

In other words, Baba is saying that the *śakti* is awakened at each of these three levels: in the *mūlādhāra,* in the heart center *(anāhata),* and in the *sahasrāra* at the crown of the head. Elsewhere, Baba indicates that although for most seekers the initial awakening takes place in the *mūlādhāra*, it can also occur in any of the three centers.* We can infer from his remarks additionally that a seeker can experience all three levels of *kuṇḍalinī:*

> As the *prāṇa-kuṇḍalinī* moves upward and comes to *cit-kuṇḍalinī* in the heart, it merges totally in *cit-kuṇḍalinī*. Then *cit-kuṇḍalinī* starts ascending higher and reaches the *sahasrāra*. It will continue to function there until it has merged in Śiva. When *cit-kuṇḍalinī* is about to merge in Śiva, it is called *parā-kuṇḍalinī*, the supreme Śakti. There, being one with God, it plays. Its main function is to make this knowledge of oneness arise in you.[155]

When I first heard Baba's description of the three levels of *kuṇḍalinī*, I found it mystifying and kept wishing he would explain more about them. Then, as my *sādhana* progressed and I continued to study Śaivism, I could intuitively sense the working of these three aspects of my inner power. I could see that not only was I changing—that is, my mind and personality were becoming more refined and subtle—but the *prāṇa-śakti* within me seemed to be changing as well. It seemed to me that the energy itself was becoming more subtle, as different from the *prāṇa-śakti* of my early experiences as water is from ice, or vapor from water. By the very positing of "three levels" of *kuṇḍalinī* with three different names, the sages indicate that the divine energy undergoes a transformation in the way it works on us as it travels on its journey of ascension.**

---

* Swami Muktananda says, "In some people, it unfolds from the base of the spine, in some it unfolds in the heart, in some it is awakened in the *sahasrāra*. It is not certain that it will be awakened only from one place; it can be awakened from any of the three." (*Siddha Path* magazine, South Fallsburg, NY: April 1979, p. 4.)

** Swami Muktananda's descriptions of the three levels of *kuṇḍalinī* were not included in any of his books; for a more detailed analysis of this schema, the reader can turn to the writings of Lakshman Joo: *Kashmir Shaivism: The Secret Supreme* (chapters 17 and 18) and *Self-Realization in Kashmir Shaivism* (chapter 5), both published by SUNY Press.

The Final Destination

It is in the *sahasrāra* that the yogi finds the ultimate bliss of *madhya-vikāsa,* the expansion of the center. As Baba Muktananda writes in his autobiography:

> When the mind is turned upward into the *sahasrāra* and becomes stable in meditation there, the sound of thunder is heard and the tongue turns up against the soft palate. Then the aspirant starts to taste a divine savor. Sometimes when the tongue is in this position, one can taste the cool nectar of the moon, and the Siddha student is full of delight and amazement. He meditates with even more enthusiasm so that he can drink more and more of the nectar.[156]

Here Baba is describing *khecarī-mudrā,* an esoteric practice in which the tongue is thrust up against the soft palate and to the back of the throat, releasing a delightful ambrosial taste in the mouth. *Khecarī-mudrā,* according to the many people who have experienced it as well as to the scriptures of Kashmir Śaivism, occurs spontaneously in advanced meditators whose *kuṇḍalinī-śakti* has been awakened. It is said to culminate in the state in which one's awareness roams *(cāra)* through the vast space *(kha)* of Consciousness, perfectly sealed in the bliss that dissolves all bondage *(mudrā).* * The sound of thunder that Baba refers to is *megha-nāda,* the final inner sound, the most subtle of the *nādas* to emanate from the mantra *haṃsa,* which itself emanates from the primordial *Oṃ.* The moon Baba speaks of is known as the lunar *maṇḍala,* a shining disc of light that sits just under the *sahasrāra* and which contains the point of

* "On the emergence of spontaneous supreme knowledge occurs that state of movement in the vast unlimited expanse of Consciousness which is the state of Śiva." (Kshemaraja's comm. on *Śiva-sūtra,* 2.5; trans. Jaideva Singh, *Śiva Sūtras: The Yoga of Supreme Identity* (1979), pp. 99-102.).

light that he describes as "the supremely beautiful Blue Pearl, as tiny as a sesame seed."[157] Baba calls this Blue Pearl the dwelling place of the Self. The lunar *maṇḍala* is experienced by yogis only when their *sādhana* has reached maturity, and it contains divine nectar, which flows through the *suṣumṇā* and fills the yogi with indescribable joy.

Abhinavagupta speaks of seven distinct states of ecstasy, culminating at the top of the *sahasrāra* in *jagadānanda,* "the bliss of the universe,"* which he describes in this way:

> That in which there is no division or limitation, for it flashes forth all around, in which Consciousness is intact [that is, in which it is Consciousness alone that expresses itself, whether as knower or means of knowledge or as known], that which increases and expands by the nectar of divine joy of absolute sovereignty [and] in which there is no need for imagination or meditation—Shambhu told me *that* was *jagadānanda.*[158]

In this context, *Shambhu* refers to Abhinavagupta's Guru, Shambhunatha. As for the means to arrive at this exalted state of *jagadānanda,* the "bliss of the world," these Kshemaraja offers to us in the next sutra.

* The seven levels of bliss denote the refinement of different aspects of *prāṇa.* When these are purified and regain their universal nature, they move progressively closer to the bliss of pure Consciousness, and therefore are nuances of *turīya,* the state of enlightenment. (Abhinavagupta, *Tantrāloka,* v. 43-54a; Italian trans., *Raniero Gnoli, Luce delle Sacre Scritture [Tantrāloka] di Abhinavagupta* (1972); English trans. Giuliana Haim.)

18

Approaches to Expanding the Center

Sutra 18

विकल्पक्षय शक्तिसंकोचविकास
वाहच्छेदाद्यन्तकोटि निभालनादय इहोपायाः

vikalpakṣaya-śaktisaṃkocavikāsa-
vāhacchedādyanta-koṭinibhālanādaya ihopāyāḥ

In this regard, the means [for expansion of the center] are
dissolution of thoughts,
contraction and expansion of one's power,
cessation of the flow [of the incoming and outgoing vital energy],
awareness of the point at the beginning and the end,
and so on.

vikalpa:	mental activity
kṣaya:	dissolution, destruction
śakti:	power
saṃkoca:	contraction
vikāsa:	expansion, unfolding
vāha:	flow
cheda:	cessation, cutting
ādi:	beginning
anta:	end
koṭi:	point, extremity
nibhālana:	awareness
ādayaḥ:	and so on; et cetera
iha:	here, in this regard
upāyāḥ:	the means

IN SUTRA 18, KSHEMARAJA identifies four specific processes by which a seeker can achieve *madhya-vikāsa,* the expansion of the center of divinity. He then ends with the term *ādaya,* the equivalent of et cetera, implying that there are other—perhaps *many* other—techniques capable of leading us to the experience of inner ecstasy. It seems his purpose is not to overwhelm us with possible practices, but rather to indicate those methods he has found most expedient and, implicitly, to invite us to select whichever of them is most convenient for us, depending on our proclivities and the level of our attainment. These practices were apparently selected for their simplicity and ease of performance, an approach that's characteristic of Śaivism: to use the least demanding means of reaching for the highest goal.

Even so, the reader should bear in mind that the practices given here are highly esoteric. The term "esoteric" doesn't mean complicated or abstruse; it implies that these techniques are accessible only to initiates. They may be easy, but only for those graced by an awakened *kuṇḍalinī.* By tradition, practices such as these either are transmitted directly from Guru to disciple or unfold naturally in a seeker without conscious effort through the unfolding of the awakened *kuṇḍalinī-śakti.* For the most part, the discussion of these practices that follows is not so much instructional as it is descriptive and explanatory. It's my intention that the reader will recognize—and be open to—processes as they occur in *sādhana* following spiritual initiation.

1. Dissolution of One's Thoughts

The first and simplest method for expanding the center is the dissolution of thoughts, *vikalpakṣaya.* It seems that to Kshemaraja, this is the quintessential method for attaining the Lord, for it is a technique he returns to again and again throughout the *Pratyabhijñā-hṛdayam.** This is how he describes it in his commentary to this sutra:

> When [a seeker] keeps his *citta* [mind] concentrated on *saṃvit* [universal Consciousness] restraining, by the method alluded to, the *vikalpas* [differentiating ideas] that obstruct staying in one's real nature, by not thinking of anything whatsoever, and thus by laying hold of the *avikalpa* [thought-free] state, he becomes used to regarding his *cit* [Consciousness] as the [real] knower, untarnished by the body , etc.[159]

This is the process of *ahaṃbhāva,* which we have, like Kshemaraja, brought up in various guises throughout this book. So, how does one fix the mind on *saṃvit?* My own favorite method is to allow my mind to gently move inward, to whatever interior experience I'm having in that moment—whatever is beyond the surface. In fact, the moment I find myself experiencing negativity, that very experience raises the question, *Are you connected?* and the process begins. The question also arises when I'm particularly pleased with the world around me: *Are you connected to what's real?* In the moment of reverie inspired in this way, I experience an opening, an *unmeṣa,* in the space of the heart. In that flashing forth of the sensation of love, all my disparate thoughts tend to dissolve. Then I can easily enter into a space of inner silence that is vibrant with light, with *saṃvit.*

Kshemaraja assures us that one who follows this practice will, within a short time, attain both the state of absorption in the Self *(turīya)* and

* Kshemaraja indicates in his commentary on sutra 18 that he gives precedence to this particular method because the originator of the Pratyabhijñā School, Utpaladeva, teaches it in his *Īśvara-pratyabhijñā-kārikā* (41.11) as an essential approach for reaching full enlightenment.

also the state of unity-awareness that lies beyond it *(turīyātīta)*. In my experience, the true effort required to keep one's mind quiet and one's attention centered on the Self is to maintain *ahaṃbhāva,* the sublime feeling of "I am."

As we assume this pristine state—unsullied by the considerations and sensations that come from having a body, a mind, a personality, and so on—then, Kshemaraja implies, with practice and in time, we become habituated to the experience of our true identity as profound inner silence: not *I am something or another,* but simply *I am.* The more one rests in a state free from thought, the more the center expands.

2. Contraction and Expansion of One's Power

The second of Kshemaraja's practices is *śaktisaṃkocavikāsa,* the contraction and expansion of one's *śakti.* Specifically, the contraction of *śakti* refers to the sublimation of energy: the energy that would otherwise flow out through the doorways of the senses is redirected to the inner Self. Kshemaraja illustrates this process with the image of a tortoise, protecting itself at the first sign of danger by contracting its head and legs and centering itself within the safety of its shell, just as the yogi who wishes to protect himself from the draining influence of the world can contract his *prāṇa-śakti,* holding it within his own being. To illustrate this process, the sage quotes the *Kaṭha Upaniṣad:*

> The Self-existent One pierced the apertures [of the senses] outward; therefore, one looks out, and not into oneself. A certain wise man in search of immortality turned his sight inward and saw the Self within.[160]

This is, of course, a renunciant's approach to *sādhana:* diverting one's attention and energy from the world and toward inner exploration. It is an undeniably valuable stance to take in spiritual work, even for those who are not renunciants. Much of what I have been able to accomplish in my own *sādhana* has come from my decision that this is my focus. Here is what Gurumayi says about this "contraction" of *śakti* and its benefits:

> Turning within is called yoga. Yoga is the divine discipline that gives a seeker the power to turn his attention within. It makes him understand the true purpose of the senses. It uncovers the glory hidden within him. It enables him to go deep into the cave of his own heart. It shows him the way to unite heaven and earth. Yoga gives a seeker the strength to uplift his energies and become mature.[161]

The expansion of one's *śakti,* in contrast to its contraction, is both a practice and a state of being. Here, the yogi directs the *prāṇa-śakti* outward, through the openings of the senses. That might sound surprising. You might ask, *Isn't that what people do all the time? Is sensory perception truly a practice that brings us to inner bliss?* It is, but only if this "expansion" of *śakti* happens in the right way. That is, only if the yogi perceiving exterior objects is able, *at the same time,* to anchor his attention on his inner center, the Self. From that perspective, the energy moving outward is seen as identical to the energy vibrating within—even though the yogi may be experiencing an invasion of sounds, smells, and other sensations.

As I've discovered on the occasions when this state has opened up within me, my awareness of the hustle and bustle continues; it is, however, now contained within a vast and silent cavern. This is the "cave of the heart" that Gurumayi describes, a space that encompasses both inner and outer or, as she puts it, both heaven and Earth. This extremely esoteric practice, known in Śaivism as *bhairavī-mudrā,* is described in a scriptural passage quoted by Kshemaraja in his commentary:

> If you project the vision and all the other powers [of the senses] simultaneously everywhere onto their respective objects by the power of awareness, while remaining firmly established in the center like a pillar of gold, you [will] shine as the One, the foundation of the universe.[162]

Kshemaraja goes on to say that this exalted state, which I have glimpsed myself once or twice as a direct result of Guru's grace, comes about gradually—and naturally—in one whose *prāṇa-śakti* is restrained "between the eyebrows by means of the power of the subtle *prāṇa.*"[163] As I mentioned earlier, this is both a practice and also a process of transformation that unfolds naturally in one whose *kuṇḍalinī* is awakened. I want to describe this very subtle process in some detail here, because I find it both humbling and awe-inspiring that so much occurs in my *sādhana* without my willing it or, often, even being aware of what is happening. I view this as a natural unfoldment of grace.

Control of the Vital Energy

Among yogis, it is widely recognized that what disturbs the mind and senses is the ceaseless activity of the vital energy, *prāṇa.* It's understood that once the yogi has calmed and controlled the *prāṇa,* the mind and senses withdraw, allowing the expansion of the great Śakti. Baba Muktananda puts it this way:

> The mind is intimately connected to the *prāṇa*. When the *prāṇa* becomes uneven, the sense of duality arises, and the mind keeps weaving new webs of thoughts and fantasies. To control the mind, to make it still and even, yogis try to control the breath. [164]

Of the five functions traditionally ascribed to *prāṇa*, the most significant in relation to the mind are the in-breath *(prāṇa)* and out-breath *(apāna)*.* As long as the in-breath and out-breath continue their normal—that is, irregular—activity, the mind will experience duality. *Haṭha-yoga* texts offer many exercises for control of the breath *(prāṇāyāma)*, and, as Baba indicates here, these can be effective methods of stilling the mind. This is not, however, what Kshemaraja is speaking of in this sutra, for the technique he recommends rests on the inner refinement of five functions of the *prāṇa-śakti*.

In the sense that Kshemaraja is using them, the terms *prāṇa* and *apāna* refer not only to the movement of the physical breath, but also to the movement of the vital energy that underlies the breath, what he calls "the power of the subtle *prāṇa*." The distinction rests on the transformation of *prāṇa* that occurs with the awakening of *kuṇḍalinī*. In the yogic scriptural tradition, the five functions that constitute the various movements of *prāṇa* are, in their dense aspect, known as airs *(vāyus)* because they circulate much as air currents do in accomplishing their vital functions in the physical and subtle bodies. When *kuṇḍalinī* becomes fully operative under the influence of this awakened *śakti*, the *vāyus* become subtle. In their dense aspect, they continue to support our

* Besides *prāṇa* and *apāna*, the five *prāṇas* and their physical functions include *samāna*, the power that distributes evenly the nourishment from food to all parts of the body; *vyāna*, the power of pervasive movement within all the *nāḍīs* of the subtle body; and *udāna*, the power that carries energy upward, giving strength and radiance to the body.

mundane life, and in their refined aspect, these vital airs become *śaktis* supporting our spiritual purification and expansion. * It is both aspects that Kshemaraja speaks of here: *prāṇa* and *apāna* moving through the nostrils and the subtle *prāṇa* and *apāna* moving through the *nāḍīs.* These distinctions apply in both the current exercise and also the next two.

The Refinement of the Vital Energies

In his discussion of the expansion of one's *śakti,* Kshemaraja makes an oblique reference to the coming together of two forces. One is the subtle *prāṇa* (which flows toward the exterior of the body in the *piṅgalā-nāḍī*) and the other is the subtle *apāna* (which flows toward the interior in the *iḍā-nāḍī*).** These come together under the influence of *samāna,* the harmonizing energy. In its mundane aspect as a vital air *(vāyu), samāna* is the power by which the body assimilates food. On the subtle level, *samāna* plays an equally significant role by bringing a stop to the constant movement of *prāṇa* and *apāna.* When *kuṇḍalinī* is awakened, the subtle aspects of *prāṇa* and *apāna* are able to unite as *samāna* in the *suṣumṇā-nāḍī,* the central channel. The result is that the mind ceases to create *vikalpas* and, spontaneously, becomes peaceful.

We can experience the effect of *samāna-śakti* during meditation when the breath comes in and out evenly through the two nostrils. We

* This view of the transmutation of energies is characteristic of Śaivism: the forces that bind us are the very forces that bring us to liberation. We could say that the powers of the refined *prāṇa-śakti* provide the internal mechanism by which mental activity is dissolved. It is this mental activity that is the basis for our sense of isolation and separation and also for the very expansion of *madhya-vikāsa* that we seek.

** The *iḍā* and *piṅgalā* are the channels that wrap around the *suṣumṇā-nāḍī* and, of all the *nāḍīs,* are the closest to it.

might also notice that as our meditation goes deeper, mental fluctuations lessen—if, indeed, any are left at all—and our breath becomes shallower. At such times, some people fear that they're suffocating; I've had that reaction several times myself. There is, however, no reason to panic. The decrease in the breath is a sign that something significant and wonderful is beginning to take place: the subtle *prāṇas* are merging in the central channel.

Once *prāṇa* and *apāna* become *samāna,* then this unified energy moves upward through the *suṣumṇā-nāḍī,* becoming *udāna-śakti,* the upward-bound energy. The refined *udāna-śakti* is the power that travels upward through the *cakras* along the central conduit. As we said, Kshemaraja speaks of "restraining the *prāṇa* between the eyebrows by means of the power of the subtle *prāṇa.*" The sage goes into an extremely technical discussion at this point. In the simplest terms, we could say that he is referring to the rise of *udāna-śakti* and the attainment of the *turīya* state in which we experience our oneness with the Self—and the bliss of *madhya-vikāsa.*[165]

3. Cessation of the Flow of the Vital Energy

The third method Kshemaraja recommends also has to do with control of the *prāṇa-śakti,* this time through mantra. The terms he uses in the sutra are *vāha,* meaning "flow," and *cheda,* meaning "cessation" or "pause." In the commentary, the sage explains that he is referring to the flow of *prāṇa* and *apāna,* the two main forms of *prāṇa-śakti,* through a very particular technique known as "voicing *anacka.*" This term can be translated as "without vowels." *Anacka* is the practice of voicing consonants without making the sounds of vowels. In Sanskrit, vowels are understood to represent the vivifying presence of Śiva, while the consonants are the aspects of Śakti that give name and form to the created things. In pronunciation, as in creation, both aspects are needed. Just try saying "pan" or "tent" or even just "do" without the vowel sounds; it simply cannot be done.

So, how does one practice voicing *anacka?* By attempting to articulate the letters inwardly without vocalizing them outwardly. In this way, the sounds of the syllables go back to their point of origin in the silence of Śiva. In other words, these subtle sounds are directed to the heart of Śiva, one's own Self. In the space of Consciousness, these powers of Śakti merge into bliss. In this process, the flow of *prāṇa* and *apāna* in the *iḍā* and *piṅgalā-nāḍīs* stops as it comes in perfect balance in the central conduit, the *suṣumṇā-nāḍī.* In his commentary, Kshemaraja quotes the *Jñāna-garbha-tantra:*

> In the heart lotus of one whose mind has been controlled—whose two *nāḍīs [iḍā* and *piṅgalā],* extending on both sides, have been stilled by the restraint brought about by sounding the vowel-less "K" and whose blinding darkness has been dispelled—arises that sprout of your knowledge. This, O [World Mother], is adequate to produce [the state of Parameśvara] even in the *paśu* [the bound soul].[166]

In the broadest sense, the practice of *anacka* arises spontaneously in meditation. Perhaps the most practical way to begin to perform this practice is simply to recognize the state when it, or something close to it, occurs. Often, while I'm silently repeating *Oṃ Namaḥ Śivāya* or *So'ham,* the syllables suddenly dissolve and I'm in a state of immense serenity. Quite naturally, in such a state, the *prāṇa* comes to rest. Besides the mantra repetition itself, no specific effort is involved in this process of casting the mantra into the silent space within. However, if one pays careful attention to mantra repetition, the syllables of the mantra naturally turn into a subtle resonance, almost as if they had lost their vowels. Then the resonance that remains, the "consonants," ultimately dissolves into the silence. Of course, the very presence of that silence is testimony that the flow of *prāṇa* and *apāna* has ceased. Then, with a quiet mind, one can experience *madhya-vikāsa,* the bliss of the center.

4. Awareness of the Beginning and Ending Point

The fourth method given is that of fixing one's attention *(nibhālana)* on the point *(koṭi)* at the beginning *(ādi)* and the end *(anta)*. Kshemaraja makes it quite clear in his commentary that his first meaning is another reference to *prāṇa-śakti,* in this case the physical breath. The "beginning" is the place where the in-breath pauses in the *hṛdaya* (by which he means not the physical heart but the center of the diaphragm), and the "end" is where the out-breath pauses outside the body, in a spot known as the *dvādaśānta.* (You determine the precise placement of the *dvādaśānta* by placing your ten fingers, one over the other, outward and arcing down from the tip of the nose, and then adding the space of two more fingers.) In terms of the breath, this practice is one of watching—simply watching—for the beginning point or the ending point of the breath, the pause that occurs when the breath itself "turns around." It's the point at which one breath has ceased and the next has not yet begun.

When Baba Muktananda referred to this practice, which he often did, he would speak about the beginning and ending points as if they were one, calling them both *hṛdaya,* both *dvādaśānta.* In *I Am That,* his book about this practice, he writes:

> Here, "heart" does not refer to the physical organ. The heart is the place where the breath merges, inside and outside. In reality, these two places are one. The duality of inner and outer space exists only because you have the sense of your physical body. The moment you transcend your body-consciousness, the inner and outer spaces merge.[167]

In his book *Secret of the Siddhas,* Baba writes of the power of this practice:

> There is no *sādhana* that can be compared to that of the *dvādaśānta.* All Siddhas have attained God in the *dvādaśānta* through *So'ham.** When a yogi has this equal vision, he understands the state of equality in which the dual state of *prāṇa* and *apāna* merges into the mysterious space, within or without. Along with that, in the same way, he dissolves all worldly objects into the mysterious Supreme Principle. Now he sees everything as inseparable from himself. By having this expanded vision of equality, he attains the supreme state.[168]

So, there is great attainment to be found in this space between the breaths.

There are other meanings in the practice as well. The term *dvādaśānta* implies that the "point at the beginning and the end" can also be the pause between two thoughts, two emotions, two physical movements, two states of mind. In fact, the "point at the beginning and the

* By *So'ham,* Baba means not so much the repetition of these mantric syllables but the pulsating awareness of "That I am" conveyed by this mantra.

end" can refer to an interstice that appears within any dichotomous activity. Any of these spaces that are bracketed by two actions can serve as an entry point into the vast realm of Consciousness.

Of course, to penetrate a space as subtle, as narrow, as that which occurs between the end of one thought and the beginning of another, or the completion of one physical motion and the onset of the next, is difficult for one in a state of normal waking consciousness. Many of us have tried—and tried and tried and tried and tried—to find this "point between" without apparent success. The key seems to lie with the control of *prāṇa* and *apāna*. This, as I mentioned before, comes naturally to one who has received an inner awakening. It is, however, a very powerful focus for one's attention. It seems to me that it is the very attempts we make to help harmonize the currents of *prāṇa-śakti* in the *iḍā* and *piṅgalā nāḍīs* that still the mind and allow us to become aware of these subtle phenomena.

5. And So On

It is in his commentary on the phrase "and so on" *(ādayaḥ)* that Kshemaraja comes to what is my own favorite section of this sutra, for here the sage recommends using any method of meditation on the Self that brings about *unmeṣa,* the expansive opening of the center. In this section, he makes a principal teaching of Kashmir Śaivism abundantly clear by quoting the following passages from the *Vijñāna-bhairava:*

> When one experiences the expansion of the joy of savor arising from the pleasure of eating and drinking, one should meditate on the perfect condition of this joy, then one would become full of great bliss.

> When a yogi mentally becomes one with the incomparable joy of song and other objects, then of such a concentrated yogi, there is identity with that [with incomparable joy], because he becomes one with it.
>
> Wherever the mind finds its satisfaction, let it be concentrated on that. In every such case, the true nature of the highest bliss will shine forth.[169]

As I indicated at the very beginning of this commentary, this process of coming to rest in joy, natural joy, is my own best-loved means of stilling my mind and experiencing bliss. Let me give an example, a moment that has remained as a treasure in my memory for some thirty years.

It was an evening shortly after I received initiation. I was alone in my mother's apartment. I prepared a simple meal, put some classical music on the stereo, and feeling very peaceful, I sat down to eat dinner. Perhaps because of my serenity, I began to eat with a certain amount of deliberation. At one point, as I took a morsel from the plate, I saw it vibrate on the fork as if it were alive. The food tasted heavenly—it was nectarean, delicious in a way that had nothing to do with cooking techniques or sauces. With every bite, I experienced ecstasy, and finally I was filled with a sense of utter plenitude. The nectar of the food seemed to have spread through my whole body.

Then the music came to my awareness. I recall—I'll never forget!—that the piece was the *Brandenburg Concerto no. 5* by Johann Sebastian Bach. As I listened, I could actually sense the music undulating through space and entering my ears. I could feel sweetness literally streaming from the music and blending with the sweetness that had already arisen in me. It was as if my inner delight were enjoying the outer delight of that beautiful sound.

In this astonishing state of open-eyed meditation, I looked at the wall in front of me, where there was a painting depicting a festival in some historic time. I'd always enjoyed that painting, but now I was perceiving the very vibrations of the colors and the lines of this much-loved scene actually move across the space of the room and enter my eyes. The rapture of my love for this painting seemed to merge with the rapture inside me until it was no longer the painting that I delighted in, but the beauty of my own joy. I could feel that the joy awakened through my senses was taking place simultaneously at the core of my being. It was as if I had been transported to the world of the gods for the most memorable meal of my life. Years later I encountered those *Vijñāna-bhairava* passages that so perfectly describe my own experience of that evening.

What is abundantly clear to me is that a living teaching such as I received that night is possible only through the grace of a spiritual teacher, a true Guru. I couldn't have "decided" to have that experience; if I had set out to have it, nothing I did or thought could possibly have made it happen. An experience such as this comes through grace. In moments of grace like this, when my heart seems to literally pour out its loving nectar, I know that a response of this magnitude, like the stilling of the mind or transformation of the *prāṇas,* can happen only in an awakened consciousness and through the grace of a spiritual master.

19

Samādhi and Its Imprint

Sutra 19

समाधिसंस्कारवति व्युत्थाने भूयो
भूयश्चिदैक्यामर्शान्नित्योदितसमाधिलाभः

***samādhi-saṃskāravati-vyutthāne
bhūyo bhūyaś cid-aikyāmarśān nityodita-samādhi-lābhaḥ***

The permanent attainment of *samādhi* [is established by] contemplating one's identity with Consciousness again and again in the state following meditation, which is full of the imprints of *samādhi.*

samādhi:	the state of absorption in the Self
saṃskāra:	mental impressions
vati:	carrying, possessing
vyutthāne:	in the arising, the state following *samādhi*
bhūyaḥ:	again
cit:	Consciousness
aikya:	oneness
āmarśān:	contemplating, dwelling upon
nitya:	always, eternal
udita:	arisen
lābhaḥ:	attainment

For me, the key term in sutra 19 is *nityodita*, "eternally emergent." This term reminds us that the joy we long for is always accessible and that, for a yogi, it isn't enough to experience joy sporadically. The goal is to become permanently established in that state of joy, to have joy coming forth from within oneself constantly and for all time. In the last two sutras, we considered the various processes that bring about the blissful expansion of the yogi's divine center *(madhya-vikāsa)*. In the present discussion, we reflect on the effort the yogi must make to become anchored in that bliss.

Self-effort in *sādhana* is a theme that Gurumayi addresses repeatedly. I like to think of it as caring for a seedling. Planting the seed may come as an act of grace, and the natural occurrence of rainfall helps it to sprout and grow. Yet, if we want some certainty that a particular plant will survive and flourish, we need to cultivate it. That may mean weeding and pruning; it may mean digging furrows to channel water through parched soil or building fences to protect a tender seedling from predators. In our *sādhana*, it's much the same: it isn't enough to receive grace; we must also cultivate this priceless gift carefully and attentively—right up to the final moments of our quest. In sutra 19, Kshemaraja tells us how we can do this. The sage says that to attain permanent *(nityodita)* absorption in the experience of the Self *(samādhi)*, we must contemplate *(āmarśān)* again and again *(bhūyo bhūyaḥ)* the impressions *(saṃskāra)* left on our consciousness in the state following meditation *(vyutthāne)* by the glimpses we've had of *samādhi*.

Let's begin by taking a look at the state of *samādhi*.

Merging with Our Own Self

Samādhi is a word as poetic as it is evocative of the highest in us. It is usually translated as "absorption in the Self," but its Sanskrit roots reveal further nuances of meaning. *Sama* means "equal, alike, united," and "focused on one point." *Dhi* signifies "mind, intelligence," and "understanding." Thus, *samādhi* is the state in which the discursive mind unites with—becomes one with—Consciousness. *Samādhi* is the fusion of the individual "I," which is embodied in the mind, and the eternal "I" of Śiva. It is the state of total integration. As Gurumayi points out, *samādhi* takes place on all levels of one's being:

> *Samādhi* is the state in which your intellect, your mind, your subconscious mind, your heart, and the ego have all come to terms with themselves. They all know what they are doing. It isn't that the heart wants one thing, the mind wants something else, and the intellect wants to do yet another thing. All these instruments, all these elements, are in agreement so there is supreme joy, the ecstatic experience; there is harmony.[170]

Thus in *samādhi,* all aspects of the mind are perfectly focused on one point, all elements of our being are absorbed in an understanding of our divine nature.

For human beings, *samādhi* is as natural as sleeping, dreaming, thinking, and all the other states of mind that we experience each day. This may sound odd, but it's a perfectly accurate statement. This is why one of the names the sages gave to *samādhi* is *turīya,* meaning "the fourth" or the fourth state of mind, acknowledging its kinship with the first three states of waking, dreaming, and deep sleep. Abhinavagupta says of *samādhi:*

> Nothing new is achieved nor is that which in reality is unmanifest revealed—[only] the idea is eradicated that the luminous being shines not.[171]

There is much that can be drawn from this short passage. The sage is telling us that the state of *samādhi* neither creates nor shows us anything that wasn't already present; *samādhi* simply erases any wrong notions we may have about the nature of reality. What I find most interesting in this statement is the implicit understanding that *samādhi* is a natural function of the mind. In other words, it is the mind—the stabilized and quiet mind—that lets go of delusion and thereby attains the state of *samādhi.* It is the mind that experiences itself as God. It is the mind that realizes its own identity with the Self. A purified mind—as I've said before—is the mirror on which Śiva reflects his perfect light, the light that brims with his overflowing bliss.

Samādhi comes as an act of grace—most often from an individual who is himself in the state of *samādhi*—and yet because it's natural to us, because it is a natural state of mind, we are all able to be in this state and to learn how to remain in it, in the same way that we might develop any skill or mental ability. We develop the capacity to remain in the state of *samādhi,* Kshemaraja tells us, by returning to the imprint that our experiences of *samādhi* have left on our waking consciousness in the state we're in following meditation—in other words, by dwelling on the memory of any glimpse of *samādhi* we may have had and by returning to our memory of it *bhūyo bhūyaḥ,* again and again.

Remembrance, Again and Again

The heart of *pratyabhijñā,* the path of recognition, is this repeated remembrance of our own highest nature. Having said this, I am now going to underscore the point by describing—returning to—another of the gems from my own *sādhana.*

Early one morning in the 1970s, I was sitting in the meditation cave at Gurudev Siddha Peeth. My attention was drawn to my physical heart, whose rhythmic movement I could both hear and feel. Then in my mind's eye, I found myself looking at a large stone *liṅgam.* A *liṅgam* is a traditional form of Lord Śiva, a pillar-shaped form. In this vision, just on the other side of the *liṅgam,* I could see a large white bull, which I recognized as Nandi, Lord Śiva's mount. Nandi was seated on the ground, as if maintaining a vigil over his adored deity.

The scene seemed oddly familiar to me, and after a few moments, I recalled where I had seen something like this before. Throughout the grounds of Gurudev Siddha Peeth, there are numerous life-sized statues of saints and deities, and this very scene of Nandi keeping watch over the *liṅgam* is depicted in a spot in the ashram's upper gardens. Almost as soon as I'd had this recollection, the form of the *liṅgam* faded away, and in its place I saw Baba Muktananda standing, his saffron silks shining as they fluttered in a light breeze. It seemed to me every pore of his body emanated joy, and I could feel waves of love surging from my own heart in response to this vision of my beloved Guru. I began to weep with love. The pull to approach Baba became irresistible, and I started to move toward him. As I got closer, Baba's form began to seem less substantial, more diffuse. Just as I put my arms out to embrace Baba, his form disappeared altogether, and I could feel the love that I knew as "Baba" fusing into my own being. From my heart, I saw a ray of white light emerge.

This marvelous light spread out in all directions, dissolving the images I'd been perceiving: the ashram grounds, Nandi, the trees, the clouds, the sky itself. The light radiated its splendor all around, absorbing the entire world into itself. In the end, there were no forms remaining. As far as I could see—in front, behind, above, below, everywhere—there was only an intense luminosity. My body had disappeared as well, and any sense I'd had of myself as an individual. All that was left was this amazing light, which was scintillating with tremendous joy. Though it was profoundly silent, it seemed that, within itself, this great light was silently murmuring, *I am, I am, I am. . .*

When I came out of this meditation, I was in a state of ecstasy, and—just as Kshemaraja recommends in this sutra—I kept that state of joy with me as long as I could. I kept thinking, *What a gift this is! What a gift!* It happened that this particular day was celebrated in India as Lord Krishna's birthday, and I was particularly grateful to have had the Lord's darshan on the Lord's birthday! So, even after I came out of the state of meditation *(vyutthāna)*, I kept contemplating *(āmarśān)* that experience again and again *(bhūyo bhūyaḥ)*. More importantly, in the years since, I've continued to recall it—or, in yogic terms, to go back to the imprint *(saṃskāra)* it has left in my memory.

One of the criteria that the Spanish saint Teresa of Avila gives for determining the authenticity of a spiritual experience is that even with the passage of time, it must retain at least some spark of its original fire.[172] I consider this quite a valid yardstick, and for me this particular experience is a proof. Some three decades have passed since that morning in the meditation cave, and yet to this day, the experience is very much alive for me. I have only to recall that moment to rekindle the extraordinary state of ecstasy it brought—and to relive that ecstasy all over again. This is true of all of my strong mystical experiences, and I am certain that everyone else has the same relationship with theirs. I have found that one of the most powerful techniques of *sādhana* is to record the times when I've been touched by grace and then to return to those instances. Kshemaraja explains that enormous benefit comes to the yogi who adopts this practice—we could call it the practice of cultivating the impressions of *samādhi*.

Samādhi as a Purification

Every time we experience the state of *samādhi*, the light of Consciousness dissolves mental impurities—our negative *saṃskāras*, our recollections of separation—and leaves in its wake its own impressions of union. Baba Muktananda used to speak of these impressions of *samādhi* as positive *saṃskāras*, for that is exactly what they are. These impressions are like energetic pathways in the mind, furrows of habit that make it increasingly easier for our consciousness to return to the experience of the Self. The imprints of *samādhi* on our normal consciousness transform the mind: *citta* becomes *citi*, the mind becomes Consciousness.

Possibly the most significant aspect of these traces is suggested by the first two syllables of *samādhi*, for *sama* is the Sanskrit word for "equanimity." It is this quality of *sama*, of deep calm, that allows one's consciousness to move through the subtle states along the path between the *ājñā-cakra* and the *sahasrāra* and on up to the *brahmarandhra,* the topmost spiritual center. In order for this process to take place, the work of inner purification has to be virtually finished: the *suṣumṇā-nāḍī* must be cleared of most karmas, the *cakras* must be functioning with openness, and the mind must have acquired great clarity, focus, and firmness.

In sutra 18, we spoke about the refinement of the *prāṇas* that Kshemaraja referred to in that sutra, including their transformation as far as the *ājñā-cakra.* As this divine energy moves into the *sahasrāra,* it is known as *udāna-śakti,* the upward-moving *prāṇa.* When it reaches this topmost center, it becomes *vyāna-śakti,* the ever-expansive power that continues beyond Self-realization and into the all-embracing Consciousness of Śiva. This is *turīyātīta,* the transcendental state, and it is here that the enlightened yogi naturally rests in his own bliss even while his senses are fully engaged with the world.

This process, and the yogic purification it implies, is the foundation of the state of *samādhi.* Yet the true means for making that state a permanent condition of the mind, Kshemaraja tells us, is our own practice of *samādhi,* of meditating again and again on our identity with supreme Consciousness. *Samādhi* is both the goal and the means to that goal.

Even if one does not enter the state of *samādhi,* the practice of meditation—sitting in a quiet place, closing the eyes, repeating the mantra—will in and of itself stamp the imprints of focus and peace and oneness on the mind. These imprints of the practice of meditation eventually make the state of meditation—*samādhi*—easier to achieve. I have seen this happen repeatedly with Siddha Yoga students who felt, sometimes for years, that "nothing" was happening in their meditation practice. With just the persistent practice of *attempting* to enter and penetrate the state of Consciousness, the mind gains in equanimity. The accumulation of meditative impressions in the student's system will in time reach a critical mass, prompting the states of *samādhi* to arise naturally.

The Unfolding of Samādhi

Kshemaraja distinguishes between two forms of *samādhi.* The experience in the meditation cave that I described previously is what the sage calls *nimīlana-samādhi,* closed-eyed absorption. In other words, one comes into this state of mergence with the Self with one's eyes closed. The second form or level of *samādhi* in this system is, as you might expect, open-eyed absorption, *unmīlana-samādhi.* This classification may sound simplistic, but as with most concepts of Śaivism, there is more to these distinctions than (if you'll pardon the pun) first meets the eye.

In drawing this paradigm, Kshemaraja was most likely inspired by the vision of the Spanda School, which describes the supreme Śakti creating the universe by pulsating rhythmically in movements of contraction and expansion, like the systole and diastole of a human heart. We have mentioned this before, in sutras 1 and 2, where these movements of the *spanda* are represented as Śiva creating the universe when he opens his eyes *(unmeṣa)* and dissolving it when he closes them *(nimeṣa).* According to Kshemaraja, the two forms of *samādhi* come about as a result of the yogi's identification with Śiva; the yogi's expression of the pulsations that characterize the opening and closing of Śiva's eyes are these two forms of absorption: *unmīlana* and *nimīlana.*[173]

Kshemaraja explains that in the beginning of his practice, a yogi experiences *nimīlana-samādhi,* that is, he becomes absorbed in the Self with his eyes closed. In this meditation, one's mind quiets and drops its identification with the body and all the attributes of individuality—and yet the purity of the Great Light is still filtered through some subtle particularities of the mind. It is an introverted practice in which the yogi can experience himself as the Self, and yet is not fused with the full infinity of Śiva. Put in technical terms, *nimīlana-samādhi* brings about the state of *turīya,* which confers *ātma-vyāpti,* the realization of the inner Self.

In time, when the yogi's practice of meditation matures, he begins to experience *unmīlana-samādhi,* open-eyed absorption. In other words, from the state of *nimīlana-samādhi,* he opens his eyes and his awareness remains absorbed in the Self even though he is in the state that comes after meditation *(vyutthāna)* with his senses fully operating. The term *vyutthāna* means "to rise" or "to wake up," which I like to think means that, in the most expansive expression of waking consciousness, one has awakened to the perception of external objects bathed in the Great Light of Consciousness. Because *vyutthāna* implies the rise of any objective perception, we can assume that, in addition to the waking state, it includes the dream and deep-sleep states as well.

Thus, the current sutra is telling us that the yogi is able to maintain his vision of total absorption in all his states of consciousness, and he does this because of the strong impressions of *samādhi* that are stored in his mind. In technical terms, *unmīlana-samādhi* opens us to the experience of *turīyātīta,* the state of *śiva-vyāpti,* in which one's subtle veil of separation is rent and one identifies with Śiva's infinite expansion throughout the universe. All traces of *mātṛkā-śakti* and their accompanying *vikalpas* are fused in the glorious "I am" of Śiva.

The Seal of Samādhi

Kshemaraja explains that at the stages just before final liberation, a yogi goes through a period of vacillation, like a tightrope walker, adjusting his balance from side to side. In this stage, the yogi swings between the internal and external states of *samādhi.* Since the yogi cannot stabilize his mind with his eyes open, he again closes his eyes, absorbing himself in the interior. He opens his eyes once again—and then closes them to return to the interior. In this way, he successively immerses himself into the two states of *samādhi,* emerging from one only to step into the other—meditating constantly in his identity with Consciousness. This movement backward and forward can last for an indefinite amount of time, depending on a yogi's level of advancement.

The name given to this blissful condition is *krama-mudrā,* which is the foundation for Kshemaraja's own commentary on sutra 19.[174] In *haṭha-yoga,* a *mudrā* is a gesture or, at times, a posture whose function is to seal one's energy and keep it from dispersing. The word *krama* is defined as "succession," or "order," and it refers in this instance to the succession of *pañca-kṛtya,* the five acts of Śiva. Now, the yogi engaged in *krama-mudrā* has already dealt with the fourth act, concealment, and he is fully immersed in the grace that is dispensed by the Lord's fifth act. These two, concealment and the bestowal of grace, are the divine actions that deal specifically with the individual. What remains are Śiva's first three actions, the cosmic acts that apply to all manifestation: creation, sustenance, and dissolution. Thus, eventually through *krama-mudrā,* the yogi assimilates what is left of the Lord's cosmic play. Through *krama-mudrā,* the yogi comes to know that this, too, is his own Self.

The process stabilizes when the yogi's perception no longer oscillates from outer *samādhi* to inner *samādhi*, but remains steady. Then the yogi experiences the Great Light penetrating the exterior just as he experiences it in the interior; he is in the same state regardless of whether his eyes are open or closed. The yogi takes delight in his own happiness, staggering with enormous joy as if he were inebriated, turning his awareness in and out over and over again as he meditates on his unmistakable identity with bliss. Kshemaraja refers to the etymology of *mudrā* to express three different aspects of the state underlying *krama-mudrā:* the manifestation of happiness, the dissolution of bondage, and—what seems most significant to me—the sealing of the universe in the state of divine luminosity.*

There are, of course, many other names and depictions for this magnificent state of perfect identity with God. Just for the joy of it, we'll explore a few of them here, with observations by *mahātmās* who are themselves established in that awareness.

Bhairavī-mudrā

One name that we mentioned in the previous sutra is *bhairavī-mudrā.* Bhairavī, for Abhinavagupta, is the form of the Goddess that projects, maintains, and retires the universe while remaining serene and immutable. In sutra 16, I give my own glimpse of how this state manifests in my spiritual master, Gurumayi. To the Siddha whose vision is permanently possessed by the gesture of Bhairavī, the world appears as

* As Jaideva Singh explains in his footnotes to Kshemaraja's commentary on sutra 19, "*Mudrā* is etymologically derived in three ways: *mudam rāti (dadāti)*, that which gives *mud* or joy; *mum drāvayati,* that which dissolves *mu* (bondage); *mudrayati iti,* that which seals up [the universe in the state of *turīya*]." (Jaideva Singh, trans. *The Doctrine of Recognition* (1990), pg. 89, fn. 189.)

a reflection in the vast field of Consciousness, as if the forms were and yet, at the same time, were not manifest. In Kshemaraja's own words:

> By penetrating into *bhairavī mudrā,* the yogi observes the vast totality of beings rising from, and dissolving into, the sky of Consciousness, like a series of reflections appearing and disappearing inside a mirror.[175]

In *bhairavī-mudrā,* the yogi feels himself in the changeless space beyond the reach of the continuous sequence of the creation, sustenance, and dissolution of the world. Anchored in this center of deep silence and complete tranquility, freed from the whirlwind of *vikalpas,* he witnesses the sequenced movement, *krama,* of Śiva's cosmic acts, with the expansion and contraction of events, times, spaces, and forms that compose the experience of the world.

Sahaja-samādhi

Baba Muktananda liked to call the highest state *sahaja-samādhi. Sahaja* means, literally, "born with" and refers to that which is natural, innate, and always the same from the beginning. In *sahaja-samādhi,* the yogi rediscovers the illumination that is his or her natural, innate condition. In describing the experience of *sahaja-samādhi,* Baba says:

> It is extraordinary to become anchored in that state in which there is no sense of differences, in which you are not subject to any agitation or change. Even if such a being were to open his eyes and see things, his *samādhi* would not be interrupted. And if he were to close his eyes, his *samādhi* would not be enhanced. If he were to speak, the silence of his mind would not be broken.

> If he were to become silent, he would not be observing a vow of silence any more strictly. Such a being, though living in the body, lives apart from it.[176]

Notice that though this great Siddha speaks of this exalted state in the most accessible and everyday terms, he specifically refers to closed-eyed and open-eyed absorption.

Pratimīlana

It is this same condition, the movement of awareness from internal to external and back again, that is described in the final aphorism of the *Śiva-sūtra: bhuyaḥ syāt pratimīlanam*—"There is, over and over again, divine awareness both inwardly and outwardly."[177] Here, the two forms of absorption in the Self, *nimīlana* and *unmīlana,* unite in one continuous flow of divine knowledge in which all traces of differentiation disappear: *pratimīlana.* Regardless of whether the yogi's eyes are open or closed, his entire being brims with ecstasy in the waking, the dream, and the deep-sleep states alike. In every moment, he knows, *I am God!* Gurumayi speaks of this glorious unity-awareness as both a goal and a means, saying:

> *Pratimīlana* is the song of the soul. The soul wants to be reunited. The *Śiva-dṛṣṭi* says, follow *sādhana* with this awareness, meditate with this awareness: *I am Śiva. My body is Śiva, my senses are Śiva, my mind is Śiva. Everything within me is Śiva. Everything about me is Śiva. Śiva is inside, Śiva is outside. I am Śiva. Śiva is me.* As you practice *sādhana* with this awareness, *pratimīlana* is experienced naturally and spontaneously. When the heart aches, it aches with the longing to be one with Śiva. It is this practice, this awareness that makes it possible.[178]

In the same way that Baba Muktananda used to illustrate the highest state by speaking of his own Guru, Gurumayi talks of the final enlightenment by describing Baba. To describe this state of *pratimīlana,* Gurumayi portrays Baba going through his day repeating "Śiva, Śiva, Śiva. . ." with every breath and in every action. She adds:

> As you practice this awareness—*I am Śiva, I am That I am, I am that Śiva*—you live in the sweet reunion, *pratimīlana.* You live in the body of the Lord.[179]

This ecstatic awareness of union with God is the keynote of yet one more name for the highest state, one that Kshemaraja uses again and again in his commentary to sutra 19, *samāveśa.*

Samāveśa

This is a term particularly characteristic of Kashmir Śaivism. *Āveśa* means "entering, penetrating," and *sama,* of course, can be read here as it is in the word *samādhi*—"equal, alike." *Samāveśa* most specifically means entering the state of Śiva and merging one's awareness with Śiva. With this expansion, the yogi not only knows his own equality with Śiva, he sees all aspects of the world as equal, as expressions of the all-pervasive Śiva.

This equality of vision reminds me of a flight I once took over the frozen landscape of the North Pole. There is only one color in that icy world: white. There are plains of snow and ice floes, there are mounds of ice—and they are all white. Everything is white. Everything made of just one substance: water, which in the process of freezing has carved a world of fantastic forms. I found this vision—this living, waking vision—to be deeply moving. In spite of the persistent roar of the airplane engines, I found that flying over this landscape gave me a sense of majestic calm, an unfathomable serenity. I felt as if I were looking at a visual representation of silence.

The experience of that flight seems to me like a glimmer of the peace that is a hallmark of *samāveśa.* In the equal vision of the highest state, naturally, the world is not frozen and lifeless but is vibrating with the luminous energy that gives form to all—even a tropical scene that is teeming with life. One who is in this state of unity-awareness does perceive the world in the way an ordinary human being does, and yet, as Baba Muktananda describes it, he also perceives the luminous bliss that permeates the world in all its intricacies. Baba once told a packed auditorium of his students that as he looked at us, what he saw was our forms as blue light. He added:

> God has granted me the vision by which I see everything with a slightly bluish tinge. In India there is a plant that grows wild in the field, and it produces small, light blue flowers. That is the color of my eyes. In the scriptures this is called the lotion of Consciousness. Tukaram Maharaj said that when this lotion of Consciousness was applied to his eyes, he could really see. First his vision was limited, and then it expanded. When it expanded he could not see the world as world any longer. He could not see people as sinners or as wicked; he could see only God's light everywhere, and everyone appeared to him to be the light of God.[180]

With this expansion of vision, of perception, as with all of these astonishing states of bliss that we have been discussing, there is no return. The impressions of *samādhi* settle indelibly in the mind and, as Kshemaraja tells us—as countless great sages tell us—our identity with Consciousness then becomes *nityodita,* "always new."

20

Mastery over the Vibrant Wheel of Powers

Sutra 20

तदा प्रकाशानन्द-
सारमहामन्त्रवीर्यात्मकपूर्णाहन्तावेशात्सदा
सर्वसर्गसंहारकारिनिजसंविद्देवताचक्रेश्वरता-
प्राप्तिर्भवतीति शिवम्

tadā prakāśānanda-
sāra-mahāmantra-vīryātmaka-pūrṇāhantāveśāt sadā
sarva-sarga-saṃhāra-kāri-nija-saṃvid
devatā-cakreśvaratā-prāptir bhavatīti śivam

Then, by entering the perfect I-ness,
whose nature is the potency of the great mantra
and the essence of the bliss of the light of Consciousness,
one attains lordship over the
wheel of the deities of Consciousness
that carry out all manifestation and reabsorption.
This is Śiva.

tadā:	then
prakāśa:	the light of Consciousness
ānanda:	bliss
sāra:	essence
mahā-mantra:	the great mantra
vīrya:	potency
ātmaka:	made of
pūrṇa:	full, perfect, complete
ahantā:	I-ness
veśāt:	by entering
sadā:	always
sarva:	all
sarga:	creation, manifestation
saṃhāra:	reabsorption
kāri:	doer
nija:	one's own
saṃvid:	Consciousness
devatā:	deities
cakra:	wheel
īśvaratā:	lordship
prāptiḥ:	attainment
bhavati:	occurs, takes place
iti:	this
śivam:	Śiva, the ultimate Reality

ONCE AFTER SEVERAL WEEKS of satsangs and workshops in Mexico, Gurumayi took a group of her students on a day trip, a little pilgrimage, to the basilica of the Virgin of Guadalupe. I'd visited this shrine of the patron saint of Mexico several times before. For me this deity represents not only the religious forms of my childhood, but also the Goddess Citiśakti of my current life path. The painting of the Virgin, framed as it is in silver and hung on a wall covered with gold leaf, seems to be surrounded by light. It always appears to me that she looks with compassion on all who come before her. On this particular visit, after paying our respects to the deity, our party sat on a pew to meditate. I closed my eyes and silently prayed, *O Mother, please grant me strength. Grant me faith and devotion so that I can serve my Guru. Grant me the ability to be open-hearted so that I can help others. Grant me wisdom. Grant me liberation.*

On our return drive, Gurumayi asked me, "Did you pray to the Virgin?" I said that I had, and she said, "What did you ask for?" I recounted my list of requests, and Gurumayi replied, "Poor lady! She's going to be very busy with you." Everyone in the car began to laugh. I felt a little uncomfortable, but I knew that some teaching would be coming my way soon, so I waited. Then Gurumayi turned to me once again and, very gently, she said, "Why didn't you ask just for liberation? With that, you obtain everything."[181]

With liberation comes everything: Gurumayi's observation is an exquisite summation of Kshemaraja's final statement in his exposition on the yoga of recognition, *Pratyabhijñā-hṛdayam.* In sutra 20, Kshemaraja tells us that with the attainment of liberation (or, in his words, "lasting *samādhi*") come all powers, all attainments—lordship over the deities of the wheel of Consciousness. Before turning to this intrinsically fascinating image of the wheel, I'd like to revisit some, by now, familiar notions. For in this final aphorism, Kshemaraja has, in the manner that we discussed in sutra 7, invoked key concepts and images that he's already introduced: the perfect I-consciousness (*pūrṇāhantā* or *pūrṇo'ham*) and the blissful effulgence (*prakāśānanda*).

Full I-Consciousness

In his commentary on sutra 20, Kshemaraja quotes the following passage from Utpaladeva to describe the total sovereignty of the yogi who has achieved the highest state:

> Resting all objective experience within one's Self is what is meant by the awareness "I am." This "resting" is called sovereignty of will, primary doership, and lordship because of the cancellation of all relational awareness and dependence on anything outside one's Self.[182]

Aham, the awareness "I am" that has been threaded through this text, is identified here by Utpaladeva as the same as having all objective experience within one's essential being. He says that this knowledge, that everything rests in one's own Self, naturally brings with it the powers of Śiva—the freedom to do and create anything. In the simplest terms, the sage is saying that when all a yogi depends on and relates to is contained in an inviolable and steady sense of "I am," he is, indeed, the Lord.

For me, the key to sutra 20 is contained in the phrase *pūrṇāhantāveśāt,* "by merging in the full I-consciousness."* *Pūrṇa* denotes perfection: that which is full, complete, accomplished.

We could say that *pūrṇa* completes us, bestowing upon us the fruition of the longing of the soul. The sutra says that the essence of *pūrṇāhantāveśāt* is the blissful and resplendent light *(prakāśānanda)* that gives rise to all forms and all perception, and it is also the potency of the great mantra *(mahāmantra-vīryātmaka).* You could say that the great *(mahā)* mantra, the eternal pulsation, is yet another name for the awareness known as *aham.* In fact, the *mahāmantra* is *aham,* and according to Abhinavagupta, all the powers of *mātṛkā-śakti,* which we discuss in sutra 12 as the evolutionary forces in the universe, arise from these two syllables, *aham.* The *"a,"* which is also the first letter of the Sanskrit alphabet, represents Śiva (the supreme Subject), and the *"ha,"* which is the last

* *Ahantā* is an abstract noun that can be rendered in English as "I-ness."

letter, represents Śakti (the creative power by which the Subject acts). Between these two sounds are arrayed all the phonemes of *mātṛkā-śakti* that mark the various aspects of Consciousness becoming both the universe and the languages by which we understand that universe. The symbol for the nasal sound *"ṃ"* is represented in Devanagarī script as a dot or point *(bindu)*,* and represents the united Śiva and Śakti as the subtle resonance of our own Self. Thus with three concise sounds, Abhinavagupta has codified all pulsations of the supreme heart of Consciousness.[183]

Kshemaraja explains the connections in this way:

> All embracing I-ness *[pūrṇāhantā]* is the mistress of all the letters from [the first] *"a"* to [the last] *"kṣa,"*** which, as the absolute power of unstruck sound, it contains and encapsulates. Thus it is a pure immutable awareness even though it has absorbed into itself every cycle of creation and destruction in the play of the Wheel of Energies, constituting the unfolding cosmic order of countless words and all they denote. It *[aham]* is the supreme level of speech, the great unspoken mantra which, eternally manifest, is the life of all beings. Here *** it is called the vibration of the Lord because it unfolds pulsating within one's own being as does the movement of this divine universe.[184]

While I would prefer not to oversimplify the final sutra, to my mind what Kshemaraja says here seems extremely fundamental: The I-consciousness, the pulsation of being that is the very ground of our

* The term *bindu* also refers to the *nīlabindu* (Blue Pearl).

** For Kshemaraja the compound phoneme *"kśa,"* which normally follows the last Sanskrit letter, indicates the end of the expansion process.

*** The word "here" refers to the Spanda School.

existence, is the one significant focus for *sādhana.* All else rests upon it—and this is Śiva.

It seems to me that this statement, the summation of the teachings we've received from Kshemaraja in this text, is irrefutable. Certainly, it encapsulates my own understanding of the spiritual path. If I were to put that understanding into one word, it would be this: *aham.* That covers it all.

Since I began to meditate and investigate my inner world, I've undergone tremendous personal transformation. Besides the obvious changes to my life circumstance and the level of my spiritual commitment, there have been improvements in my character, a quieting of my mind, a refinement of my intellect, an expansion of love, and more. Over the years, I've had insights into universal truths, challenges to my views of reality, and astonishing glimpses of subtle realms. Yet with all of these attainments and experiences—which are to me more precious than rare gemstones—there is one awareness that threads through and holds them together: the pulsation of my own being. Everything in *sādhana* points back to that one vibration: the perfectly full "I am," *aham,* the heart of my being. From this one, transcendental heart, comes all the potency *(vīrya)* of the universe. Abhinavagupta writes:

> For one immersed in such an uncreated heart, no matter what he does, how he breathes and thinks, everything is considered [mantra] recitation.[185]

The uncreated heart, the pulse that exists prior to creation, is itself the origin of all worlds, all beings, all things both subtle and manifest; and the one who is immersed in this primal vibration is himself a living scripture.

Bhagawan Nityananda was not a teacher in the most familiar sense of that word, and yet his immersion in the primordial pulsation of being was, from the accounts of people who spent time in his presence, absolute and total. The vibrations of pure Consciousness emanated so strongly from this holy being that his devotees would spend days traveling to his ashram in Ganeshpuri for the opportunity to stand just for a moment in his presence. Though Bhagawan Nityananda often spoke to those who came, very little of what he said was recorded at the time, and so very few of his teachings have survived. One that is dependably his echoes the seminal instruction of this sutra:

> The heart is the hub of all sacred places; go there and roam.[186]

Bhagawan Nityananda speaks here of the transcendental heart, the pulsation that underlies our lives, and by calling it a "hub," he's intimating that the heart is the center, the focal point, of the wheel of Consciousness.

The Wheel of Consciousness

When I envisage the wheel of energies, the wheel of Consciousness, I think of the sunflowers that grow in my homeland. In the Spanish language, the sunflower is known as a *girasol,* literally "sun-turner." This is a reference to the sunflower's almost magical ability to pivot its massive head as much as 180 degrees in one day so that it is always facing the sun. A field of sunflowers faces east at dawn and west at sunset, just as the wheel of energy Kshemaraja refers to in sutra 20 both draws from the light and moves toward it.

While the sutra speaks of one wheel, this should be understood as the primary wheel, the *cakra* of *cakras,* rather than the *only* wheel—for the created universe is full of *cakras,* of wheels and cycles of all kinds. In the Indian tradition, life itself is seen as a wheel, the wheel of *saṃsāra,* of recurring birth and death. The Indian sages represent history in terms of cycles, with each age giving rise to the next and the sequence of ages coming around again in an immense, ordered progression. We can all see that, in our own lives, there are the cycles of the seasons and the round of holidays that constitute our year. Closer to Kshemaraja's point are the planets of a solar system, which, each on its own axis, circle the sun. The energies of living tissue function in much the same way: there are constellations of atoms, each with its own system of protons and neutrons held in their orbits by an all-powerful nucleus.

The turning of the wheel can be viewed as an archetypal movement of life, and it is a particularly compelling symbol when applied to the circle that Kshemaraja is invoking in sutra 20: the whirling vortex of energies that constitute the subtle human system. This wheel is composed of four concentric circles around the Self, which is its heart. The innermost circle is related to the individual perceiver; the next circle is the psychic instrument; the next is the senses; and the outermost is connected with external objects. The sutra says that, once we are established in the heart of Consciousness as a result of lasting *samādhi,* we secure the attainment *(prāpti)* that bestows sovereignty over the deities of the wheel of powers *(saṃvid devatā-cakreśvaratā).* These deities represent the instruments and energies that bring to fruition the processes of emanation and reabsorption of the universe and make possible our lives as individuals.

Kshemaraja has a particular interest in the esoteric expressions of the Krama School, according to which the forces that generate our bodies and the world are grouped in wheels or clusters of energies. The sage has built upon his own Guru's image of *aham,* portraying it as the *mahāmantra* at the center of an array of powers, ordered in circles and able to create, maintain, and dissolve our individual existence. Thus, the awareness "I am" is the nucleus of this wheel of Consciousness, this *citi-cakra,* with all the powers of the universe whirling round at its command.

So mighty is the "I am" for Kshemaraja that he personifies this force as a goddess, calling her Vāmeśvarī, the power that commands all the other powers, the great Goddess of Consciousness who creates from her very being the forms of the universe. The name Vāmeśvarī is sometimes associated by commentators with the root *vam,* which is "to emit, project, expel." Vāmeśvarī, the central deity of the wheel of *citi-cakra,* emits the universe from her own essence, which is of course the luminous resonance of "I am."Reigning within the heart of the circle of powers, Vāmeśvarī embodies the silent and immutable depths of the Great Void, from which all the movements of the *spanda* arise; the sequence of events as well as eternity itself all abide within her vast cosmic order. The deities of Consciousness, *saṃvid-devatā,* radiate from and revolve around the heart of the supreme Goddess, each carrying out her own sphere of functions, the sum of which is our reciprocal relation with our world.* The pulsations

* In describing the *saṃvid-devatā* revolving around the goddess Vāmeśvarī, the tradition speaks of four distinct circles of energies from which our entire existence as individuals is projected. In describing these "certain dynamic forms of Śakti, who is known in different spheres by different names," Swami Muktananda writes, "When she moves in the inner sky of Consciousness, she is called Khecarī. When she moves through the fourfold psychic instrument, she is known as Gocarī. When she moves in different directions [through the sense organs], she is Dikcarī. And when she moves on the earth [creating various objects], she is known as Bhūcarī." (Swami Muktananda, *Nothing Exists That Is Not Śiva* (1997), p. 25).

vibrate from the axes of the divine wheel, emanating from and returning to the center like the rhythm of the human heart.

Every human being in the universe is an embodiment of this vibrant wheel of powers, a microcosm of the divine order. By understanding these phenomena, a seeker begins to comprehend not only how the disparate forces of the universe all emanate from the one *śakti* but also how, in mastering these forces, a yogi can achieve universal mastery. These circles of powers intertwine in our lives, creating a huge matrix of vibrational frequencies that pulsate with vitality and creative potential. The events of our personal lives, and, no less, the movements of human history, take form from the continuous interactions among the forces of these conscious circles.

The name Vāmeśvarī is also associated with *vāmācāra,* which means "the reverse, the opposite course," which I have always associated with the establishment of identities in us that are contrary to the Truth. This power thereby deceives us into ignorance of who we truly are. With Vāmeśvarī's formidable array of forces working to hide the universal pervasion of Consciousness, we become the puppets of our fears and desires. The *tattvas* associated with these power-bearing *cakras* are accompanied by their respective forces. These forces are none other than the phonemes composing *mātṛkā.* It is *mātṛkā,* you may recall, that fosters delusion, contracting into the three bodies with their respective states of awareness and giving rise to thoughts and articulated speech that are filled with ignorance. Whirling within the constrictive circles of Vāmeśvarī and her forces, we, thus, throw ourselves into *saṃsāra,* the cycle of life and death.

This cycle of "reversal" is turned around once again, however, once we have embarked on the road to enlightenment—the road to recognition. Then the Goddess reveals her benevolent face as the grace-bestowing power. Her circles of energies begin to work to restore to us the vision of Śiva, and the accompanying *mātṛkā-śakti* creates thoughts that allow us to enter the realm of light.*

Thus, depending on how we identify with these forces emanating from the one Śakti, the wheel of powers can be the source of either bondage or liberation. Bondage arises from attachment to our individual appearance and mental concepts, to our words and interrelations with people and incidents of life. Liberation is to experience those very things as the play of Consciousness. The core of this experience, as Kshemaraja explains it, consists of fusion with the divine effulgence:

> Nothing can manifest unless it enters the light of the highest Reality. And the highest Lord is full of the flow of bliss, because he is free from all desire, because he is fully perfect, because he is the essence of absolute freedom, and because he has attained to the state of full universal ecstasy. He has made his own the entire world consisting of word and indicated object, by reflecting on the entire assemblage of illumined words from "*a*" to "*kṣa*."[187]

One who has entered the vast heart of Consciousness and has become united with it, has become the Lord of the Wheel *(cakravartī)* and rules the deities that emanate and reabsorb the entire universe. In Kshemaraja's view:

* The yogi who has achieved mastery over these energies ceases to be deluded by them. For the one who is their lord, they become liberating powers: *khecarī* allows the Self to roam the vast expanse of Consciousness without restriction; *gocarī* affirms the understanding that everything is only one essence; *dikcarī* perceives objects as identical to Consciousness; and *bhūcarī* supports the experience of the world as part of our Self.

> He who has become the independent ruler of the *citi-cakra* and the great Lord, being served by the groups of deities, is a rare being who surpasses all.[188]

The Recognition of Our Own Heart

At the beginning of his *Īśvara-pratyabhijñā-kārikā,* the inspiration for the text we've been studying, Utpaladeva clarifies the purpose of these teachings:

> Having somehow attained the position of a servant of the great Lord Maheśvara, and being now desirous to do [the greatest] good to other people as well, I am presently expounding the doctrine of his recognition; that is, on one hand, the source of the attainment of all affluence of divine powers [literally riches] and that can, on the other hand, be achieved through the attainment of such divine affluence.[189]

Utpaladeva, having attained the goal of yoga, says that he wishes to serve by sharing his insight with others: Everything comes from one's recognition of the Great Lord, Śiva. With that recognition, we attain mastery over the innumerable powers natural to the Lord, enjoying the same sovereignty as the Lord himself.

Recognition arises when our cognitive understanding of the Lord's glorious nature and our mystical experience of our own Self come together in a flash, in a moment of revelation, and we know: *I am God.* The difference between the intellectual understanding and the experience of recognition lies in having full *aiśvarya,* lordship, over the powers that, in and of themselves, make us identical to the Supreme Lord. Such is the splendor of recognition!

Now we have come full circle, returning to the evocative term that provides a name for the core of teachings we've been contemplating: *pratyabhijñā.* To look at this word, etymologically, as we have at so many others, can give us a greater understanding of its full import. The Sanskrit prefix *prati* means "again, toward, back, in return"; *abhi* has a similar connotation, indicating "going toward, approaching"; and *jñā* means "to know." So, the word *abhijñā* could be defined as "to approach knowledge" and in this sense *pratyabhijñā* clearly conveys a return toward knowledge.

Given our course of study, we might ask, *What is it that returns to knowledge? What is it that seeks to remember? What is the act of remembering? And what is the nature of that knowledge that's remembered?*

As we said in the very beginning, in the entire universe there is one knower, one knowledge, and one known. *Pratyabhijñā,* then, is the knowledge of the knower turning back to know itself. The light of the Self reflects on itself, always turning to its own rapturous presence as the only knowledge that exists. In the impeccable space of our own heart, love adores love, bliss revels in bliss, light shines on light, every action is an act of worship, and all perceptions are forms of meditation. Not having to depend on anything other than our Self, we can live immersed in complete freedom and overflowing fullness. For us, the world can appear as the play of light and shadow enacted by *citiśakti.*

Thanks to the powerful grace of this self-reflective vibration at the heart of Consciousness, the efforts we make to return to the knowledge of our own Self do bear fruit. As a yogic practice, *pratyabhijñā* involves a persistent and steady return of our awareness, over and again, to the ever-present movement of the *spanda* that vibrates in all our actions and all our thoughts. In my own practice, I experience recognition as an alert and vital sweetness, an actual inner sensation, that reminds me of the free and playful energy that is the driving force behind all that I know and do. This power expresses itself through the veil of my personality and character traits, and these do sometimes inspire me to speak or act nonsensically. There are other times when this power is unfiltered, and then it radiates from me, literally pours out, as pure love, as love that takes delight in my own existence and in everything and everyone else's.

Throughout this book I've specified various practices as aids in approaching the sublime experience. The most significant of these, the practice that we have turned to again and again, is the remembrance of the essential "I am" that pulsates as our very heart.

We translated the title of Kshemaraja's text as *The Heart of Recognition,* and this seems serviceable since he clearly intended to expound on the core of the teachings on recognition as taught by Utpaladeva. At the same time, it occurs to me that Kshemaraja has left us a little room for interpretation. In his title, the sage joins the words *pratyabhijñā* and *hṛdayam* without a verb to connect them, and this very association gives the two words equal weight. Thus, *The Heart of Recognition* could just as easily be called *The Recognition That IS the Heart*—for this is the essence of the sage's approach and of the *sādhana* he describes. It may also be construed as *The Heart That Is Recognition,* for the heart does consist solely of a state of recognition.[190]

Kshemaraja ends sutra 20 with the observation, *iti śivam,* "This is Śiva," and writes toward the end of his commentary:

> The word *iti* in the sutra connotes conclusion. The word *Śiva* in the sutra means that whatever is the body of the above text is Śiva, because it is a means to the attainment of Śiva. It is Śiva also because it has come from Śiva, because it is not different from the true nature of Śiva, and because it is indeed Śiva.[191]

With this message the *Pratyabhijñā-hṛdayam* comes to a rapid close. The sage ends by giving us his blessing—*śubham astu,* "Let there be prosperity!"[192] As the term *śubham* conveys a sense of splendor and beauty, auspiciousness and goodness, Kshemaraja is saying a great deal here. I feel it is his wish that the teachings contained herein inspire in us an overflowing abundance, a recognition of Consciousness, and the certainty that we are, in truth, Śiva, the Lord.

And because it is my experience and firm conviction that all such exalted attainments come through the grace of one's spiritual teacher, I close my commentary with my own blessing for the reader—"Triumph to the true Guru, the great sovereign!"

Sadgurunāth mahārāj kī jay!

Epilogue

On a Visit to Kashmir

IN SEPTEMBER 1982, in the last month of his life, Baba Muktananda took a final pilgrimage to Kashmir in northernmost India, to the mountainous terrain that was home to the sages of Kashmir Śaivism. Baba said that he arranged this trip so that he could show Gurumayi the birthplace of the philosophy he so loved. I was fortunate enough to be among the dozen or so people accompanying Baba and Gurumayi.

We were driving through the Kashmiri flatlands, I recall, along avenues bordered by graceful poplars, when we saw a lofty mountain with pine-forested hillsides and icy peaks. Someone said, "That is Mahadeva Mountain," and I could feel a thrill of excitement in my heart. According to tradition among Kashmiri scholars, it was at the base of Mahadeva Mountain in the ninth century that the sage Vasugupta was directed in a dream to a massive boulder. As he stood before it, the rock overturned as if by divine will and revealed, inscribed on its underside, the seventy-seven aphorisms that comprise the seminal text of this system, the *Śiva-sūtra.*

The boulder itself was wide and tremendously high, about the size of a one-bedroom cottage, and it stood just at the edge of a sparkling brook. At Baba's direction, we mounted this rock and, for the next several hours, we sat atop it in the brilliant morning sunlight, chanting various Śaiva scriptures. I have always thought it significant that Baba had us begin by singing the twenty sutras of the *Pratyabhijñā-hṛdayam.*

In Kashmir, we frequently went on outings to places sacred to the Śaiva tradition. We visited the *Śiva-sūtra* rock a number of times; we went to Parimahal, which is where the sage Maheshvarananda received the revelation that became his great work, the *Mahārtha-mañjarī;* and we also saw various Śaiva and Śakta temples in the area. In one of these temples, there is a large *Śiva-liṅgam,* an emblematic image of Śiva in the form of a stone about a foot and a half thick, which is not mounted on a pedestal but stands alone in the temple garden. It is called the Kaliṅgam; in the Kashmiri language, the word *ka* means "eleven." The custom here is to gather eleven people who put their index fingers under the rock as lightly as possible and then, concentrating intently, repeat, *"ka, ka, ka"*—and together lift the rock, each using only one finger. We did this several times, and each time we lifted the rock—waist high! It was light as a feather.

When we were in Kashmir, a couple of us started joking about trying to lift the *Śiva-sūtra* rock with a car jack, and someone reported this conversation to Baba. At first he laughed. Then his mood shifted, and he said to me, "You cannot lift the *Śiva-sūtra* rock in that way. Only Lord Śiva is able to lift that rock." He paused, and added, "The sutras are there." [193] I have no doubt that in this moment, Baba was referring to all levels of subtlety; he was saying that the sutras are physically etched on the underside of that rock and that they live as a beacon to guide us on our inner journey. To this day, I continue to be inspired by his implicit faith in the veracity of the scriptures.

At one point, Lakshman Joo, who is thought to have been the last of the lineage of the Kashmiri Śaiva scholars, paid a visit to Baba. It was clear from the way Baba greeted him—the way he pulled him close and hugged him and wrapped him in a beautiful warm shawl—that he had great respect for Lakshman Joo and gratitude for all that he had done for Kashmir Śaivism. Lakshman Joo embodied the teachings and preserved them and had presented them to countless people over the years.

Baba and Lakshman Joo spoke in Hindi, so I couldn't make out much of the conversation, and yet from the names I recognized—Parimahal, Maheshvarananda, Vasugupta—I knew they were discussing the Śaiva sages of old and the holy sites they had left, places we had been visiting with Baba in the preceding days. The other thing I could hear in the conversation, in the very timbre of their voices, was their enthusiasm for the subject and the deep affection of one philosopher for another, an exchange of love in which it seemed to me that all levels of creation, from the highest to the most elemental, are known in the moment and are recognized, blissfully, for what they truly are.

In the words of Utpaladeva:

> I roar! Oh, and I dance!
> My heart's desires are fulfilled
> Now that you, Lord,
> Infinitely splendid,
> Have come to me.
>
> In that state, O Lord,
> Where nothing else is to be known or done,
> Neither yoga
> Nor intellectual understanding
> Is to be sought after,
> For the only thing that remains and flourishes
> Is absolute Consciousness.
>
> Whose voice ever rings
> With the eternal sound *Śiva*
> Escapes spontaneously
> The cruel grip of undefeatable, endless sorrows.[194]

This sublime perspective of the sage is available to us all.

Appendix A

The Lineage of Masters:

Guru-paramparā

IN MOST SPIRITUAL TRADITIONS OF INDIA, knowledge is transmitted through a *guru-paramparā*, a lineage of masters. The term *paramparā* means, literally, "uninterrupted row," implying that each successive master has received the capability to fulfill that function from the one who preceded him or her in the lineage. The authority of a spiritual master is thus founded on tradition. When you consider that a Guru is one who can awaken students' spiritual potential, impart unity awareness to them, and guide them in assimilating these principles of universal oneness in even the most minute aspects of their lives—guide them to a state of full God-realization—then it's clear that this is a role requiring arduous preparation and rigorous testing. The establishment of an individual on the seat of a spiritual *paramparā* implies a passage of power that links that individual to an established line of masters and, through them, to the supreme Power. As Baba Muktananda once said in reply to a question about the need for a spiritual lineage, "How can you have a son without a father?"[195] Elsewhere, he said:

> All the power lies in the lineage. If you trace the line of the Siddhas back to its source you find that it is Maheśa, the Supreme Being, who is the source, the primal Lord from whom all the Siddhas, all the true Gurus have descended.
>
> While describing the nature of the Supreme Being, the sages say that the Supreme Being is the One from whom this universe emanates, the One who becomes the universe, who unfolds the universe, who, in spite of becoming the universe, remains immutable, and who in his innermost nature is pure consciousness and bliss. This primal Lord, this Supreme Being is the original Guru, the primal Guru, and all other Gurus have descended from him.[196]

This tradition of the *guru-paramparā* exists in spiritual paths throughout the world—in Japan, China, Turkey, Egypt, Morocco, and historically in Tibet and throughout the Middle East—and many of these, it seems, trace their lines, as Baba does, right back to the supreme Power or to a transcendental state. This is certainly true in India and in the two distinct *guru-paramparās* to which we refer in the preceding pages: that of the Siddha Yoga tradition and of the Pratyabhijñā School. In order to provide a proper context for understanding this book, I will say a bit more here about each of these lineages.

The Pratyabhijñā Lineage

In the final chapter of his *Śiva-dṛṣṭi,* the ninth-century sage Somananda mentions the various masters of what became the lineage of the Kashmiri Śaiva Pratyabhijñā School. Somananda traces the origin of this lineage to Śiva who, at the onset of the present age of Kali Yuga, appeared as Śrīkanthanātha (the Lord of the Auspicious Blue Throat) to the sage Durvasas. Śrīkanthanātha gave the sage the power of *śaktipāta-dīkṣā,* enabling him to initiate students by a direct bestowal of divine grace, and out of compassion for humankind entering into darker times, he also dictated to Durvasas the Śaiva Āgamas, the scriptures that were the basis for the text we have been studying here. Of these texts, those in the nondualist current were called the sixty-four Bhairava Tantras, all of which make the point that God has both created and become the universe and everything in it. In the words of the twentieth-century sage Lakshman Joo, who claims direct descent from this lineage:

> Śrīkanthanātha told him [Durvasas] that he was to expand the thought of the Bhairava Tantras in all of the universe without restriction to caste, colour, or creed.[197]

Following Durvasas, these teachings of nondualism and the power of granting divine initiation were passed on to nineteen masters in succession until the line reached Somananda, who is the first of this lineage to be quoted in these pages. Somananda initiated Utpaladeva, who was succeeded in turn by Lakshmanagupta. Abhinavagupta, who belonged to a different though related *paramparā,* received the teachings of Pratyabhijñā from Lakshmanagupta and passed them on to his disciple Kshemaraja, the author of the text we're studying here.[198]

The Siddha Yoga Lineage

The Siddha masters belong to a *guru-paramparā* originating in Lord Śiva personified as Maheśa, as Baba Muktananda says earlier, or as Paramaśiva (Supreme Śiva) or Ādiguru (the primordial master), as Baba says elsewhere. He indicates that this line of Siddha masters includes some of the most brilliant exponents of the sacred tradition of India: Vasishtha, Vyasa, Suka Muni, Gaudapada, and others. As it can happen with a lineage where the primary transmission is the inner awakening itself, the manifestation of this *paramparā* becomes at times almost impossible to trace historically, as the initiation can come in a dream or in meditation from a Siddha operating from another plane of existence. Writing of this tradition, one Western scholar has said that, at its heart, the Siddha lineage is a mystical concept of connection to the primordial Guru, Śiva:

> In this sense, the connection to the siddha lineage is one that occurs atemporally and even ahistorically. It is the assertion of a mystical and synchronic connection to Śiva as the fountainhead of all siddhas, a connection that occurs at every instant, both within and beyond time. In this sense, a true siddha experiences a direct linkage to the foundational source of the lineage, here understood or personified as the deity Śiva, symbolic of the absolute Consciousness itself.[199]

The line of Siddhas apparently disappears for some length of time, resurging in the twentieth and twenty-first centuries with the three contemporary Gurus of what has come to be known as the Siddha Yoga lineage.

Swami Chidvilasananda

The living Siddha Yoga master is Swami Chidvilasananda, who is widely known as Gurumayi. The name Gurumayi means "one who embodies the Guru." Born in the South Indian state of Karnataka in 1955, Gurumayi met her Guru, Swami Muktananda, at the age of five, and from that point forward, he played an active role in guiding her education, both secular and scriptural. For the last eight years of Baba Muktananda's life, Gurumayi served as his translator, forging a bridge of understanding between him and his thousands of Western students in his private meetings with them, his public lectures, and his books.

Gurumayi took monastic vows in May 1982, and when Baba Muktananda died in October of that year, she began to carry on his work—until, ultimately, she transformed and expanded it into a far-reaching mission with a *rasa,* a flavor, of her own. Gurumayi is a *śaktipāta-guru,* and in her global broadcast Intensives, she gives spiritual initiation to seekers by the thousands, to seekers all over the world. Through her lectures and books, Gurumayi translates the essential teachings of India's subtlest philosophies into words that are accessible to modern minds, inspiring hundreds of thousands of her students to bring these profound teachings into every aspect of their lives.

Years ago, in a conversation with a group of her students, Gurumayi made an aphoristic statement that has stayed with me ever since. She said, "Siddha Yoga is about learning and serving." I've pondered these words and have come to the conclusion that the sort of study Gurumayi was speaking of involves the examination of one's own heart and that for her, true service is the willingness to be transformed by that exploration, to let one's own love inspire all of one's words and actions. In *My Lord Loves a Pure Heart,* a collection of her talks, Gurumayi has said:

> In every respect, from the ordinary to the sublime, the quality of your heart is what matters most. To live a decent life you have to have a good heart. If you want to know God, you have to have a heart that is pure as well as steady, one that is capable of holding grace and never wavers from its purpose. Even after the physical body perishes, truly, the heart is what lives on.[200]

Gurumayi is enormously creative in guiding her students. She is always finding new means of presentation, so that not only do seekers hear or read her timeless teachings, but also we translate them into our own words and actions, and ultimately we hold them as beacons to illumine and transform the dark corners of our minds. Gurumayi gives lectures, and she also writes poetry, composes music, and sings; she presents the teachings to people from every walk of life and from every culture, and she also spends much of her time working with children and young adults, teaching them through drama and music, through stories and the visual arts.

Under Gurumayi's influence, the Siddha Yoga ashrams have become places of retreat for spiritual practice and study, offering refuge to people engaged in meeting the demands of modern urban life. She established The PRASAD Project to assist those in need in India, Mexico, the United States, Australia, France, Italy, and Spain with medical and dental care and community development. Gurumayi also created the Muktabodha Indological Research Institute, dedicated to preserving and disseminating the sacred texts and religious traditions of India.

Swami Muktananda

Siddha Yoga meditation was introduced in the West—and, in fact, the name "Siddha Yoga" was first applied to this lineage—by Swami Muktananda, who occupied the seat of the Siddha Yoga Guru from 1961 to 1982. Born in 1908, also in the region of Karnataka, he left home in his early teens, becoming a monk and wandering as a sadhu, a mendicant, across the entire length and breadth of India several times, traveling mostly on foot. For more than a quarter of a century, Swami Muktananda traveled in this way from one ashram to the next so that he could study the scriptures of Vedānta, Yoga, and Śaivism from competent teachers. He was, he said later, always looking for his Guru. It was in 1947 that he received the grace of *śaktipāta* from Bhagawan Nityananda. After nine years of intense *sādhana* under Nityananda's subtle guidance, Baba Muktananda became fully Self-realized, an attainment his Guru proclaimed publicly, calling out, "Swami Muktananda, Swami Muktananda, Swami Muktananda, Swami Muktananda! He is the greatest of all. Hey, he has become supreme Śiva. He has become the supreme Lord."[201]

It was on the express direction of Bhagawan Nityananda, that Baba Muktananda settled near Ganeshpuri and began to build the Siddha Yoga ashram that later would become Gurudev Siddha Peeth. It was also on the command of his Guru that Baba Muktananda took the Siddha Yoga teachings and the gift of *śaktipāta* across India and later, on three international tours, to the West.

Soon after I met him in 1972, Baba said to me, "I'm going to create a meditation revolution. If you like, you can come along and help me." I did accompany him, and for the next ten years, I watched as thousands of people received *śaktipāta* initiation and began to meditate, discovering in themselves the hidden treasure of an expanded *kuṇḍalinī* energy. Baba Muktananda expounded on the subtleties of the spiritual journey in his lectures and in his autobiography, *Play of Consciousness,* where he describes his own process of inner expansion in great detail. Baba did much to bring the precepts of Kashmir Śaivism to the public, presenting it widely in the West, and through his books and lectures, he laid a blueprint for Siddha Yoga practice, establishing the canon of teachings that distinguishes this path.

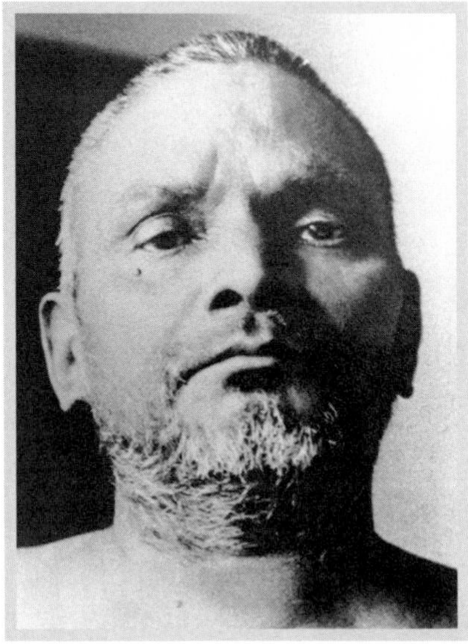

Bhagawan Nityananda

Bhagawan Nityananda is considered the father of the Siddha Yoga path in our present age. An unconventional ascetic, or *avadhūta,* he was born near the end of the nineteenth century in the South Indian state of Kerala. Little is known of his family or his youth, nor is it known who gave him spiritual initiation. According to Baba Muktananda, Bhagawan Nityananda was born in the state of complete illumination.[202] Though he honored the head of the house in which he was reared as his Guru, Nityananda was already perfectly illumined and so he must have had a master before entering this world. Bhagawan Nityananda was an example of what the sage Abhinavagupta calls a *saṃsiddhika-guru* (a thoroughly accomplished master), the name given one born as a perfected being with an intuitive knowledge of the meaning of the scriptures.

Nityananda was an extraordinary being, and for this reason people used to call him Bhagawan, which means not only "the lord," but also "adorable" and "divinely glorious." From an early age he began his work as a spiritual master, sharing with villagers his expanded state as well as his power to cure their illnesses and perform miraculous deeds that would benefit their day-to-day lives. Later, he established places to feed village children who would have otherwise gone without sustenance.

In the mid-1930s Bhagawan Nityananda settled at the Tansa River Valley in the state of Maharashtra, a move that led to the eventual growth of the village of Ganeshpuri. Bhagawan Nityananda spoke very little and, except for a loincloth, rarely wore clothing. Despite his simple, rustic appearance, when people approached him, they felt deep peace and many had marvelous experiences of the inner world. His core teaching was, "The heart is the hub of all sacred places; go there and roam." This message perfectly describes what Bhagawan Nityananda represents as a spiritual master: the fundamental need for everyone to go within and access the Self, heart, and center of our life and our universe. To this day, this profound statement continues to be the most essential Siddha Yoga teaching.

Appendix B

The Principles of Creation:

Tattvas

THE COSMOS AND EVERYTHING in it are an expression of Paramaśiva, who assumes form by moving through thirty-four distinct stages of subtlety known as the *tattvas,* or principles of creation. For a more detailed description of this map of Consciousness, please see the commentary on sutra 4. While the thirty-four *tattvas* listed on these two pages and the innumerable forms that arise from them appear to be different, each from the other, in truth they are all only Paramaśiva.

Paramaśiva
Śiva/Śakti ("I/am")

1. *sadāśiva* ("I am this")

2. *īśvara* ("This I am")

3. *śuddha-vidyā* ("I am this; this I am")

4. *māyā* (illusion)

5. *kalā* (limited authorship)

6. *vidyā* (limited knowledge)	7. *rāga* (desire)	8. *kāla* (time)	9. *niyati* (causality, space, form)

10-11. *puruṣa/prakṛti* (individual subject/object)

12. *buddhi* (intellect)

13. *ahaṃkāra* (ego)

14. *manas* (thinking faculty)

15-19. *jñānendriyas*	(powers of sense perception)
ghrāṇendriya	(smelling)
rasanendriya	(tasting)
cakṣurindriya	(seeing)
sparśanendriya	(feeling by touch)
śravanendriya	(hearing)

20-24. *karmendriyas*	(powers of action)
vāgindriya	(speaking)
hastendriya	(handling)
pādendriya	(moving)
pāyvindriya	(elimination)
upasthendriya	(reproduction)

25-29. *tanmātras* (elements of perception)

śabda	*sparśa*	*rūpa*	*rasa*	*gandha*
(sound)	(touch)	(form)	(taste)	(smell)

30-34. *mahā-bhūtas* (gross elements)

ākāśa	*vāyu*	*tejas*	*āpaḥ*	*pṛthivī*
(ether)	(air)	(fire)	(water)	(earth)

Appendix C

The Perceivers: *Pramātās*

THE PERCEIVERS *(pramātās)* are seven categories that include the main experiencing subjects in the universe and describe their modes of perception. Each of these levels of experience is available to a human being.

In the pure creation, the highest three *tattvas,* the perceivers have bodies made of pure Consciousness. In the impure creation, the perceivers have bodies composed of the various principles under *māyā-tattva* that are found at the level where they exist.

The *sakalas,* the least evolved of the perceivers, include not only human beings but also gods and other celestials as well as animals, plants, and minerals. Among the *sakalas,* only those in human bodies are capable of developing knowledge of the Self.

Perceiver	Field of Perception	What is Perceived
śiva-pramātā (knower of Śiva)	Śiva/Śakti	The entire universe as one with the light of Consciousness.
mantra-maheśvara (great lord of mantra)	*sadāśiva-tattva*	The entire universe as vaguely distinct from the Self.
mantreśvara (lord of mantra)	*īśvara-tattva*	The entire universe, even more prominent and more distinct than the Self and yet identical with it.
mantra or ***vidyeśvara*** (lord of knowledge)	*śuddha-vidyā-tattva*	Vast portions of the universe as simultaneously different from and identical with the Self.
vijñānakala (inert in knowledge)	between the pure and impure creations	The universe as separate and different from the Self—possesses knowledge of the Self without the power of agency; has only *āṇava-mala.*
pralayākala (inert in dissolution)	*māyā-tattva*	Only the void of *māyā*—lacks awareness of the Self; has *ānava* and *māyīyā malas,* but no *kārma-mala.*
sakala (embodied)	all *tattvas* under *māyā*	The universe as separate and different from its own body—often lacks knowledge of the Self; usually possesses all three *malas.*

Notes

Introduction (pp. 1–20)

1. Kshemaraja, *Pratyabhijñā-hṛdaya,* trans. Jaideva Singh, *The Doctrine of Recognition: A Translation of the Pratyabhijñā-hṛdayam* (Albany: SUNY Press, 1990), pp. 42–43.
2. Badarayana, *Brahma-sūtra* I.1.3
3. From the author's notes.
4. Gurumayi Chidvilasananda, *Courage and Contentment* (South Fallsburg: SYDA Foundation, 1999), pg. 56. From a talk given on August 2, 1997, in South Fallsburg, New York.
5. Swami Muktananda, from a talk given on January 21, 1981; unpublished transcript.
6. Swami Muktananda, *Siddha Path,* September 1978, p. 9.
7. Gurumayi Chidvilasananda, *Resonate with Stillness* (South Fallsburg: SYDA Foundation, 1995), quote for February 21.
8. From the author's notes.
9. Abhinavagupta, *Īśvara-pratyabhijñā-kārikā-vimarśinī,* comm. on verse 1; trans. K. C. Pandey, *Doctrine of Divine Recognition* Vol. III (Delhi: Motilal Banarsidass, 1954), pp. 6-7.
10. Kshemaraja, *Pratyabhijñā-hṛdayam,* introductory prayer from *Shri Rudram: Namakam, Chamakam and Shiva Ārati* (South Fallsburg: SYDA Foundation, 1989).

Sutra 1 (pp. 21–44)

11. Swami Muktananda, *From the Finite to the Infinite* (South Fallsburg: SYDA Foundation, 1994), p. 28.
12. Gurumayi Chidvilasananda, *Smile, Smile, Smile!* (South Fallsburg: SYDA Foundation, 1999), p. 24.
13. Utpaladeva, *Īśvara-pratyabhijñā-kārikā* I.1.4; trans. B. N. Pandit, *Īśvara Pratyabhijñā Kārikā of Utpaladeva: Verses on the Recognition of the Lord* (New Delhi: Publication forthcoming).
14. Punyanandanatha, *Kāma-kalā-vilāsa* v. 2; trans. Sir John Woodroffe, *Kāmakalāvilāsa* (Madras: Ganesh & Co., 1953), p. 6.
15. Gurumayi Chidvilasananda, *The Yoga of Discipline* (South Fallsburg: SYDA Foundation, 1996), p. 80.

16. Swami Muktananda, *Where Are You Going?* (South Fallsburg: SYDA Foundation, 1994), pg. 5.
17. Kshemaraja, *Pratyabhijñā-hṛdayam,* comm. on sutra 1; trans. Jaideva Singh, *The Doctrine of Recognition* (1990), p. 45.
18. Kshemaraja, *Pratyabhijñā-hṛdayam,* comm. on sutra 1; trans. Jaideva Singh, *The Doctrine of Recognition* (1990), p. 46.
19. Swami Muktananda, *Mukteshwari: Aphorisms by Swami Muktananda* (South Fallsburg: SYDA Foundation, 1995), vv. 57, 61.
20. Abhinavagupta, *Paramārtha-sāra,* 26; trans., Douglas Renfrew Brooks, *The Paramārthasāra, or The Essence of Ultimate Reality of the Great Lord, The Master Abhinavagupta* (Rochester: unpublished manuscript).
21. Kshemaraja, *Parāprāveśika,* pp.1–2; trans. Jaideva Singh, *The Doctrine of Recognition* (1990), p. 103, n. 5.
22. Abhinavagupta, *Īśvara-pratyabhijñā-vivṛti-vimarśinī* I, p. 710; trans. Mark S. G. Dyczkowski, *The Doctrine of Vibration: An Analysis of the Practices of Kashmir Śaivism* (Albany: SUNY Press, 1987), p. 63.
23. *Vijñāna-bhairava,* v. 106; trans. Jaideva Singh, *The Doctrine of Recognition* (1990), p. 48.

Sutra 2 (pp. 51–65)

24. *Vijñāna-bhairava,* v. 110; trans. Jaideva Singh, *The Yoga of Delight, Wonder, and Astonishment: A Translation of the Vijñānabhairava* (Delhi: Motilal Banarsidass, 1991), p. 99.
25. Abhinavagupta, *Paramārtha-sāra* v.12–13; trans. Douglas Renfrew Brooks, *The Paramārthasāra* (unpublished manuscript).
26. Swami Muktananda, *Secret of the Siddhas* (South Fallsburg: SYDA Foundation, 1994), p. 111.
27. Swami Muktananda, *Play of Consciousness* (South Fallsburg: SYDA Foundation, 2000), p. 207.
28. Gurumayi Chidvilasananda, from a question and answer session June 5, 1987; unpublished transcript.
29. Swami Chidvilasananda, *Transformation: On Tour with Gurumayi Chidvilasananda, Vol. 3* (South Fallsburg: SYDA Foundation, 1987), p. 276.
30. Jaideva Singh quotes this passage from Abhinavagupta's *Tantrāloka* (3.100) in his Introduction to his commentarial translation of *Pratyabhijñā-hṛdayam: The Doctrine of Recognition* (1990), p. 8.
31. Kshemaraja's comm. on Utpaladeva's *Śiva-stotrāvalī;* trans. Jaideva Singh, *The Doctrine of Recognition* (1990), p. 11.

Sutra 3 (pp. 67–85)

32. I heard Professor Paul E. Muller-Ortega use this term in a talk he gave in 1999 in a course for staff members at Shree Muktananda Ashram in South Fallsburg, New York.
33. *Ābhāsa-vada* is explained throughout books 1 and 2 of Utpaladeva's *Īśvara-pratyabhijñā-kārikā* as the operation of the Lord's two principal forces of manifestation: *jñāna-śakti,* the power of knowledge, and *kriya-śakti,* the power of action.
34. Utpaladeva, *Īśvara-pratyabhijñā-kārikā* 4.1.1; trans. B. N. Pandit, *Īśvara Pratyabhijñā Kārikā of Utpaladeva* (New Delhi: Publication forthcoming).
35. Swami Muktananda, *Secret of the Siddhas* (1994), p. 106.
36. From the author's notes.
37. Utapaladeva, *Īśvara-pratyabhijñā-kārikā* 2.4.1; trans. B. N. Pandit, *Īśvara Pratyabhijñā Kārikā of Utpaladeva* (New Delhi: Publication forthcoming).

Sutra 4 (pp. 87–108)

38. Kshemaraja, *Pratyabhijñā-hṛdayam;* trans. Jaideva Singh, *The Doctrine of Recognition* (1990), p. 53.
39. Swami Lakshman Jee [Joo], *Kashmir Shaivism: The Secret Supreme* (Albany: Universal Shaiva Trust, 1988), p. 1.
40. Abhinavagupta, *Tantrāloka* 4.240–4.243a; Italian trans. Raniero Gnoli, *Luce delle Sacre Scritture [Tantrāloka] di Abhinavagupta,* Classici delle Religioni, seizione prima, Le religioni orientali (Turin: Unione Tipografico-Editrice Torinese, 1972); English trans. Giuliana Haim.
41. Abhinavagupta, *Tantrāloka* 13.110b–13.112a, trans. Paul E. Muller-Ortega, *Meditation Revolution: A History and Theology of the Siddha Yoga Lineage* (South Fallsburg: Agama Press, 1997), p. 440.
42. From Martin Heidegger's note on his title *Holzwege,* which is a term referring to the uncharted paths through a wood; trans. by Julian Young and Kenneth Hayens, *Off the Beaten Track* by Martin Heidegger (Cambridge, England: Cambridge University Press, 2002).
43. Utpaladeva describes the seven *pramātās,* or perceivers, in book 3 of *Īśvara-pratyabhijñā-kārikā;* trans. B. N. Pandit, *Īśvara Pratyabhijñā Kārikā of Utpaladeva* (New Delhi: Publication forthcoming).
44. Abhinavagupta, *Para-triṃśikā-vivaraṇa,* trans. Mark S. G. Dyczkowski, *The Doctrine of Vibration* (1987), p. 88.
45. *Śiva-sūtra* 3.14; translation in Swami Muktananda, *Nothing Exists That Is Not Śiva: Commentaries on the Śiva Sūtra, Vijñānabhairava, Gurugītā, and Other Sacred Texts* (South Fallsburg: SYDA Foundation, 1997), p. 44.

46. *Maitrī Upaniṣad* 6.7–8; trans. S. Radhakrishnan, *The Principal Upaniṣads* (Atlantic Highlands: Humanities Press, 1978), pp. 821–22.

Sutra 5 (pp. 109–126)

47. Kshemaraja, *Pratyabhijñā-hṛdayam;* trans. Jaideva Singh, *The Doctrine of Recognition* (1990), p. 56.
48. Swami Muktananda, *Nothing Exists That Is Not Śiva* (1997), p. 53.
49. Gurumayi Chidvilasananda, from a talk given June 10, 1984; unpublished transcript.
50. *Spanda-kārikā* vi, p. 164; trans. Mark S. G. Dyczkowski, *The Doctrine of Vibration* (1987), p. 126.
51. See Kshemaraja's commentary on aphorisms 8, 9, and 10 in the first section of the *Śiva-sūtra;* trans. Jaideva Singh, *Śiva Sutras: The Yoga of Supreme Identity* (Delhi: Motilal Banarsidass, 1979), pp. 41–47.
52. Swami Muktananda, *From the Finite to the Infinite* (1994), p. 375.
53. *Maitrī Upaniṣad* 6.34; trans. S. Radhakrishnan, *The Principal Upaniṣads* (1953), p. 845.
54. *Vijñāna-bhairava* v.116; trans. Jaideva Singh, *The Yoga of Delight, Wonder, and Astonishment* (1991), p. 103.

Sutra 6 (pp. 127–146)

55. *Spanda-kārikā* 46; trans. Mark S. G. Dyczkowski, *The Stanzas on Vibration* (Albany: SUNY Press, 1992), p. 122.
56. Swami Muktananda, from a talk given January 14, 1981; unpublished transcript, p. 1.
57. Gurumayi Chidvilasananda, *My Lord Loves a Pure Heart* (South Fallsburg: SYDA Foundation, 1994), p. 136.
58. Maheshvarananda, *Mahārtha-mañjarī* 21; trans. Mark S. G. Dyczkowski, *The Doctrine of Vibration* (1987), p. 136.
59. *Conversations with Swami Muktananda: The Early Years* (South Fallsburg: SYDA Foundation, 1998), pp. 90–91.
60. Swami Muktananda, from a talk given January 14, 1981; unpublished transcript, p. 2.
61. Gurumayi Chidvilasananda, from a talk given February 23, 1991, unpublished transcript, p. 11.
62. Abhinavagupta, *Īśvara-pratyabhijñā-vimarśinī,* trans. K. A. S. Iyer and K. C. Pandey; *Īśvara Pratyabhijñā Vimarśinī of Abhinavagupta: Doctrine of Divine Recognition* Vol. III (Delhi: Motilal Banarsidass, 1986), p. 6.

Sutra 7 (pp. 147–163)

63. Kshemaraja, *Pratyabhijñā-hṛdayam,* introductory comment to sutra 7; trans. Jaideva Singh, *The Doctrine of Recognition* (1990), p. 58.
64. Abhinavagupta, *Tantrāloka* 12. 6–8; trans. Mark S. G. Dyczkowski, *The Doctrine of Vibration* (1987), p. 140.
65. Gurumayi Chivilasananda, from a talk given June 28, 2000; unpublished transcript, p. 3.
66. Kshemaraja, *Pratyabhijñā-hṛdayam,* comm. on sutra 7; trans. Jaideva Singh, *The Doctrine of Recognition* (1990), p. 59.

Sutra 8 (pp. 165–175)

67. Kshemaraja, *Pratyabhijñā-hṛdayam,* comm. on sutra 8; trans. Jaideva Singh, *The Doctrine of Recognition* (1990), p. 62.
68. Swami Muktananda, *Satsang with Baba,* Vol. III (Ganeshpuri, India: SYDA Foundation, 1977), pp. 227–28.
69. *Chāndogya Upaniṣad* 8.7–12; trans. Patrick Olivelle, *Upaniṣads* (Oxford and New York: Oxford University Press, 1996), pp. 171–75.
70. Gurumayi Chidvilasananda, *Kindle My Heart* (South Fallsburg: SYDA Foundation, 1996), p. 162.
71. Kshemaraja, *Pratyabhijñā-hṛdayam,* comm. on sutra 8; trans. Jaideva Singh, *The Doctrine of Recognition* (1990), p. 63.

Sutra 9 (pp. 177–199)

72. Kshemaraja, *Pratyabhijñā-hṛdayam,* comm. on sutra 9; trans. Jaideva Singh, *The Doctrine of Recognition* (1990), pp. 63–64.
73. Kshemaraja, *Pratyabhijñā-hṛdayam,* comm. on sutra 9; trans. Jaideva Singh, *The Doctrine of Recognition* (1990), p. 64.
74. Abhinavagupta, *Paramārtha-sāra* v. 92; trans. Douglas Renfrew Brooks, *The Paramārthasāra* (unpublished manuscript).
75. *Śiva Purāṇa, Rudra Saṃhita* 5.42.16–19; trans. in Ancient Indian Tradition and Mythology Series, Vol. 2, *Śiva-Purāṇa, Part II* (Delhi: Motilal Banarsidass, 1970), pp. 980–81.
76. Kshemaraja, *Pratyabhijñā-hṛdayam* comm. on sutra 4; trans. Jaideva Singh, *The Doctrine of Recognition* (1990), pp. 52–53.
77. Gurumayi Chidvilasananda, "The Flashing Forth of the Supreme: A Talk by Gurumayi Chidvilasananda," *DARSHAN,* No. 39, June 1990 (South Fallsburg: SYDA Foundation), p. 76.

78. *Bhagavad-gītā* 4.17; trans. Swami Muktananda, "A Force Called Destiny: Questions and Answers with Baba Muktananda," *DARSHAN,* No. 54, September, 1991, p. 32.
79. Abhinavagupta's exposition on the workings of karma can be found in *Tantrāloka,* 9.98b–146; Italian trans. Raniero Gnoli, *Luce delle Sacre Scritture [Tantrāloka] di Abhinavagupta* (1972); Engish trans. Giuliana Haim.
80. Abhinavagupta, *Tantrāloka* 9.98b–146; Italian trans. Raniero Gnoli, *Luce delle Sacre Scritture [Tantrāloka] di Abhinavagupta* (1972); Engish trans. Giuliana Haim.
81. *Saṁvitprakāśa* 3.2; quoted by Bhagavadutpala, *Spanda-pradīpikā,* p. 88; trans. Mark S. G. Dyczkowski, *The Stanzas of Vibration* (1992), p. 143.
82. A full rendition of this story can be found in *Vasishtha's Yoga,* trans. Swami Venkatesananda (Albany: SUNY Press, 1993), pp. 55-92.
83. These observations were made by my colleague and fellow monk, Swami Anantananda, who holds a doctorate degree in biology and has an ongoing interest in matters relating to science.

Sutra 10 (pp. 201–216)

84. *Svacchandra-tantra,* 1.3; trans. Jaideva Singh, *The Doctrine of Recognition* (1990), p. 66.
85. Kshemaraja, *Pratyabhijñā-hṛdayam,* comm. on sutra 10; trans. Jaideva Singh, *The Doctrine of Recognition* (1990), p. 67.
86. Kshemaraja, *Pratyabhijñā-hṛdayam,* comm. on sutra 10; trans. Jaideva Singh, *The Doctrine of Recognition* (1990), p. 67.
87. Abhinavagupta, *Tantrāloka* 14.24–5; trans. Mark S. G. Dyczkowski, *The Stanzas on Vibration* (1992), p. 179.
88. Utpaladeva, *Śiva-stotrāvalī,* v. 12; trans. Constantina Rhodes Bailly, *Shaiva Devotional Songs of Kashmir: A Translation of Utpaladeva's Shivastotravali,* (Albany: SUNY Press, 1987), p. 108.
89. *Śiva-sūtra* 2.6; trans. Swami Muktananda, *Nothing Exists That Is Not Śiva* (1997), p. 33.
90. Kshemaraja comm. on *Śiva-sūtra* 2.6; trans. Jaideva Singh, *Śiva Sutras* (1979), p. 103.
91. *Kulārṇava-tantra* 13.51–52; trans. Ram Kumar Rai *Kulārṇava Tantra* (Varanasi: Prachya Prakashan, 1983), p. 249.
92. Swami Muktananda, *Play of Consciousness* (2000), p. 101.
93. Bhagavadutpala, *Spanda-pradīpikā,* stanza 32 of *Spanda-kārikā;* trans. Mark S. G. Dyczkowski, *The Doctrine of Vibration* (1987), p. 166.
94. *Kulārṇava-tantra* 14.3; trans. Ram Kumar Rai, *Kulārṇava Tantrā* (1983), p. 262.
95. *Mantriśiro-bhairava-tantra,* quoted by Kshemaraja in his comm. on *Śiva-sūtra* 2.6; trans. Jaideva Singh, *Śiva Sutras* (1979), p. 103.
96. Swami Muktananda, *Satsang with Baba, Vol. III* (1977), p 282.

97. Swami Muktananda, *Paramartha Katha Prasang* (Ganeshpuri, India: SYDA Foundation, 1981) p. 182.
98. Swami Muktananda, *Satsang with Baba, Vol. IV* (Ganeshpuri, India: SYDA Foundation, 1978), p 293.
99. Swami Muktananda, *Where Are You Going?* (1994), p. 152.

Sutra 11 (pp. 217–219)

100. Kshemaraja, *Pratyabhijñā-hṛdayam,* comm. on sutra 11; trans. Jaideva Singh, *The Doctrine of Recognition* (1990), pp. 68–69.
101. Kshemaraja, *Pratyabhijñā-hṛdayam,* comm. on sutra 11; trans. Jaideva Singh, *The Doctrine of Recognition* (1990), p. 68.
102. Kshemaraja, *Pratyabhijñā-hṛdayam,* comm. on sutra 11; trans. Jaideva Singh, *The Doctrine of Recognition* (1990), p. 69.

Sutra 12 (pp. 231–253)

103. Kshemaraja, *Pratyabhijna-hṛdayam,* sutra 12; trans. Jaideva Singh, *The Doctrine of Recognition* (1990), p. 70.
104. Swami Muktananda, from a talk given on March 11, 1981; unpublished transcript.
105. Swami Muktananda, *From the Finite to the Infinite* (1994), p. 402.
106. It is Abhinavagupta who makes the most decisive of all the delineations, primarily in his *Parā-triṃśikā-vivaraṇa* and also in *Īśvara-pratyabhijñā-kārikā-vimarśinī* and *Tantrāloka.* For material in this chapter, I am indebted to Jaideva Singh's translation of the *Parā-triṃśikā-vivaraṇa,* appearing in his *Abhinavagupta: A Trident of Wisdom* (Albany: SUNY Press, 1989), and to Andre Padoux, the author of *Vāc: The Concept of the Word in Selected Hindu Tantras,* trans. Jacques Gontier (Albany: SUNY Press, 1990).
107. John 1.1–3, *The New Jerusalem Bible: Reader's Edition* (New York: Doubleday, 1990), p. 1243.
108. *Sāma-veda, Tandya Mahā Brāhmana* 20.14.2; trans. Raimundo Panikkar, *The Vedic Experience,* (Pondicherry: All India Books, 1977), p. 107.
109. Genesis, 1.3-11, *The New Jerusalem Bible* (1990), p. 5.
110. *Īśvara-pratyabhijñā-kārikā* 1.5.13–4; trans. Mark S. G. Dyczkowski, *The Doctrine of Vibration* (1987), p. 196.
111. Swami Muktananda, *Mystery of the Mind* (South Fallsburg: SYDA Foundation, 1981), p. 30.
112. Abhinavagupta, *Parā-triṃśikā-vivaraṇa;* trans. Andre Padoux, *Vāc* (1990), p. 212.
113. Swami Chidvilasananda, *The Yoga of Discipline* (1996), p. 146.

114. From the author's notes.
115. *Śiva-sūtra* 2.3; trans. by Jaideva Singh, *Śiva Sutras* (1979), p. 88.
116. *Śiva-sūtra-vimarśinī*, Kshemaraja's comm. on sutra 2.6; trans. by Jaideva Singh, *Śiva Sutras* (1979), p. 103.
117. Swami Muktananda, *Selected Essays* (South Fallsburg: SYDA Foundation, 1995), p. 89–90.
118. Swami Muktananda, "Japa in the Four Bodies," *Light on the Path* (South Fallsburg: SYDA Foundation, 1994), pp. 63–71.

Sutra 13 (pp. 255–270)

119. Swami Chidvilasananda, *The Yoga of Discipline* (1996), p. 196.
120. Swami Muktananda, *Satsang with Baba, Vol. III* (1977), p. 53.
121. Swami Muktananda, *Secret of the Siddhas* (1994), p. 81.
122. Abhinavagupta, *Anuttarāṣñikā* 2; trans. Jaideva Singh, *Śiva Sutras* (1979), p. xxxiv.
123. *Vijñāna-bhairava* v.124; trans. Jaideva Singh, *The Yoga of Delight, Wonder, and Astonishment* (1991), p. 111.
124. Jayaratha's commentary to Abhinavagupta's *Tantrāloka* II; trans. Deba Brata SenSharma, *The Philosophy of Sadhana*, (Albany: SUNY Press, 1990), p. 113.
125. *Ratna-mālā*, quoted by Maheshvarananda in *Mahārtha-mañjarī*, p. 166, trans., Mark S. G. Dyczkowski, *The Doctrine of Vibration* (1987), p. 178.
126. Gurumayi Chidvilasananda, "With Grace You'll Scale the Heights," *DARSHAN*, No. 91, September 1994, p. 41.

Sutra 14 (pp. 271–279)

127. Gurumayi Chidvilasananda, "The Flashing Forth of the Supreme," *DARSHAN*, No. 39, June 1990, p. 84.
128. *Śiva-sūtra*, 2.9; trans. Swami Muktananda, *Nothing Exists That Is Not Śiva* (1997), p. 36.
129. Abhinavagupta, *Tantrāloka*, 3.259b–264; trans. Paul Muller-Ortega, *The Triadic Heart of Śiva: Kaula Tantricism of Abhinavagupta in the Non-dual Shaivism of Kashmir* (Albany: SUNY Press, 1989), p. 195.
130. Gurumayi Chidvilasananda, from a question and answer session on August 6, 1986; unpublished transcript.

Sutra 15 (pp. 281–287)

131. From SYDA Foundation Shakti Punja archives, South Fallsburg, N.Y.
132. Abhinavagupta, *Tantrāloka* 3.283–85, trans. Mark S. G. Dyczkowski, *The Doctrine of Vibration* (1987), p. 189.

Sutra 16 (pp. 289–303)

133. Swami Muktananda, *From the Finite to the Infinite* (1994), p. 3.
134. *Śiva-sūtra* 1.7; trans. Jaideva Singh, *Śiva Śutras* (1979), pp. 36–37.
135. Quoted by Maheshvarananda in *Mahārtha-mañjarī*, p. 24; trans. Mark S .G. Dyczkowski, *The Doctrine of Vibration* (1987), p. 123.
136. Abhinavagupta uses this term in his *Parā-triśikā-laghuvṛtti*; see Paul E. Muller-Ortega, *The Triadic Heart of Śiva* (1979), pp. 140-141.
137. *Spanda-kārikā* 2.5; trans. Paul Muller-Ortega, *Śambhu-mahārtha-tantra: The Book of Inquiry into the Great Meaning, the Great Purpose, the Great Treasure of Lord Śiva* (unpublished manuscript).
138. Gurumayi Chidvilasananda, quoted in Peter Hayes, *The Supreme Adventure: The Yoga of Perfection* (London: HarperCollins, 1994), pp. 178-179.
139. Abhinavagupta, *Paramārtha-sāra* vv. 58–59; trans. Douglas Renfrew Brooks, *The Paramārthasāra* (unpublished manuscript).
140. Maheshvarananda, *Mahārtha-mañjarī* v. 21; French trans. Lilian Silburn, *La Maharthamañjarī de Maheshvarananda avec des extraits du Parimala* (Paris: Editions de Bocard, 1968); English trans. Cynthia Franklin.
141. Maheshvarananda, *Mahārtha-mañjarī* v. 22; French trans. Lilian Silburn, *La Maharthamañjarī de Maheshvarananda avec des extraits du Parimala*; English trans. Cynthia Franklin.
142. Utpaladeva, *Īśvara-pratyabhijñā-kārikā* IV, 1.12; trans. B. N. Pandit, *Īśvara Pratyabhijñā Kārikā of Utpaladeva* (New Delhi: Publication forthcoming).
143. Swami Muktananda, *From the Finite to the Infinite* (1994), p. 468.
144. Swami Muktananda, *Secret of the Siddhas* (1994), pp. 24–25.
145. Paul E. Muller-Ortega, "The Siddha: Paradoxical Exemplar of Indian Spirituality," *Meditation Revolution* (1997), pp. 174–75.
146. Abhinavagupta, *Tantrāloka* 2.35-8; Italian trans. Raniero Gnoli, *Luce delle Sacre Scritture [Tantrāloka] di Abhinavagupta* (1972); English trans. Guiliana Haim.
147. *Śiva-sūtra* 3.13; trans. Jaideva Singh, *Śiva Sutras* (1979), pp. 158–60. The final translation is from Swami Muktananda, *Nothing Exists That Is Not Śiva* (1997), p. 43.
148. Gurumayi Chidvilasananda, *Inner Treasures* (South Fallsburg: SYDA Foundation, 1995), p. 8.

Sutra 17 (pp. 305–317)

149. Kshemaraja, *Pratyabhijña-hṛdayam*, comm. on sutra 17; trans. Jaideva Singh, *The Doctrine of Recognition* (1990), p. 80.
150. *Praśna Upaniṣad* 3.6; trans. Patrick Olivelle, *Upaniṣads* (1996), pg. 283.

151. Swami Muktananda, *Secret of the Siddhas* (1994), p. 13.

152. Kshemaraja, *Pratyabhijñā-hṛdayam,* comm. on sutra 17; trans., Jaideva Singh, *The Doctrine of Recognition* (1990), p. 81.

153. Gurumayi Chidvilasananda, *Inner Treasures* (1995), p. 72.

154. Swami Muktananda, quoted in "Letter from Melbourne," *Siddha Path* magazine, October, 1978, p. 12. The original source for this classification is found in the Āgamas of the *kula-śāstra,* the system taught to Abhinavagupta by his Guru, Shambhunatha.

155. Swami Muktananda, quoted in "Letter from Oakland," *Siddha Path* magazine, April 1979, p. 4.

156. Swami Muktananda, *Play of Consciousness* (2000), p. 173.

157. Swami Muktananda, *From the Finite to the Infinite* (1994), p. 96.

158. Abhinavagupta, *Tantrāloka* v. 50b–52a; trans. Jaideva Singh, *The Doctrine of Recognition* (1990), p. 157.

Sutra 18 (pp. 319–335)

159. Kshemaraja, *Pratyabhijñā-hṛdayam,* comm. on sutra 18; trans. Jaideva Singh, *The Doctrine of Recognition* (1990), p. 82.

160. *Kaṭha Upaniṣad* 4.1; trans. Patrick Olivelle, *Upaniṣads* (1996), p. 240.

161. Swami Chidvilasananda, *The Yoga of Discipline* (1996), p. 5.

162. *Kakṣyā-stotra,* quoted by Kshemaraja in his commentary on sutra 18 of *Pratyabhijñā-hṛdayam;* trans. Mark S .G. Dyczkowski, *The Doctrine of Vibration* (1987), p. 158.

163. Kshemaraja, *Pratyabhijñā-hṛdayam,* comm. on sutra 18; trans. Jaideva Singh, *The Doctrine of Recognition* (1990), p. 84.

164. Swami Muktananda, *Kundalini: The Secret of Life* (South Fallsburg: SYDA Foundation, 1994), p. 34.

165. Kshemaraja follows Utpaladeva's interpretation of these forms of *prāṇa-śakti* as expressed in *Īśvara-pratyabhijñā-kārikā* 3.2.19–20.

166. *Jñāna-garbha-tantrā;* trans. Jaideva Singh, *The Doctrine of Recognition* (1990), pp. 85–86.

167. Swami Muktananda, *I Am That: The Science of Hamsa from the Vijnana Bhairava* (South Fallsburg: SYDA Foundation, 1992), p. 41.

168. Swami Muktananda, *Secret of the Siddhas* (1994), p. 201.

169. *Vijñāna-bhairava,* v.72–74; trans., Jaideva Singh, *The Doctrine of Recognition* (1990), p. 87.

Sutra 19 (pp. 337–355)

170. Gurumayi Chidvilasananda, "All This Is God! All This Is God!" *DARSHAN*, No. 60 March 1992, p. 42.
171. Abhinavagupta, *Īśvara-pratyabhijñā-kārikā-vinarśinī*, v. II, p. 129; trans. Mark S. G. Dyczkowski, *The Doctrine of Vibration* (1987), p. 194.
172. St. Teresa of Avila, *Interior Castle*; trans. E. Allison Peers (New York: Image Books, 1972).
173. Mark S .G. Dyczkowski, *The Doctrine of Vibration* (1987), p. 30.
174. As stated in his commentary, Kshemaraja adopted this term from the *Krama-sūtra*, a Krama School text that is no longer extant.
175. Kshemaraja, *Spanda-nirṇaya*, p. 25; trans. Mark S. G. Dyczkowski, *The Doctrine of Vibration* (1987), p. 159.
176. Swami Muktananda, *From the Finite to the Infinite* (1994), p. 507.
177. Jaideva Singh, *Śiva Sutras* (1979), p. 230.
178. Gurumayi Chidvilasananda, from a talk, given June 11, 1989; unpublished transcript.
179. Gurumayi Chidvilasananda, from a talk, given June 11, 1989; unpublished transcript.
180. Swami Muktananda, *From the Finite to the Infinite* (1994), pp. 141–2. The flower described is known as "morning glory."

Sutra 20 (pp. 357–371)

181. From the author's notes.
182. Utpaladeva, *Ajaḍa-pramātṛ-siddhi* vv. 22–23; quoted by Kshemaraja in his comm. on sutra 20, *Pratyabhijñā-hṛdayam;* trans. Jaideva Singh, *The Doctrine of Recognition* (1990), p. 92.
183. My summary of the symbology of the letters of *aham,* which I must admit was bold in its brevity, is based on Abhinavagupta's discussion, threaded throughout his *Parā-triśikā-vivaraṇa* [trans. Jaideva Singh, *Abhinavagupta: A Trident of Wisdom: Translation of Paratrisika Vivarana* (Albany: SUNY Press, 1989)] and appearing in chapter 3 of his *Tantrāloka* and *Tantra-sāra.* I also drew from Mark S. G. Dyczkowski's discussion of this topic in his *The Doctrine of Vibration* (1987), p. 186.
184. Kshemaraja, *Spanda-nirnaya;* trans. Mark S. G. Dyczkowski, *The Doctrine of Vibration* (1987), p. 202.
185. Abhinavagupta, *Tantrāloka*, 4.194; Italian trans. Raniero Gnoli, *Luce delle Sacre Scritture [Tantrāloka] di Abhinavagupta* (1972); English trans. Giuliana Heim.
186. Baba Muktananda often quoted this passage as Bhagawan Nityananda's essential teaching.

187. Kshemaraja, *Pratyabhijñā-hṛdayam,* comm. to sutra 20; trans. Jaideva Singh, *The Doctrine of Recognition* (1990), pp. 91-92.
188. Kshemaraja quoted by himself in his comm. on *Pratyabhijñā-hṛdayam* sutra 20; trans. Jaideva Singh, *The Doctrine of Recognition* (1990), p. 94.
189. Utpaladeva, *Īśvara-pratyabhijñā-kārikā,* 1.1.1; trans. B. N. Pandit, *Īśvara Pratyabhijñā Kārikā of Utpaladeva* (New Delhi: Publication forthcoming).
190. I owe these observations to a conversation with Carlos G. Pomeda, who wrote on this subject in an MA dissertation entitled "The Heart of Recognition" at the University of California at Berkeley.
191. Kshemaraja, *Pratyabhijñā-hṛdayam,* comm. on sutra 20; trans. Jaideva Singh, *The Doctrine of Recognition* (1990), pp. 94–95.
192. Kshemaraja, *Pratyabhijñā-hṛdayam,* comm. on sutra 20; trans. Carlos G. Pomeda.

Epilogue (pp. 372–375)

193. From the author's notes.
194. Utpaladeva, *Śiva-stotrāvalī,* Third Song, v. 11–13; trans. Constantina Rhodes Bailly, *Shaiva Devotional Songs of Kashmir* (1987), pp. 40–41.

Appendix A (pp. 376–385)

195. Swami Muktananda, *Satsang with Baba, Vol. V* (Ganeshpuri, India: SYDA Foundation, 1978), p. 110.
196. Swami Muktananda, *Satsang with Baba, Vol. IV* (1978), p. 10.
197. Swami Lakshman Jee [Joo], *Kashmir Shaivism* (1988), p. 92.
198. Swami Lakshman Jee, *Kashmir Shaivism* (1988), pp. 89–95.
199. Paul E. Muller Ortega, "The Siddha: Paradoxical Exemplar of Indian Spirituality," *Meditation Revolution* (1997), p. 192.
200. Swami Chidvilasananda, *My Lord Loves a Pure Heart* (1994), pp. 132–33.
201. From an interview with Rajgiri Gosavi, 1990; SYDA Foundation Shakti Punja archives, South Fallsburg, N.Y.
202. Swami Muktananda, *Secret of the Siddhas* (1994), p. 208.

A Note on the Sanskrit

Throughout the text, names of individuals, places, and geographical features do not include diacritical markings. Otherwise, the standard international transliteration scheme for South Asian languages has been used. This includes Sanskrit words in quotes from the Siddha Yoga Gurus even though—since the transliteration style has varied considerably in Siddha Yoga publications over the years—these terms often appear in a different style in their published sources.

Also, to simplify pronunciation, when long Sanskrit words are combined to form a term or phrase, a hyphen has been employed, as in, for instance, the title of the work we are studying.

For readers not familiar with Sanskrit, the following is a guide for pronunciation.

Vowels

Sanskrit vowels are categorized as either long or short. In English transliteration, the long vowels are indicated with a macron, a horizontal line over the vowel, with the exception of the *e* and the *ai*, and the *o* and the *au*, which are always long.

Short:	Long:	
a as in cup	*ā* as in father	*ai* as in aisle
i as in give	*e* as in save	*au* as in cow
u as in full	*ī* as in seen	*ū* as in school
	o as in know	

Consonants

The main differences between Sanskrit and English pronunciation of consonants are in the aspirated and retroflexive letters.

The aspirated letters have a definite h sound. The Sanskrit letter *kh* is pronounced as in inkhorn; the *th* as in boathouse; the *ph* as in loophole.

The retroflexes are pronounced with the tip of the tongue touching the hard palate; *ṭ*, for instance, is pronounced as in ant; *ḍ* as in end.

The sibilants are *ś*, *ṣ*, and *s*. The *ś* is pronounced as sh but with the tongue touching the soft palate; the *ṣ* as sh with the tongue touching the hard palate; the *s* as in history.

Other distinctive consonants are these:

c as in church	*ṃ* is a strong nasal
ch as in pitch-hook	*ḥ* is a strong aspiration
ñ as in canyon	

Double consonants take an extra stress.

Glossary

Āgama: Revealed Śaivite scripture.

Bhairava: A name of Śiva, or supreme Consciousness.

Bhairavī: A name of Śakti, or the dynamic manifestation of supreme Consciousness.

Cakra: A center of energy located in the subtle system of the human being. Six major cakras lie within the *suṣumṇā nāḍī,* or central channel, of the subtle body. When awakened, *kuṇḍalinī śakti* flows upward through the cakras to the highest spiritual center, the *sahasrāra,* at the crown of the head.

Citi: Supreme awareness. The creative power of universal Consciousness, variously personified as a goddess (Citi) and understood as an impersonal force *(citi).*

Knowledge, triad of: The relationship between the knowing subject *(pramātā),* the object known *(prameya),* and the means of perception *(pramāṇa).*

Kuṇḍalinī: Spiritual energy that lies dormant at the base of the spine until, when awakened and guided by a Siddha master, it brings about spiritual purification in the yogi. Also depicted as a goddess, Kundalini.

Mala (lit., stain or impurity): The term in Indian philosophy that describes how the individual's experience of pure Consciousness is limited by identification with separation *(āṇava-mala),* difference *(māyīya-mala),* and a sense of doership *(kārma-mala).*

Māyā: The power that veils the true nature of the Self and projects the experience of multiplicity.

Nāḍī: A conduit of the subtle body; part of a branching network of such channels. The three main *nāḍīs* are the *suṣumṇā,* the central channel, which is the pathway of the awakened *kuṇḍalinī,* and the *iḍā* and *piṅgalā,* which flank the *suṣumṇā* on either side.

Nondualism: The philosophical perspective holding that, in the ultimate analysis, all reality is one.

Paramaśiva: Supreme Śiva; a name for the one, all-pervasive supreme Reality.

Prakāśa: Light; light of Consciousness.

Prakṛti: The principle of nature; a force that provides the material for creation.

Psychic instrument, threefold *(antakharana):* The word-forming faculty *(manas),* which has the capacity to think; the ego *(ahaṃkāra),* which creates the experience of limited individuality; and the intellect *(buddhi),* which has the power to discriminate.

Puruṣa: The individual Self, manifest when the divine principle becomes a limited being.

Sādhana: Spiritual discipline and practice; the spiritual path.

Sādhaka: One who engages in sustained spiritual practice.

Śakti: The name of the dynamic aspect of absolute Reality; that power personified as a goddess (Śakti); the creative force of the universe (*śakti*).

Śaktipāta: Descent of grace; yogic initiation by a Siddha master.

Samādhi: The state of full meditative absorption in God.

Saṃsāra: The soul's cycle of birth, mutability, death, and rebirth.

Saṃskāra: A karmic impression stored in the subtle body.

Saṅgham: A community of devotees who follow a shared body of teachings and practices.

Satsang: A Hindi term meaning "the company of saints and devotees; a gathering of seekers for the purpose of chanting, meditating, and receiving scriptural teachings."

Siddha: A fully enlightened yogi.

Śiva: The name of the static aspect of absolute Reality; a name given absolute Reality personified as a god (Śiva); the illuminative principle of Reality *(śiva)*.

Spanda: The divine pulse, or vibration, of energy that creates and pervades all of life.

Sutra: Scriptural aphorism; any work consisting of aphorisms.

Tantra (lit. extension): A scripture or body of scriptures that explains religious doctrine or practice. Originating within Hinduism, Buddhism, and Jainism around the fourth century C.E., Tantric texts promote a world-view that all reality is a manifestation of the divine principle.

Tattva: In Indian philosophy, one of the principles of creation, each principle designating a particular step in the process of universal manifestation from pure Consciousness to matter; that which is the essence of a stage of manifestation.

Trika: A system of Kashmir Śaivite philosophy positing both the immanence and transcendence of the supreme Self.

Vikalpa: A movement of the mind; a differentiated perception.

Vimarśa: The faculty of awareness.

Index

Transliterated Sanskrit words have been alphabetized according to their spelling, without regard to diacritical marks. For example, Śakti is listed as if it were spelled "Sakti." References to footnotes are expressed as, for example, 125fn* (= asterisked footnote on page 125).

A

Ābhāsa, 73–85, 196, 221–22

Ābhāsana, 221–22

Abhinavagupta, 1–2, 220
- on *aham,* 360–61
- on language learning, 244
- and pathless path, 267
- on speech, 239, 241, 242, 244
- on *upayas,* 260fn*

Abhinavagupta, quoted on:
- *ahaṃbhāva,* 145–46
- experience of liberation, 293, 295, 300–1, 317, 362
- fire of Consciousness, 277
- five cosmic actions, 207
- I-Consciousness, 287
- impure and pure creation, 97
- liberation of yogis, 267
- nature of reality, 56
- perceiving, 45
- physical body, 155
- reasons for creation, 64
- *samādhi,* 342
- *śāmbhavopāya,* 266
- *tattvas,* 106
- transmigration, 182

Absorption. *See Samādhi*

Action,
- five powers of, 100–1, 155
- limited, 99
- *See also Kārma-mala; Kriyā-śakti; Pañca-kṛtya*

Actions, five cosmic. *See Pañca-kṛtya*

Āgamas (revealed scriptures), 12, 95, 213, 214, 313
- on knowing, 44–45

Aham (I am), 122, 296, 370
- in a contemplation, 146
- at different levels, 104, 245
- as goal of yoga, 360–62, 365
- in pure creation, 94, 95, 96
- as vibration of *Parā-vāc,* 238
- *See also Ahaṃbhāva*

Ahaṃbhāva (I-feeling), 145–46, 278
- as central to *sādhana,* 359–62
- in dissolving thoughts, 323–24
- revealed through mantra, 250, 253
- as *śiva-vyāpti,* 286–87

D

I

J

K

while in *samādhi*, 348
See also Pramāṇa; Pramātā(s); Vikalpas
Piṅgalā-nāḍī, 328–330
Powers, divine, 143fn*, 158
Practice, spiritual. *See Sādhana;* Spiritual Practices, specific
Prakāśa (light of Consciousness), 27–33
etymology of, 27
as Śiva, 31–33
See also Light
Prakṛti (nature), 99, 143, 152
Pramāṇa (knowing, perceiving), 44–46, 48, 132–34, 264
as Consciousness, 133
and individual identities, 132–33
See also Knowledge; Perception; *Pramātā(s); Prameya*
Pramātā (knower), 43–46, 48–49, 57, 133, 158, Appendix C
etymology of, 45
at seven levels, 72, 103–5, Appendix C
universe contained in, 90–92
See also Perception; *Pramāṇa*
Prameya (known object), 43–46, 48, 243, 262
See also Perception; *Pramāṇa; Pratibimba*
Prāṇa (vital energy), 151, 326–29
harmonizing *(samāna)*, 153, 328–29
and mind, 326–29
See also Prāṇa-śakti
Prāṇas, five, 153–54, 326–29
Prāṇa-śakti, 153, 309–10, 325–31
See also Prāṇa
Pratibimba (reflection of object), 56–60
Pratimīlana, 352–53
Pratyabhijñā (recognition), 16–18, 369
Psychic instrument, 100, 136–42, 154, 364
after liberation, 296–97
as cause of transmigration, 192–93
See also Ego; *Buddhi; Manas;* Mind
Pulsation. *See Spanda*
Purification:
of *cakras*, 312
by *kuṇḍalinī*, 310–15
of mind, 258–70
by *samādhi*, 345–37
Pūrṇo'ham-vimarśa, 145, 250, 253. *See also Ahaṃbhāva*
Puruṣa (individual), 99–100
Puryaṣṭaka (subtle body), 151, 152, 154, 156

Q

Qualities, three. *See Guṇas*

R

Rajas (guṇa), 143. *See also Guṇas*
Rakti (enjoyment), 222–23
Reality, supreme. *See* Citi; *Cidānanda;* Paramaśiva; Śiva
Reincarnation. *See* Transmigration

S

Sadāśiva-tattva, 95–96, 116, 184, 245
Sādhaka, 270
See also Sādhana

Y

Suggested Reading

This list of references, by no means exhaustive, is meant to assist readers who wish to continue to expand their knowledge of Siddha Yoga and Kashmir Śaivism.

Books on Siddha Yoga

Swami Chidvilasananda

Courage and Contentment: A Collection of Talks on Spiritual Life. South Fallsburg, N.Y.: SYDA Foundation, 1999.

Enthusiasm. South Fallsburg, N.Y.: SYDA Foundation, 1997.

My Lord Loves A Pure Heart: The Yoga of Divine Virtues. South Fallsburg, N.Y.: SYDA Foundation, 1994.

The Yoga of Discipline. South Fallsburg, N.Y.: SYDA Foundation, 1996.

Swami Muktananda

I Am That: The Science of Hamsa from the Vijñānabhairava. South Fallsburg, N.Y.: SYDA Foundation, 1992.

From the Finite to the Infinite. South Fallsburg, N.Y.: SYDA Foundation, 1994.

Kundalini: The Secret of Life. South Fallsburg, N.Y.: SYDA Foundation, 1994.

Nothing Exists That Is Not Śiva: Commentaries on the Śiva Sūtra, Vijñānabhairava, Gurugītā, and Other Sacred Texts. South Fallsburg, N.Y.: SYDA Foundation, 1997.

Play of Consciousness. South Fallsburg, N.Y.: SYDA Foundation, 2000.

Secret of the Siddhas. South Fallsburg, N.Y.: SYDA Foundation, 1980.

Other Authors

Brooks, Durgananda, Muller-Ortega, Mahony, Bailly, Sabarathnam. *Meditation Revolution: A History and Theology of the Siddha Yoga Lineage.* South Fallsburg, N.Y.: Agama Press, Muktabodha Indological Research Institute, 1997.

Kripananda, Swami. *The Guru's Sandals: Threshold of the Formless.* South Fallsburg, N.Y.: SYDA Foundation, 1997.

——. *The Sacred Power: A Seeker's Guide to Kundalini.* South Fallsburg, N.Y.: SYDA Foundation, 1995.

Translated Texts of Kashmir Śaivism

Bailly, Constantina Rhodes ed. & trans. *Shaiva Devotional Songs of Kashmir: A Translation and Study of Utpaladeva's Shivastotravali.* Albany, N.Y.: SUNY Press, 1987.

Dyczkowski, Mark S. G. ed. & trans. *The Aphorisms of Śiva: The Śiva Sūtra with Bhaskara's Commentary, the Vārttika.* Albany, N.Y.: SUNY Press, 1992.

——. *The Stanzas on Vibration: The Spandakārikā with Four Commentaries.* Albany, N.Y.: SUNY Press, 1992.

Gnoli, Raniero ed. & Italian trans. *Essenza dei Tantra (Tantrasāra) d'Abhinavagupta.* Torino: Editore Boringhieri, 1968.

——. *Luce dei Tantra (Tantrāloka).* Milano: Adelphi Edizioni, 1999.

Iyer, K. A. S. and K. C. Pandey ed. & trans. *Īśvara Pratyabhijñā Vimarśinī of Abhinavagupta: Doctrine of Divine Recognition* (3 vol.). Delhi: Motilal Banarsidass, 1986.

Pandit, B. N. ed. & trans. *The Essence of the Exact Reality or Paramārthasāra of Abhinavagupta.* Delhi: Munshiram Manoharlal, 1991.

Sen Sharma, Debabrata ed. & trans. *Ṣaṭtriṁśattattvā-sandoha (A Text of Trika Philosophy of Kashmir): With the Commentary by Rājānaka Ānanda Kavi.* Kurukshetra, India: B. N. Chakravarty University, 1977.

Singh, Jaideva ed. & trans. *Abhinavagupta: A Trident of Wisdom, Translation of Parātrīśikā Vivaraṇa.* Albany, N.Y.: SUNY Press, 1989.

——. *The Doctrine of Recognition: A Translation of the Pratyabhijñāhṛdayam.* Albany, N.Y.: SUNY Press, 1990.

——. *The Yoga of Delight, Wonder, and Astonishment: A Translation of the Vijñāna-bhairava.* Albany, N.Y.: SUNY Press, 1991.

——. *The Yoga of Vibration and Divine Pulsation: A Translation of the Spanda Kārikās with Kṣemarāja's Commentary, the Spanda Nirṇaya.* Albany, N.Y.: SUNY Press, 1992.

——. *Śiva Sūtras: The Yoga of Supreme Identity,* Delhi: Motilal Banarsidass, 2003.

Torella, Raffaele ed. & trans. *The Īśvarapratyabhijñākārikā of Utpaladeva: With the Author's Vṛtti,* critical edition and annotated translation. Roma: Istituto Italiano Per Il Medio Ed Estremo Oriente, 1994.

General Works on Śaivism

Alper, Harvey. *Mantra.* Albany, N.Y.: SUNY Press, 1989.

Chatterji, J. C. *Kashmir Shaivism.* Albany, N.Y.: SUNY Press, 1986.

Dyczkowski, Mark S. G. *The Doctrine of Vibration: An Analysis of the Doctrines and Practices of Kashmir Shaivism.* Albany, N.Y.: SUNY Press, 1987.

Muller-Ortega, Paul Eduardo. *The Triadic Heart of Śiva: Kaula Tantricism of Abhinavagupta in the Non-Dual Shaivism of Kashmir.* Albany, N.Y.: SUNY Press, 1989.

Lakshman Jee, Swami. *Kashmir Shaivism: The Secret Supreme.* Albany, N.Y.: SUNY Press, 1988.

Lakshmanjoo Raina, Swami. *Lectures on Practice and Discipline in Kashmir Shaivism.* Albany, N.Y.: Universal Shaiva Trust, 1982.

Lakshmanjoo, Swami. *Self Realization in Kashmir Shaivism: The Oral Teachings of Swami Lakshmanjoo.* John Hughes ed. Albany, N.Y.: SUNY Press, 1994.

Padoux, Andre. *Vāc: The Concept of the Word in Selected Hindu Tantras.* trans. Jacques Gontier. Albany, N.Y.: SUNY Press, 1990.

Pandey, K.C. *Abhinavagupta: An Historical and Philosophical Study.* Varanasi, India: The Chowkhamba Sanskrit Studies, 1963.

———. *An Outline of History of Śaiva Philosophy.* Delhi: Motilal Banarsidass, 1986.

Pandit, B. N. *The Mirror of Self-Supremacy or Svātantrya Darpana.* Delhi: Munshiram Manoharlal, 1993.

———. *Specific Aspects of Kashmir Śaivism.* Delhi: Munshiram Manoharlal, 1997.

Rastogi, Navjivan. *Introduction to the Tantrāloka: A Study in Structure.* Delhi: Motilal Banarsidass, 1987.

———. *The Krama Tantricism of Kashmir: Historical and General Sources.* Delhi: Motilal Banarsidass, 1979.

Sen Sharma, Debabrata. *The Philosophy of Sadhana: With Special Reference to the Trika Philosophy of Kashmir.* Albany, N.Y.: SUNY Press, 1990.

You can learn more about the teachings and practices of Siddha Yoga meditation by contacting

SYDA Foundation
PO Box 600, 371 Brickman Rd.
South Fallsburg, NY 12779-0600, USA
Tel: (845) 434-2000
or
Gurudev Siddha Peeth
P.O. Ganeshpuri, PIN 401 206
District Thana, Maharashtra, India

Please visit our website at www.siddhayoga.org

For further information on books in print by Swami Muktananda and Gurumayi Chidvilasananda, editions in translation, and audio and video recordings, please contact

Siddha Yoga Bookstore
PO Box 600, 371 Brickman Rd.
South Fallsburg, NY 12779-0600, USA
Tel: (845) 434-2000 ext. 1700

Call toll-free from the United States and Canada: 888-422-3334
Fax toll-free from the United States and Canada: 888-422-3339

Pratyabhijñā-hṛdayam

Sutra Pronunciation Guide CD

with

Vedamurti Shri Vivek Godbole

In traditions throughout the world, oral recitation is viewed as a significant facet of scriptural study. In India, it is considered particularly auspicious for a student to repeat a sutra or verse in the language in which the text was originally written. The *Pratyabhijñā-hṛdayam* is recited, as are most of India's scriptures, in Sanskrit.

So that the reader may have a complete learning experience of this text, we are including a CD recording of the twenty sutras. This CD is an exceptional learning tool, and has been designed to aid students at every level of familiarity with Sanskrit pronunciation. Each sutra has a corresponding track (tracks 1–20), recorded in the following sequence:

- a model recitation (for listening only).
- single words or short phrases (with spaces for repetition) repeated twice.
- three slow-pace recitations (with spaces for repetition).
- three regular-pace recitations (with spaces for repetition).

Track 21 compiles all the sutras, recited in consecutive order at regular pace with spaces for repetition.

Vedamurti Shri Vivek Godbole

Pronunciation of the *Pratyabhijñā-hṛdayam* sutras is presented here by Vedamurti Shri Vivek Godbole, a Brahmin priest and the director of the Swami Muktananda Vedashala in Satara, India. The Vedashala (school of Vedic study) is sponsored by the Muktabodha Institute to prepare young men for the Brahmanic priesthood. Over the years, Vedamurti Shri Vivek Godbole has performed thousands of Vedic ceremonies, including numerous rites at both Gurudev Siddha Peeth in Ganeshpuri, India, and Shree Muktananda Ashram in South Fallsburg, New York.